The Role of Economic Advisers in Developing Countries

Lauchlin Currie

CONTRIBUTIONS IN ECONOMICS AND
ECONOMIC HISTORY,
NUMBER 44

GREENWOOD PRESS

Westport, Connecticut • London, England

Library of Congress Cataloging in Publication Data

Currie, Lauchlin Bernard.
   The role of economic advisers in developing countries.

   (Contributions in economics and economic history,
ISSN 0084-9235 ; no. 44
      Bibliography: p.   ↻
      Includes index.
      1. Economic assistance. 2. Underdeveloped areas—
Consultants. I. Title. II. Series.
HC60.C835   338.91′09172′4   81-6623
ISBN 0-313-23064-1 (lib. bdg.)   AACR2

Library of Congress Catalog Card Number: 81-6623
ISBN: 0-313-23064-1
ISSN: 0084-9235

First published in 1981

Greenwood Press
A division of Congressional Information Service, Inc.
88 Post Road West
Westport, Connectict 06881

Printed in the United States of America

10 9 8 7 6 5 4 3 2 1

CONTENTS

TABLES

ACKNOWLEDGMENTS

The Twentieth Century Fund supported the research for this work and made available the services of Roger Sandilands for two periods during which he collaborated first in the basic research and later in lengthy discussions of the content, especially the theoretical basis of the appraisal and lessons. Among other tasks, he prepared the first and longer draft of the chapter on the controversial steel works. I cannot acknowledge my debt to him too warmly. I also wish particularly to express my appreciation for the advice, criticisms, and suggestions of Murray Rossant, Carol Barker, and Gary Nickerson of the Fund's staff. I also profited from various helpful suggestions made by readers of the first draft of the manuscript and the later, most efficient work of the editor, Beverly Goldberg, and finally of Associate Director John Booth in arranging for publication.

I appreciate the assistance of the Ford Foundation in making available files relating to some of its work in Colombia and especially the help afforded by Reed Hertford of the Foundation's staff; Lester Gordon of the Harvard Advisory Service and former members of the Harvard Advisory Service in Colombia—Richard Mallon, Stanley Nicholson, Clive Gray, Richard Bird, and V. L. Bassie; officials of AID in both Bogotá and Washington, especially Margaret Krantz of the Washington office; the help provided by Jorge Ruiz Lara of the staff of the Interamerican Development

Bank; and the helpful collaboration of Ernesto Franco Holguin, Colombian Executive Director of the World Bank, and Juan M. Cock-Londoño in the office of the Executive Director of the International Monetary Fund (IMF) for Colombia in supplying factual information.

The Departamento Nacional de Planeación of Colombia and particularly its director during the major part of the study, John Naranjo, provided working facilities and were most generous in granting access to files and permitting references to them.

Resources for the Future, Inc., Washington, D.C., in conjunction with the Latin American Institute for Economic and Social Planning (ILPES), Santiago, funded a study in 1977 that I directed for the Instituto de Estudios Colombianos, Bogotá, which provided me material on the course of growth in Colombia and on agricultural data, cited in this study.

I am also indebted to Margaret de Vries, historian of the IMF, and to William Diebold, of the Foreign Policy Association, for a careful reading and comments on the chapter on monetary and exchange advice; and to Albert Berry of the University of Toronto for similar work on the chapter on the Harvard Advisory Mission's work in Colombia. For the conclusions, of course, I take responsibility.

My secretary, Alicia de Téllez, as always, performed miracles in deciphering my crabbed script and in keeping abreast of the work of my two jobs. She was assisted in the closing stages by the highly efficient work of Gisela de Rosas. To both of them I owe a great debt for converting a disordered into at least a readable manuscript.

PREFACE

The present study is the outgrowth of my long experience as a professional economic adviser and occasionally as a recipient of economic advice from others, serving in many different situations and capacities. The views expressed herein and the judgments made are unavoidably influenced by this experience. My role in the formulation of the overall economic recovery policy of the New Deal, first as assistant to the chairman of the Board of Governors of the Federal Reserve System and later as assistant to President Roosevelt, is a matter of record* and the experience will be drawn upon briefly at different places in the text.

---

*The story of this experience is told in some detail in Byrd Jones, "Lauchlin Currie, Pump Priming and New Deal Fiscal Policy, 1934-1936"; L. Currie, "Recollections and Comments on New Deal Fiscal Policy"; and two hitherto unpublished memoranda of 1935 by L. Currie, "Federal Income-Increasing Expenditures, 1932-35" and "Comments on Pump Priming" (the former with Martin Krost), in a package in *History of Political Economy*, October 1978, and in the same journal, 1980, "The Causes of the Recession of 1973," L. Currie (written in 1938) with commentary by Byrd Jones. See also Herbert Stein, *The Fiscal Revolution in America* (Chicago: University of Chicago Press, 1969); Robert Lekachman, *The Age of Keynes* (London: Penguin Books, 1967); Kenneth Galbraith, "How Keynes came to America," in *Economics, Peace and Laughter* (Boston, Mass.: Houghton Mifflin, 1975); Alan Sweezy and L. Currie in *The Second Crisis of Economic Theory*, ed. Rendigs Fels (Morristown, N.J.: The General Learning Press, 1972), and other references given by Jones.

I organized and recruited the World Bank's first study mission to any country (Colombia, in 1949), then edited and wrote much of the subsequent report, and took an active part in the implementation of its recommendations. Thereafter I advised the Colombian government intermittently in many different capacities and over a long period of time, both in official capacities and as a private consultant, both as a foreigner and later as a national. Hence, I had an opportunity—an almost unique one—of both advising and dealing with advisers. Indeed, as these lines are being written, I am still an adviser of the head of the Colombian Government Planning Agency.

What is not so well known but what is an essential part of the story is my administrative and diplomatic experience. From 1942 to 1944, I acted as *de facto* director of the Foreign Economic Administration (the director spent most of his time in his other post as head of the Federal Deposit Insurance Corporation), whose farflung operations ranged from the selection of bombing targets to civilian lend lease, and the administration of areas liberated from the enemy. In this work, I made my own decisions and had my own staff of economic advisers. In 1941-1942, I handled all lend lease aid to China, making two trips for many hours of negotiations with Chiang Kai-Shek, and in early 1945, I negotiated the first War Time Trade Agreement with Switzerland, with the aid and advice of technicians from the U.S. Treasury and the Department of State.

My own professional background is also a bit of a mixture. My economic theory training was strictly classical, since, at the London School of Economics, I was profoundly influenced by Edwin Cannan, an author of a standard book on theories of production and distribution, and later, at Harvard, by Frank Taussig, who was the author of the standard economic textbook of the 1920s. On the other hand, I was also influenced by the early writings of J.M. Keynes, taking to heart his insistence on the fallacy of composition in private and public accounting, and by Allyn Young at Harvard who steered me into monetary theory and whose writings, while few, are still seminal and can be read with great profit today. So the reader of this book will find this mixture of theoretical training and experience in advice-giving reflected in my general appraisal of advice.

At the beginning and throughout my career, I taught economics at various universities and published a good deal, in this way charging and recharging my intellectual batteries. Almost equally valuable for the work of advising were the interludes of business and farming experience. When, in the course of this book, I write of agricultural policy in less developed countries (LDCs), I am able to draw not only on the literature and the advice given but also on my own first-hand experience as a dairy farmer in a developing country over a ten-year period.

However, this book is neither a history nor an autobiography. The basic motivation and objective is to appraise the enormous outpouring of advice from many different sources and in many different forms, and attempt to derive some generalizations therefrom. On a few occasions, I have injected a more personal note. Policy decisions are obviously made by individuals as we know them. Interpersonal relations, conflicts, motivations, personal and frequently unconscious, all must aid or contend with logic and the public weal. Yet, in official histories of economic policy decisions, this complex interplay is apt to be simplified and deemphasized, and the decisions take on an appearance of inevitability—the outcome of logical reasoning that certainly was not apparent to the actors involved. I have tried to take account of the silent and deep-rooted operation of economic forces as well as the elements of chance and the role of particular individuals and pressure groups at particular times. Economic theory deals with economic behavior in the mass; economic policy, and its accompanying advice, must necessarily deal with and be influenced by particular individuals, groups, and cultural characteristics of nations. In short, I have tried to strike a balance between the general and the particular and between personal and societal interests.

The book, I fear, is rather critical in tone. I regret this fact, but actually, in view of the record of lost opportunities of the past thirty years, it is difficult not to be critical. Moreover, since the motivation of the work was to improve advice and to accelerate, if possible, the process of development, naturally the bias had to be on the critical side. I hasten to add that the appraisal would have been much less critical if the treatment had been confined to individual projects. If any reader feels that my critical sense weakens when I treat of my own work, let me add that I may hold the world's record for the number of recommendations rejected. The *coups* and *tours de force* I mention have been the exception rather than the rule.

The giving (and seeking) of economic advice to and by lesser developed countries are important parts of the general process of transferring technology. My final very general conclusion to the effect that the transfer and adaptation of this particular type of technology can proceed no faster than the rise in the general level of administration, competence, knowledge, and good-will, while it is a bit sober, is fortunately subject to some qualifications. It is also my belief that under favorable circumstances and assuming the right kind of advice, progress can be accelerated, and it is this possibility that creates the eternal hope and excitement for the practitioners of the art. This is one reason why this work includes a discussion on learning from the experience of other countries.

Advisers nevertheless face many frustrations and must generally accept the fact that recognition and credit generally go to the formulators of policy, who bear the responsibility, rather than to the advisers. Advisers are expected to maintain a low profile. They are expendable, the turnover is rapid, and they are often blamed for the miscarriage of advice. This is an unavoidable occupational hazard for those who advise directly rather than through the channels of international organizations or in scholarly journals and in teaching. But this latter channel is a bit remote from the rapid events on the firing line of policy formulation. It is an exacting profession since it requires not only the intellectual equipment of a good economist but also almost indefinable elements of judgment and idealism on what is or can be made acceptable, desirable, and feasible. To recommend only what is acceptable is to be sterile; to attempt too much is to lead a short and not even a merry life. Drawing the line is difficult. In my own case, I have probably erred on the side of pushing too hard too rapidly, and I sometimes think I might have had more impact if I had not aroused so much heated opposition. But another general conclusion I think a reader of this book cannot escape is that to bring about a significant change in national policies and institutions is no small task.

Lauchlin Currie
Bogotá, Colombia
February 1981

PART 1
THE PROBLEM AND ITS SETTING

1
AN APPRAISAL
OF ECONOMIC ADVICE
TO DEVELOPING COUNTRIES

Although the giving of advice must have a history as long as the making of decisions, only in recent times has it mushroomed into a major, full-time activity. This is especially true in regard to giving economic advice.[1] Since 1950, there have been literally thousands of missions, teams, individuals, analyses, and position papers of multilateral agencies concerned with the study of less developed countries (LDCs). Behind or accompanying these have been billions of dollars of "aid." Accompanying aid, in turn, has been the training of hundreds of thousands of students, abroad and in their own countries, in advanced economics courses. Although they frequently act anonymously, "advisers" attached to international, bilateral, or national institutions have played a most important role, laying down conditions to be accepted and followed if loans or other forms of assistance are to be granted. Then there have been the books, articles in the thousands, conferences, and international meetings, addressed to both the practical and theoretical aspects of helping the developing countries develop faster.

Despite, or perhaps because of, the length of time spent giving economic advice and the number of people involved, there is no agreement on the nature of the problem of development and its solution. The diagnoses and prescriptions differ widely, rather more than less as time has passed, and there have been few attempts to appraise the overall effort. There is, however, a growing general dissatisfaction with the results attained to date. There is hardly an international conference in which this dissatisfaction, and even resentment, are not voiced by representatives of LDCs, evoking irritation and, at times, guilty consciences on the part of spokesmen for more developed countries.

Despite the considerable disagreement on policy, during the 1950s and early 1960s, there was general agreement on a loose definition of "development" in terms of the growth targets set in the First Decade of Development and in the Alliance for Progress (5.5 percent rate of growth in gross national product and 2.5 percent per capita). In the late 1960s, attitudes changed. Thereby growth targets were no longer satisfactory to the LDCs, and assertions were frequently made—and not often challenged—that despite statistical growth, distribution was worsening, with most or all gains going to a small minority. In 1970, Robert Asher wrote that "dissatisfaction, disenchantment and xenophobia are rampant."[2] The chorus swelled in numerous world conferences, finding expression in impassioned speeches, ringing denunciations, and demands for a New International Economic Order.[3]

Virtually all organizations engaged in international and bilateral lending and aid subscribed to the new view. The Pearson Report, funded by the World Bank, called for greatly increased contributions from the more developed countries.[4] The International Labor Organization (ILO) initiated a World Employment Program and organized five large country missions, each of which issued a report stressing a lack of progress and urging a change of emphasis from growth to distribution.[5] The recommendations of another group, the Rio Project (Reshaping the International Order), cover a vast field and propose a number of drastic changes in the international economic order (for example, a World Treasury financed by world taxes and the world community's ownership of natural resources).[6] Perhaps the most influential supporter of the new emphasis on distribution was Robert McNamara, president of the World Bank.

At least some of this dissatisfaction may be discounted. As John White has ably argued, all aid agencies whose existence depends on appropriations have an obvious interest in presenting the need for more funds in urgent terms.[7] The interest of lending agencies in making loans is likewise obvious. Politicians in developing countries and delegates from such countries to international meetings served their own self-interest when they stressed the harsh contrasts between life in lesser and more developed countries.[8]

Economic advice-giving is a field in which normative considerations naturally influence thinking. Extreme contrasts of wealth and poverty are repugnant, and hunger and privation excite compassion. There is a tendency to concentrate on and generalize from the hardest cases and to dismiss the success stories as atypical and hence irrelevant, or to attribute the success solely to the large amount of foreign capital. There is also a tendency to insist that countries with highly skewed income distributions should be denied aid. When dealing with countries other than their own, many liberals become radicals and make proposals—such as the expropriation (if necessary without compensation) and redistribution of land—that would never be made for more developed countries.

A statistical anomaly also contributes to the overstatement of the problem. Comparisons of both absolute levels of income and growth in income are customarily made in terms of U.S. dollars at current rates of exchange. But in terms of real purchasing power—command over calories, warmth, clothing, shelter, and services—this comparative measure exaggerates the gap. As early as 1968, Everett Hagen proposed that a multiplier of 3 be applied to the product figure of countries with per capita incomes of between US$0-125 and a progressively smaller multiplier be used until per capita incomes of $1,500 are attained.[9] Hagen's multiplier calls attention to the fact that the greater the apparent difference in income, the greater the statistical exaggeration of the difference. A corollary, however, is that equal rates of growth of poor and rich countries probably overstate the rate of growth of the poor country in terms of buying power for goods and services.[10] In short, the gap between richer and poorer countries, while often large, is less than appears when current quantitative measurements are used, though not in terms of rates and growth.

Still, the gaps in production and consumption per capita are high and in some cases growing, as demonstrated by physical consumption per capita of energy, water, metals, and even space. Even more sobering is the virtual certainty that per capita levels will continue to rise in the advanced industrial countries, such as their making up the Organization for Economic Cooperation and Development (OECD), while most LDCs must contend with a further large growth in population. Even with the revised calculations, Kravis, Heston, and Summers conclude that "the least productive half of the people produce only 12% of world output" (other than centrally planned economies) and that the average real per capita gross domestic product (GDP) of the more developed countries (MDCs) is 6.4 times that of the LDCs.[11]

Insofar as many mistakes are being made and better policies could be adopted, dissatisfaction with the results of economic advice-giving is to the good. Unfortunately, however, disputes over advice have confused the issue and diffused the objectives, with a consequent lessening of the contribution that economics could make. A comparison of the recent literature on development with the literature related to the economic problems of the more developed countries reveals to what extent normative attitudes have influenced economic thinking on development. There appears to be a tacit agreement that much of current economic analysis is inapplicable to developing countries. In part, it is this widespread feeling that accounts for the wide disparity and disagreement in policies recommended by economists to the governments of LDCs. It is the bias of this book that the tools of economic analysis and the corpus of relevant economic theory are applicable to developed and developing countries alike.

The record of the past thirty years has been unsatisfactory on the whole. We should be able to do much better, to improve our understanding of the nature of the problem, to better diagnose its causes, and to arrive at a closer agreement on the appropriate solutions or policies to be followed. A desirable step in this direction would be an objective appraisal of the past and current economic advice tendered LDCs.

Such an appraisal should take precedence over continued data gathering, refinement, and analysis in the form of pilot studies, demonstration projects, and proposals for a vast "direct attack on poverty." Enough data have been accumulated already, and sufficient explanations and solutions proposed, to make it highly unlikely that startling new facts or theories will be brought to light by further missions, studies, and conferences. What is necessary is a careful analysis of what we know and what has been proposed. The goal should be a greater consensus on appropriate objectives and policies.

2
BASES FOR
APPRAISAL OF ADVICE

To evaluate the appropriateness of economic advice and the success or failure of economic policies, we must have in mind specific objectives. Determining how worthwhile the objectives of policy are and the relative priorities to be given different objectives is as important as the appropriateness of the policies recommended for their attainment. It is precisely in this field, however, that serious differences have arisen that are the source of much of the disarray in advice-giving.

We can all agree that "development" is desirable. The difficulty is that there is considerable disagreement on what constitutes development. Growth? In per capita or gross or net income? How much and how fast? Distribution? If so, of income or of consumption? Is a lessening of differences in consumption more desirable than greater equality of income? Should we aim first at satisfying basic human needs? What *are* basic human needs? Can we meet them by leveling up rather than leveling down? Should a distinction be made between "absolute" or "critical" poverty and relative poverty? Or should the objective be a lessening of the differences in per capita income between countries?

Obviously, there is room for much difference of opinion here. But this listing by no means exhausts the issues. What weight should be given to price stability or avoidance or lessening of inflation? If avoidance of some rise in the cost of living is incompatible with full employment and/or more rapid growth, at what point should the tradeoff be made? It is easy enough to be in favor of growth, of employment, of efficiency, of equality, of stability, of lessening gaps and differences of a sectoral, regional, or international nature, of well-being, of balance, of integration, and of consistency, but such a diffusion of objectives can only result in no objectives or, more accurately, in forced compromises that leave nobody satisfied. The necessity of establishing priorities appears unavoidable, and consciously setting the priorities is obviously preferable. Some of the objectives may be compatible, but others are incompatible, and the simultaneous pursuit of incompatible objectives can be self-defeating and lead either to a frustrating paralysis or to highly disruptive conflicts.

A very different objective, rarely listed as such, is the furthering of the careers of particular leaders in particular posts. It can be decisive in the acceptance or rejection of advice. The first problem, then, is to find a basic definition of development.

Until fairly recently, the term "development" was used interchangeably with "growth," especially with regard to per capita income. There were, however, awkward exceptions to this general practice. For a considerable period, Argentina, with a relatively high income per capita but torn by internal strife, was still considered a less developed country, while there was no hestitation in including Japan in the more developed category, even when its income per capita was below that of the Argentine. More recently, some of the oil-rich countries have been included. Evidently, a high income per capita was a necessary but not sufficient condition to merit the accolade of development, making it apparent that the classification rested also on a qualitative distinction. The distinction turned on whether or not the countries in question evidenced a relatively greater degree of dominance over the economic, political, and social environment, so that they were able to deal with new problems more or less satisfactorily as they arose. I shall, therefore, mean by "development": the ability to manage, control, or dominate the environment.[1]

Objectives and Criteria of Development

There has been some tendency in recent years to rank countries in terms of distribution of income. The data on income distribution, however, especially in LDCs, are of very doubtful reliability, and very different results can be obtained by varying the percentages of the population at the top and the bottom of the income scale or by the appearance of a few very rich individuals. The fact that virtually all of what are generally listed as more developed countries (with higher growth rates) enjoy a higher degree of equality than do LDCs suggests that high growth rates facilitate progress toward greater equality, probably because it is easier to redistribute the benefits of growth than it is to redistribute existing wealth, and better tax administration generally accompanies and characterizes more developed countries. The most that can be said, therefore, is that greater equality should constitute one of the objectives of policy for LDCs insofar as it can be obtained without excessive retardation in the rate of growth.

This observation should not be interpreted as suggesting that nothing need be done to assure better distribution. While powerful economic forces are at work to bring about greater equality in incomes from work (competition, mobility, universal and obligatory education), this is not so evident in incomes from ownership, and positive intervention by the state is essential. (This is particularly the case with the ownership of land, especially urban and suburban land.) But intervention is easier and is likely to be more effective the more rapid the rate of growth.

It may be noted in passing that more equitable distribution as an objective overlaps that of greater price stability, since instability or inflation gives rise to wide changes in relative incomes. Savers as a class receive a negative rate of return, and borrowers as a class obtain a windfall gain in negative rates of interest, when adjustment is made for the fall in the purchasing power of money. Some groups, especially organized labor, are able to defend and increase their real income, but others experience great difficulty in securing adequate adjustments. The gains and losses are arbitrary and occur quite independently of conscious policy to secure better distribution. The benefits of a "direct" attack on distribution may be completely nullified by the inequities created by a failure to attain greater stability—an important element in the "indirect" approach to distribution.

Recently, there has been increasing emphasis, as a policy objective, on meeting the basic human needs of a community. Jacob

Viner was an early advocate of this view,[2] and I also proposed in 1961 and 1966 that the improvement in the lot of the lower 50 percent of income groups be the primary objective of policy.[3] It is now proposed that this objective can be attained most effectively by making the absolute poor a target group to be aided by *direct* action rather than by the more indirect action of economic forces and transfer payments. A new twist on aiding the poor introduces a new criterion of policy. A direct attack on poverty may well be self-defeating if it results in a decline in growth. Examples that come to mind are rent controls that lead to a decline in building; fixing the prices of necessities below the cost of production, which dries up output; and encouraging auto-construction (self-built) shanty towns in the peripheries of large cities, which results in an unsatisfactory and, in the longer run, costlier urban design. The list could be indefinitely extended.

Another worthy objective is providing more and better remunerated employment, the achievement of which would both promote growth and ensure better distribution. Like the objective of meeting "basic human needs," however, this goal when approached directly is in danger of becoming identified with the creation of employment for its own sake, with the retention of more people in rural areas than is economically necessary, and with the promotion of labor-intensive methods of production.

Finally, a widely held objective is to accelerate growth, not so much as an end in itself, but as a means of lessening the gap in per capita income between the more and less developed countries, so that more countries may be able to make the transition to the more developed category. This certainly is possible and desirable for some countries, especially in Latin America, but since the more developed countries are also growing, the attainment of the objective would require a great effort and the achievement of much higher growth rates (and decline in rates of population increase) than has occurred in most countries in the past few decades. It runs counter to the current tendency to disparage growth as a strategy.

Implicit in these various objectives is a growth in welfare and/or a lessening of "illfare." But there is much less assurance now than a few years ago that after a certain degree of affluence has been attained, there exists any close correlation of well-being with continued growth. The fact, and it is a fact, that most people would like to have an increase in income does not necessarily mean that when the increase is attained they are any happier for it. After basic human needs are satisfied, the driving force underlying economic incentives to work, to save, and to improve is not so much the direct satisfaction that consumption can yield as it is anticipated satisfaction of *social* wants—the desire to be respected or to gain status and not to fall behind in the eyes of others. Societies in which an individual's worth is linked with a growing income may be said to be "growth bound" or, to use a less charged phrase, "growth conditioned." In such societies, a lack of growth can occasion much unhappiness and dissatisfaction.

To be sure, increases in goods and services may not yield additional satisfaction. But that may be beside the point. The important thing in growth-conditioned societies is that people think it will. The deprivation effect that remains after incomes and salaries increase does not diminish the desire ("compulsion" is hardly too strong a term) to seek still higher incomes. Growth facilitates steady advances in real income, better employment opportunities, more openings for those joining the labor force, and the possibility of more frequent promotions. Thus, any government that attempts to lessen inequality at the expense of growth will quickly lose popularity, because of the recession and unemployment involved.

Fortunately, growth and better distribution need not be in conflict. The history of the currently more developed countries suggests that it is possible to pursue both objectives simultaneously and successfully, although if the absolute poor are very much in the minority and are diffused, they may not possess sufficient political power to win attention, and their aspirations may run counter to those of the more numerous and better organized employed.[4] That political and economic difficulties exist is implied by the statement that, as of 1969, it would have required only some $10 billion a year in the United States to raise all persons above the statistical poverty line.[5]

It will be noted that I have refrained from making the distinction that more and less developed economies depend on welfare, well-being, or degree of happiness, even though well-being is presumably the underlying objective of economic, political, and social systems. We may be reasonably sure that a sick or a (chronically) hungry person does not possess well-being, but paradoxically, we cannot affirm that a healthy and well-fed person possesses it. One of the main reasons for a lack of consensus among economists is this qualitative factor. We can secure a large measure of consensus on what constitutes efficiency and even, though less, on how to be more efficient. But not on how to be happier. Beyond the "pain economy," we should recognize that economists have no particular competency in matters of well-being, which is a subject whose study must be shared with other disciplines.

We do not need to aim for psychic well-being to justify accelerating the process of transformation from less to more developed societies. Welfare may be the ultimate aim of development, but it may be prudent to place initial emphasis on something much more fundamental, which is survival in the modern world. There can be no turning back to a subsistence, do-it-yourself society; the numbers are vastly greater and new wants have been created. The task now is to learn to resolve the problems that science and technology have created, and to aim for better control and greater dominance over the political, social, economic, and demographic environment. If we stress, therefore, a criterion on which we can speak with most competence—that of efficiency—and combine it with better distribution, we may be making a more useful contribution than by seeking to encompass the fields of all the social sciences.

A corollary of this discussion is the conclusion stressed by many writers that development is a process rather than a state. There is no country that can claim to be fully developed in the sense of a complete and rational dominance over its environment in all its aspects. I have elsewhere argued[6] that existing economic motivations in non-pain economies do not satisfy the social needs of man and that some of us should now be thinking of a state of noneconomic motivations and the painful transition that an eventual steady economic state implies. But this is for the future. Meanwhile, and especially for LDCs, rapid growth is necessary or at least desirable to attain a *more* developed status and a sense of going places and doing things. The fact that there are probably many unhappy people and much frustration in Scandinavian countries does not make them any less desirable intermediate models for

LDCs. If we are eventually to substitute noneconomic for economic motivations, the lead must probably be taken by "welfare states" rather than by the LDCs.

Conclusions on Objectives

Enough has been said here to indicate the grounds for choosing as objectives in developing countries the attainment of high rates of growth, the relief or abolition of "absolute" poverty (basic human needs), and the lessening of inequality in ways that are compatible with high rates of growth, such as fuller and more productive employment through greater mobility under conditions of relative price stability. These objectives, then, can in turn be adopted as some of the criteria to be used in evaluating the work of advisers.

There will be many occasions to call attention to the pursuit of incompatible objectives or, more generally, to the use of incompatible policies to achieve objectives that might otherwise be reconciled and be pursued simultaneously. In other words, and in some cases, the incompatibility may inhere in the means proposed rather than in the ends. In treating lessons from success stories, I shall have occasion to stress the striking results in some countries of a strong dedication to the single objective of high and sustained growth.

This stress should not be interpreted as meaning that the goal of policy should be any specific rate in the growth of the GNP. While the overall objective should be strong growth, the emphasis and short-term criteria can be sectoral, in securing a fuller mobilization of resources under conditions of price stability and in the advocacy of policies that favor economic growth. Relationships are not so constant and unchanging, however, as to admit of fine tuning in precise quantitative terms. The same is true of measures to ensure that a substantial part of the fruits of growth flow through to the poorer sections of the community. Advice to policymakers should be more concerned with the tendency or direction of movement. Relationships between variables change, what is feasible changes, time is always pressing, and opportunities must be seized as presented.

In other words, the actual and precise rate of growth is not a target in itself but is a result of other policies designed to secure bet-

ter and fuller utilization of resources and greater mobility. The
Japanese, for example, continually exceeded the growth targets of
their yearly plans and simply kept revising the plans and the targets. Similarly, Colombia's Plan of the Four Strategies for 1971-
1974 emphasized the importance of growth but avoided specific
targets. (See Chapter 4.) In answer to the queries, how much?
and how long? the answer given was for as much as is feasible
and for as long as wide gaps persist.[7] This formula avoided placing
sole reliance on a constant capital/output ratio and allowed for
greater flexibility in overcoming bottlenecks and in adopting
policies to changing conditions. What is sacrificed in apparent rigor
and precision will be more than compensated by the gain in realism
and feasibility.

For recommendations bearing more directly on allocation of
resources, especially specific projects, the criterion of cost-benefit
analysis is now generally followed. In cases of commercial investment or public works by public bodies, however, decisions often
turn on noneconomic considerations, such as providing employment in a depressed area. Judgment must be exercised on whether
the proposed project is sufficiently important to be made an issue.
The economist must be especially concerned with opportunity cost
and with the type of financing proposed.[8]

There is a large and growing literature on financial and technical
assistance, on what constitutes "assistance," and on what is the
precise relation of financial aid to development. Again, there is a
lack of consensus that is particularly awkward for the theme of the
present study, for "advice" is so closely linked to both technical and
financial assistance. Much of what is called aid consists simply of
loans at interest rates and maturities that are a little lower and
somewhat longer than the commercial market or suppliers can offer
because of the more favorable terms multilateral and bilateral agencies can secure. Are the beneficent effects of official aid and the
dangerous consequences of private borrowing matters solely of
these differences in terms? Or is the difference to be found in the
selection of projects to be financed and the general nonfinancial
terms laid down by the lenders? Since the differences in the financial terms of "hard loans" are not so great, presumably the reason
that official lending is presumed to be beneficent, and private lend-

ing suspect, is that the aid agencies either know better or are in a position to be more objective in the matter of allocation of resources and the safe limits on borrowing capacity than are national governments.

Until at least fairly recently, the criterion of success in aid-giving was economic growth, particularly if it appeared to be self-sustaining, and the quantity of aid was linked directly to the amount of growth. Thus, the Pearson Report leaned heavily on the necessity of more aid to increase growth and lessen the "gap." Similarly, Robert Asher, writing at the same time, affirmed that "virtually all the success stories in foreign aid—success in the limited, previously discussed, sense of raising per capita income and improved capacity to import, are stories of generous amounts of assistance."[9] This point of view rested in the final analysis on the exchange constraint argument and was challenged on these grounds by P. T. Bauer and B. S. Yamey, T. J. Byres, Keith Griffin, Harry Johnson, and Michael Lipton.[10] The criticisms covered a wide field, but there appears to be a consensus that the dependence of growth on a greater abundance of foreign exchange had not been established. Nevertheless, the "official" view prevailed, and per capita growth targets were moved up to 3-4 percent per annum, which in turn provided criteria for increased foreign aid.

In the meantime, objectives had shifted to giving priority to meeting directly the basic needs of the absolute poor. This presented economic advisers with a problem, as the basic needs of the very poor are very large, and the lending agencies could not very well be converted into purely philanthropic organizations. One solution was to keep the per capita growth target and add onto it an additional sum,[11] which called for much higher aid requirements (around $30 billion annually by 1980).[12] Hence, the new objective weakened the previous arguments for aid (growth) but increased requirements.

Something about Colombia

Although the major emphasis in what follows will be on cases and lessons applicable to less developed countries in general, there are many specific references to advice-giving in Colombia. With its close neighbor, Venezuela, Colombia lies in the extreme north of the South American continent but fronts on both the Atlantic (Caribbean) and Pacific oceans and is traversed by three north-south ranges of the Andes. The population is young, having increased rapidly from 11 million in 1951 to an estimated 25 million or so in 1978 (the last census was in 1973). Since 1964, and correlated with the growth in urban population and size of cities, there has been a marked fall in the birth rate, so that the rate of increase in population slowed from 3.2 percent per annum to around 2.0 percent in 1979. The accompanying major transformation from a rural, agricultural society to an urban, industrialized one has been proceeding with the rural percentage falling from 61 percent in 1951 to 39 percent in 1964. (It is still lower today.)

In these major transformations, with accompanying changes in education, income, and cultural characteristics, Colombia has been following a well-marked pattern of development. The unusual abundance of smaller cities, often thought to be an advantage, is probably the result of the extremely difficult terrain which, until the 1950s, gave a large measure of protection to local industries. Following the great transport revolution of the 1950s-1960s, with the economies of scale thus made possible, growth assumed the more customary pattern of greater concentration in some six cities.

Colombia has maintained a federal and democratic form of government modeled on the American separation of powers. But "states of emergency" and the invocation of martial law are the rule rather than the exception, and the states and municipalities, with their appointed governors and mayors, exercise little independent authority. Hence, the descriptive term "federal" may be a bit misleading. During the period under discussion (1950-1978), there was a period of military dictatorship (1953–1957) followed by a caretaker government of the armed forces (1957). This administration turned the government back to the civilians in 1958, with an agreement under which the two major parties were to participate in the government for a period of sixteen years, with the presidency alternating between the two parties every four years. The arrangement tended to lessen differences, and the participation persisted even after the legal alternation of presidents ceased in 1978.

Even so, economic policies were subject to considerable and

abrupt changes with changes in administration. The early years of the period corresponded with widespread violence in rural regions, and the great eastern plains in particular were roamed by armed bands who pillaged and burned and brought economic life to a standstill.

Colombia has an abundance of agricultural lands and climates. The great resources of hydroelectric power arising from the combination of heavy rains and mountainous terrain compensate for the high transport costs caused by this same terrain and in part for the recent insufficiency of petroleum resources, as do offshore discoveries of large natural gas reserves. Coal deposits appear to be large. In coming years, the place of coffee in exports will probably be increasingly assumed by manufactured exports, other agricultural produce, coal, nickel, and phosphates. The country on the whole has abundant natural resources; a modern manufacturing, agricultural, construction, and transport base; and well-trained cadres of professionals in all fields. The constraints on growth appear to be due not to lack of potential, therefore, but to inadequate exploitation of resources. In this respect, Colombia appears to resemble many other less developed countries.

Since its choice as the first country to be studied by a full-dress mission of the World Bank in 1949, Colombia has been considered representative of countries in its general per capita income group and has been a favorite of loan and assistance agencies and the scene of many trials and experiments.

The rate of growth of the GDP, ranging by periods between 4 and 7 percent per annum, would generally be considered satisfactory (Table 1). In a later chapter, I shall have occasion to delve a little more deeply into the significance of the persistence of growth despite periods of violence, military dictatorship, chronic and growing inflation, abrupt changes in plans and policies, massive devaluations, and a chronically overvalued currency for all exports except coffee.

Table 2, relating to estimated GDP per capita in recent years, brings out clearly the powerful impact of the birth rate and productivity on trends in per capita income. The notable increase in per capita income in the period 1970-1974 was the combined result of higher productivity, more workers, and fewer dependents. Note,

Table 1
GDP GEOMETRIC ANNUAL RATES OF GROWTH
(Percentage)

Sector	1950-1953	1953-1957	1958-1962	1962-1966	1966-1970	1970-1974	1975-1977
1. Agriculture	2.72	3.59	3.06	2.35	4.85	4.70	3.2
1. Fishing	3.97	14.10	20.80	4.42	14.08	1.19	9.7
3. Forestry	6.11	8.34	2.93	2.41	4.71	7.68	6.5
4. Mining	5.40	4.44	2.89	5.90	3.04	0.08	4.7
5. Manufacturing	6.41	6.98	6.83	5.50	6.33	8.01	4.9
6. Construction	8.44	8.22	6.16	2.31	10.93	5.68	3.8
7. Commerce	7.21	1.78	6.66	5.78	5.57	6.92	4.8
8. Transport	10.70	4.87	8.16	5.34	5.99	7.45	6.9
9. Communication	9.57	9.80	10.57	9.91	9.26	13.99	11.3
10. Elect., W. Gas	9.34	9.89	13.33	6.78	9.72	9.79	6.6
11. Banking	8.49	6.53	16.12	6.81	9.41	12.57	12.2
12. Rents	2.21	5.14	10.04	7.32	6.05	6.22	6.3
13. Other services	3.18	4.58	3.89	4.76	5.48	6.90	6.4
14. Government	9.10	1.00	5.31	5.31	5.09	6.75	2.7
Total (overall rate)	5.16	4.26	5.49	4.60	5.85	6.65	4.6

Source: Banco de la República.

Table 2
GROWTH IN POPULATION, GDP, AND PER
CAPITA INCOME
COLOMBIA, 1971–1977

	1971	1972	1973	1974	1975	1976	1977
GDP	5.8	7.8	7.1	6.0	3.8	4.6	4.8
Population	2.5	2.4	2.3	2.3	2.2	2.1	2.0
Per Capita Income	3.3	5.4	4.8	3.7	1.6	2.5	2.8

Source: Banco de la República; Departamento Nacional de Planeación.

however, the much lower rate of growth in income per capita in the period 1974-1977, despite the estimated continued fall in the rate of population increase.

The almost stationary rural population and the rapid and substantial decline in the proportion it formed of the total population, together with more or less constant agricultural-nonagricultural terms of trade and increasing agricultural exports, indicate a great growth in productivity in agriculture that permitted the release of manpower for the production of other things. This was not, as is often stated, offset by growing urban unemployment or disguised unemployment. The same proportion of the urban work force was working after the great urban growth up to 1973 as twenty-five years previously. In this development, Colombia is again believed to be typical, at least of LDCs in Latin America.

Despite the progress made in many fields, and the speed with which the society was being transformed, the bulk of Colombia's population appeared to remain dissatisfied. Distribution remained highly skewed; inflation, with its arbitrary distribution of gains and losses, grew beyond control (Table 3); personal and property security diminished; tax evasion increased, along with law enforcement in general; and the growing of narcotics for export tended to corrupt the public service that was touched by this traffic. There was little pride of achievement, as well as much cynicism and political apathy (with, however, a growth in nationalism as distinguished from patriotism). Foreign investment, in the mid-1970s, was tolerated rather than actively sought. In many of these negative findings, Colombia is likewise believed to be typical of many developing countries.

Table 3
INFLATION IN COLOMBIA, 1971-1978

(Percentage Rise in National Index of Prices)

1971	1972	1973	1974	1975	1976	1977	1978
12.4	14.1	22.1	25.2	17.5	25.4	27.5	19.7

Source: Departamento Administrativo Nacional de Estadística (DANE), Monthly Bulletins.

PART 2
MACROECONOMIC ADVICE

3
ADVICE ON GROWTH AND DEVELOPMENT

The theory of growth subscribed to by the person or organization offering advice often is the foundation for the advice given to developing countries on the general subject of growth. This is more often implicit than explicit, one of those things assumed to be so self-evident as not to require specific treatment. Yet, much of the divergence in macroeconomic advice is traceable to profound theoretical differences. It appears expedient, therefore, to begin my treatment of macroeconomic advice by outlining briefly the several theories of the nature of the growth process and to follow them with a discussion of my own orientation.

Following this introduction, I propose to examine critically the various explanations given for unsatisfactory growth rates and the advice that has been offered to LDCs, elaborating on both the more and the less sophisticated views mentioned earlier.

The Nature of Economic Growth

The recognition that growth is closely related to efficiency goes back to the origins of economic reasoning. It was Adam Smith who set forth the thesis that "the wealth of nations" (read "national income") is dependent upon specialization and division of labor; the extent to which it pays to specialize in production depends upon the size of the market. The greater the volume of sales (in physical terms), the more it pays to specialize.

Although this thesis became incorporated into economic theory, its full implications were not completely grasped until the twentieth century. Capital was treated as an exogenous variable, and inventions were seen as fortunate accidents. In 1928, Allyn Young updated the Smith thesis, expanding the "division of labor" to include the use of labor to produce capital goods and the specialization of operations by firms.[1] He combined Marshall's "external economies of scale" with internal economies arising from the growing volume of (physical) operations. The most profitable combination of factors became a function not only of the size of the market but also of the relative cost of the factors, the ideal being to make the lowest paid labor "scarce," increasing its value and encouraging the use of more machinery. Growth became demand-induced (by the market), either cumulative and progressive or self-perpetuating. The basic assumption to adopt for allocation and price theory was a chronic state of increasing returns. The trend would always be away from equilibrium (unchanging resources, production, and the state of the arts); with varying degrees of elasticity of supply and demand, growth must be unequal in different sectors.

In order to get to real processes behind the monetary veil, Young had assumed no interruption in the flow of money from production to demand. Unfortunately, his notable paper appeared just on the eve of the worst such interruption that the modern world had experienced, and this assumption became manifestly invalid during the Great Depression.

The possibility that investment opportunities (in money terms) would not be sufficient to provide outlets for the volume of saving (in money terms) at full employment became a cornerstone of Keynesian theorizing. An increase in production and employment was still demand-induced, but the demand became purely monetary instead of real. The Smith-Young thesis now appeared to be of only theoretical interest.

With the recovery of relatively full employment, interest in real phenomena revived, but instead of returning to the Smith-Young theory, economists concentrated on the classical and narrower relations of capital to output embodied in the new equations of Harrod and Domar (1944-1945). It was, I believe, Ragnar Nurske who first used this relationship to explain growth in developing countries.[2]

Nurske set forth two vicious circles besetting developing countries: one (demand) of poverty—small markets—low productivity—
poverty, the other (supply) of low savings—inadequate capital—
low productivity—small savings—inadequate capital. Most of his
book was devoted to an elaboration of the latter sequence. Writers
on development in the 1950s and 1960s followed Nurske's lead,
subscribing in one form or another to the capital gap and the
exchange gap; the explanation of underdevelopment became largely identified with the existence of these "constraints." The prevailing emphasis on the stimulation of exports was not so much to
encourage internal activity directly as to overcome the exchange
constraint.

Although there was almost universal agreement that savings
were scanty and capital formation inadequate, fewer efforts were
made to increase domestic savings—that was considered too difficult—than to better utilize existing savings. This led to a large
literature on the misallocation of savings due to various "distortions" arising from inequality in incomes, prices set below the
market, an overvalued rate of exchange, or the maintenance of low
interest rates.

The preoccupation with constraints and distortions tended to
give emphasis to elements on the supply side. The possibility of
inadequate demand was generally dismissed. As demand was identified with monetary demand, the existence of chronic inflation
appeared to indicate that demand was if anything excessive, and in
any case that the *wants* in developing countries were insatiable.

Until this point, I have been referring to what I might call the
more sophisticated theories on the nature of the growth process. A
less sophisticated view assumed that the mobility mechanism was
inoperative and that more remunerative work must be provided
people where they were and for what they were doing. This led to a
policy of dualism: agrarian reform in the countryside and, in the
cities, state intervention in industry, to promote labor-intensive
techniques.

It is interesting to note that both the more and the less sophisticated explanations of continued poverty, too slow growth
and open or disguised unemployment, assumed an inadequate
and/or misapplied stock of capital, little attention was devoted to

the possibility of increasing it except by foreign borrowing. The neoclassical equilibrium analyses on which policy was based took for granted an unchanging volume of capital and state of the arts, which, though a useful analytical device, is dangerously untrue. The major concern is growth per capita, which requires increased real output per worker as a result of greater efficiency. The benefits can be seen in increased output at lower real cost of particular articles and services if the price elasticity of demand for such articles is high, or, if the demand is relatively inelastic, in a release of manpower to make other things.

If the market is small or stationary, an increase in output per worker depends on the replacement of capacity by more efficient equipment and on finding ways of reducing costs. The *rate* of growth resulting from such types of improvement may be positive but low. A large, and especially a rapidly growing, market is required to expand capacity rapidly and to secure the internal and external economies of scale that result therefrom.[3] But this larger market must be in real or physical terms. The faster the growth in the market, the more it pays to be technical, to invest in research, and to increase the capital per worker. Generally, the higher the output per worker, the higher the remuneration per worker in real terms. The greater the mobility, the more uniform the rise in workers' incomes; it will pay to specialize in more and more sectors. As Young stated, the ideal is to make the least remunerative labor "scarce." Hence, the growth process contains within itself a tendency to equalize incomes from work. To this extent, it is a theory of distribution as well as a theory of production.

Little of the knowledge necessary to increase efficiency in developing countries is completely new. There is a vast reservoir of unutilized knowledge, little of which is privately owned and covered by patents. Most of it can be copied, or learned, or is incorporated in existing equipment. Costly research into new products and new ways of making things can for the most part be left to very large companies in the most technically advanced countries.

The question then becomes, why is more of the existing technical knowledge and equipment not taken over by developing countries? The main and all-embracing answer is a paradoxical "it does not pay." It does not pay because the domestic market is small or is not growing rapidly. It is difficult and often risky to break into the external market. For some countries, the benign circle of self-perpetuating growth is opposed by the vicious circle of self-perpetuating poverty.

It is at this point that I would differ with the many other macroeconomic advisers who, from varying viewpoints, all stress the role of capital. Those who stress constraints on output point to the inadequacy of capital formation. Those who stress the existence of distortions (especially of price) link such distortions to a poor use of inadequate capital. Still others find the explanation for unemployment in lack of capital to provide sufficient jobs. But the Smith-Young approach places the stress on markets or real demand. It tends to make the volume of savings and the use of capital more a consequence than a cause of growth.

The adequacy or inadequacy of capital is relative to the demand for it. The smaller or more stagnant the growth in the market, the less demand. The lower the wages, the less incentive to use capital. The more rapid the growth of the market, the more rapid can be the growth of income, saving, and consumption. The growth in consumption is a necessary condition (apart from import substitution) for the incentive to enlarge plant and capacity.

In short, the matter of emphasis on the constraints on the supply side or on inadequate size or rate of growth on the demand side is not a quibble over words. Thinking of supply and demand as just two blades of a pair of scissors is a misleading analogy for present purposes. The difference in emphasis will lead to widely differing advice in policy.

Two caveats are in order. The concept of demand relevant to the Smith-Young approach is real demand or output. This point must be emphasized for, since Keynes, the word "demand" has connoted purely monetary demand. The demand discussed here, especially for developing countries, is a money demand that arises from and is matched by an increase in real output. Demand arising from purely monetary causes will most likely quickly exhaust itself in higher prices and provide no stimulus to output and growth.

The second caveat is that stressing real demand for advising and policy purposes does not mean that there is not a need for increased savings, for increasing training, for greater mobility and competition, and for the correction of distortions that lead to a faulty use of productive resources. It is a matter of emphasis and of concentration of limited time, interest, and effort in the most strategic factors—the key logs in a log jam.

Growth may tend to be self-perpetuating but at a constant rate. To raise this rate requires concentration on sectors that are subject to exogenous stimuli, for whose products the demand is latent rather than actual, and that have a high income elasticity of demand to spur continued growth. The overall rate of growth is the sum of weighted sectoral rates, but these rates are influenced by the overall rates. The task is to break into this interacting circle to raise certain sectoral rates and in this way raise the overall rate. This differs from the more conventional concern embodied in the phrase "demand management," as, instead of relying on market forces in general, it is at pains to ensure that the increase in demand arises out of actual production.

In light of the foregoing analysis, the emphasis on exports and the frequent recurrence of export-led booms is more a case of utilizing a leading sector than of breaking exchange constraints. The real lesson which export-led booms should teach us is not that of pressing for more exports to secure imports, but rather the more comprehensive one of exploiting leading sectors in general.

Businessmen have long been keenly aware of the importance of markets. The concern with maintaining or increasing one's "share of the market" is not, as some academic writers appear to think, a mild manifestation of megalomania, but a policy with a sound economic base. A firm that can grow rapidly by enlarging its share of the market, particularly if the market itself is growing, can avail itself of many internal economies of scale. If it grows less rapidly than its competitors, it will find itself at a continually growing disadvantage. The more rapidly physical production grows, the more profitable becomes increased specialization and use of capital. Adam Smith would have no difficulty understanding such assertions.

Constraints on the Side of Supply

The widely held view that slow or stagnant growth is caused by constraints on production arising from inadequate capital formation is supported by the fact that capital, properly used, *does* make labor more productive. The less developed a country, the less, generally, is capital per worker; imports tend to equal exports, quantitative restrictions are imposed on the use of proceeds of exports, and a fairly constant relation exists between imports and the GNP. It appears reasonable, therefore, that increased capital, either from internal saving or from foreign earnings or borrowings, should increase output. The assumed relationship, calculated in countless models, offers the theoretical justification for increasing public investment, borrowing abroad, promoting exports to purchase more imports, and improving the allocation of scarce capital.

Despite this powerful case, doubts arise. The fact that production *could* be checked by the lack of some essential elements, such as energy in the form of petroleum products, does not mean that ordinarily it *is*. Other, less essential, things can be foregone. The relation between imports and the GDP has changed in various countries, as has the relation between savings, capital formation, and output, especially in terms of incremental changes. And the relationship varies in different countries. Statistically, the explanation proves too much. It can be used to explain a 2-percent, 5-percent, or 10-percent rate of growth.

The case is also open to theoretical criticism. It is forced to assume that all capital is equally fruitful in increasing production—that, for example, a road from nowhere to nowhere is as productive as a road between two large cities. It is forced to assume that there is effective demand for all uses of capital, intermediate goods, and raw materials held in check only by physical inability to increase productive capacity, and that this holds true at *all rates* of *growth*. Finally, it is forced to assume a distinction between current operating expenses and investment in public accounts that is extremely tenuous. A schoolhouse or a hospital is capital; a teacher's or a doctor's salary is a bureaucratic expense. And yet, such is the power of semantics that there exists a strong conviction that public investment should be increased while the bureaucracy should be cut.

Even more significant is the doubt, raised in the previous chapters, that capital, in a true sense of the term, is much more scarce in a developing than in a more developed country. In Colombia, it is true, successful private companies have refrained from expanding capacity in the face of increasing real demand, but this condition appears to be more a result of past experience of stop and go and uncertain prospects of sustained growth than of real inability to expand. There are constant complaints of lack of credit and of "asphyxiation," but these must be taken with a large grain of salt. In general, business finances its expansion and replacement out of internal cash flows, and the percentage of national gross saving in this form (around 11 percent) does not differ appreciably from the percentage in the United States. Much personal saving is also a semiautomatic function of income. Consequently, the more rapid the rate of growth, the higher, in absolute terms (and usually in relative terms), becomes the volume of savings available for capital formation. Interest rates, in real terms after allowance for the depreciation of the value of money, are a poor measure of the abundance or scarcity of capital equipment, and comparisons in absolute terms as between countries may only reflect differences in volume of output and techniques employed, and the techniques, as was argued earlier, depend in turn on the volume of production and the market. Current expenditures on manufacturing equipment represent an astonishingly small proportion of the GNP in the United States, for example, a country that uses what are generally considered to be highly capital-intensive methods. (See discussion below, pp. 35–37).

Opposed to these considerations are rather staggering estimates of the financing required for urban services, particularly hydroelectric power, which, it is held, can only be secured by borrowing. But this may simply reflect an inability to work out ways and means of channeling an excess favorable balance of payments into the financing of these particular requirements. From 1976 to 1979, while heavy foreign loans were being negotiated in Colombia, the international reserves of the central bank were increased from zero to US$4 billion. And, after all, loans must presumably be repaid from current earnings.

The argument is not that an exchange constraint cannot arise and cannot affect production, but that this is an insufficient explanation for actual past and current rates of growth in developing countries. The mere fact that some of these countries were able to attain and sustain rates of growth of 10 percent or more per annum without borrowing suggests that the constraint exercised by lack of capital is, in most cases, potential rather than actual. In short, the capital constraint explanation of underdevelopment is too easy. Its use generally leads to excessive reliance on borrowing. Even in cases where an exchange constraint appears to be imposing an actual impediment to increased production, this effect can be eased by varying the components of domestic investment from products with heavy import content to those with much less.[4]

Distortions

Closely allied to capital and exchange constraints as an explanation of underdevelopment or low rates of growth is the existence of a multitude of distortions (defined as resulting in a product mix smaller than and different from one that would prevail under perfectly functioning market forces). Generally, writers who stress constraints also stress distortions.

Again, the case is difficult to disprove, as unquestionably distortions do abound in developing countries. In Colombia, for many years, the exchange rate was overvalued and interest rates were maintained at levels too low to encourage personal savings, leading to excessive demand for loans. A favorite curative measure was the imposition of price controls of various sorts, almost always set at levels that failed to encourage production. Elitist groups of workers created variations in wage scales and costs that were different from what could have occurred with perfect mobility. The list is very long, and I have myself frequently criticized measures that create such distortions and have advised their removal or alleviation.

Nevertheless, the existence of distortions (which appear in abundance in highly developed countries as well) is inadequate as an explanation of underdevelopment. The term is too broad to be very useful. Inflation, for example, which results in so many distortions, can itself be caused by distortions arising from highly organized groups that force monetary expansion to prevent unemployment. Indeed, the looseness of the term can make it appear that the main characteristic of the lesser developed countries is the existence of too many and too serious distortions. If all are given equal importance and attempts are made to correct all these distortions, there is no possibility of being effective. To be effective, advice must be selective. Priorities must be established and followed.

The distortion explanation as a basis for advising corrective measures is therefore not so much invalid as, again, too easy and too nonselective. The existing obstacles to the development of leading sectors whose rapid growth can pull the whole economy up after them may be called distortions. But for the purposes of macroeconomic advice, it will be more effective to use different terminology and to be highly selective in treating the particular distortions that appear to be of key significance.

It should be noted, however, that not all interventions in the market create distortions. Some correct them, and the answer to others may depend on whether one adopts a short-term, static view or a longer-term, more dynamic view. For example, the maintenance of a fixed exchange rate when relative domestic costs of production are rising may create a serious distortion. Corrective intervention that departs from immediate comparative advantage in such a case would take the form of protectionism, or of subsidies to encourage exports. While open to obvious abuse, the careful use of these measures may be desirable to create a larger, more diversified market and to secure the economies of scale.

Capital and Employment

I turn now to the somewhat less sophisticated arguments that link the inadequacy of capital to the existence of unemployment and that tend to advise measures to restrain migration, to spread the work, and to promote less capital-intensive techniques. Rarely is the more obvious measure of increasing saving advocated, possibly because a measure of this type is believed to result in worse distribution. The same is true of foreign private investment, which, it is often held, is prejudicial to national interests.

The widespread belief that capital is necessary to set people to work appears to be based on the division of the capital of an industry or sector by the number of workers. The resulting figure is then stated to be the amount of capital necessary to provide employment; of course, the industries that utilize capital-intensive methods come out very badly in such a ranking.[5] The existence of a lump sum of capital is assumed; therefore, it follows that, if more is used in capital-intensive processes, there is less for labor-intensive processes, and employment suffers.

Frequently, "industry" is taken as synonymous with the nonagricultural sector in a simple two-sector model. The capital requirements to provide employment for the natural increase in the urban work force plus the migrants are then calculated. The resulting aggregate capital requirements are so high that it appears that there is not enough capital to provide for the addition to the work force. The conclusion follows that migration should be restrained and that the labor-intensive industries and the "informal sector" should be favored while the capital-intensive industries are discouraged. In this version, services are usually either ignored or dismissed as being so low paid as to constitute disguised unemployment.

The conclusion in effect calls for the substitution of less efficient for more efficient processes and a reduction in mobility. Yet, in order to accelerate the rate of growth, the very opposite policy should be pursued. Either something is wrong with the diagnosis, or LDCs must reconcile themselves to lower rates of growth in order to maintain full employment. A third possibility might be to increase capital by saving more or borrowing more from abroad (the two-gap model).

There also appears to be some lack of clarity in speaking of the process of "capital formation." Part of the difficulty arises from thinking of capital on the one hand as homogeneous and divisible and, on the other, as limited in supply or as a fixed lump sum. The combination of these largely implicit simplifications leads to the idea of "spreading" a limited "supply" of capital more or less evenly over a range of productive activities. But only capital in a strictly monetary sense is homogeneous. The act of capital formation, involving the current use of labor, organization, materials, and equipment created largely in the past, is specific, and in the very act of formation the new capital becomes indivisible. Moreover, the current supply of capital is not fixed but is the product of the use of the real resources currently devoted to capital formation. This product can be varied by varying the total of resources and the efficiency of their use. So capital is elastic in supply, depending on many factors that enter into the calculations of promoters and investors.

An objection will be raised to the effect that devoting more labor to making things means foregoing current consumption, i.e., saving, and the capacity of a poor economy to save is strictly limited. But this is inconsistent with the whole concept embodied in the use of the terms "unemployment" and "disguised unemployment." It is easy to see that self- or auto-construction of a house in one's "spare" time entails no decrease in consumption, although, by definition, the addition to capital (the house) is matched by increasing saving (since the house is not immediately "consumed" but is used only over a long period). By the same reasoning, putting virtually all the unemployed and underemployed to work building houses or public works of all kinds, so long as the lost production (presumably, and by definition, small) can be made up by the existing employed, can greatly increase capital formation (and saving) without decreasing consumption. If, for example, the modern sector of agriculture can in a single harvest season produce the agricultural goods formerly produced by a large number of traditional or subsistence farmers, no decline in consumption need occur. (Of course, if such farmers secure jobs in the formation of "capital," and, even more evidently, if the jobs they secure are to produce other consumer goods, consumption is even less likely to decline.)

It will probably be argued at this point that an agricultural "surplus" of "wage goods" must first be accumulated before workers can be withdrawn from agriculture, and the abstention of consumption of such a surplus constitutes an act of saving. This might be true if such a static, step-by-step approach were necessary in real life. In the actual world, a number of things can proceed simultaneously—decisions to invest, increasing agricultural productivity, additions to the work force, and so forth. The *prior* accumulation of capital, resulting from increased saving or abstention from current consumption, is not a necessary precondition of increasing employment.[6]

Labor is seldom paid wages in advance of production. A worker's current production adds to the stock of the employer, and when he is paid money wages, the employer simply exchanges one form of capital (money) for another form (increased inventories). In other words, wage payments do not deplete the existing stock of capital and do not require a prior accumulation of capital. If a prior accumulation of capital were required to employ labor, labor would never, since the beginning of time, have been able to work to produce capital. Similarly, if capital were the constraint on employment, we should expect the unemployment rate to be always higher in capital-poor than in capital-rich countries. No such neat correlation exists.

We may turn, then, to the next point in the alleged relation of capital to employment—the quantity of capital to provide one man-year of employment. This, again, appears to be a case of excessive simplification. If one adopts the view that generally the most efficient technique will be the criterion of investment, this will determine the factor proportions used, given interest costs, wage rates, and other factors that influence entrepreneurial judgments on what enters into and constitutes efficiency or least cost per unit. A further assumption is that the final composition of consumer demand will reflect varying degrees of income elasticity of demand and varying income distributions, and the size and growth of demand will determine the economies of scale and the extent to which specialization is economic. To meet this final demand most efficiently will call for different proportions of capital and labor in a large number of fields and, as explained above, the use of labor and equipment in the production of various kinds of goods and services, consumers' and producers', called the factor proportions mix.

At this point, it becomes important to pay attention to economic history and to current national accounts. In the period of growth in the United States most closely akin to current growth in developing countries, over half the new urban jobs created were in services.[7] From 1966 to 1976, the increase in nonagricultural employment in the United States was 15.1 million. Of this total, 0.4 million were in jobs in manufacturing, mining, construction, transportation, and public utilities; and 14.7 million were in services, wholesale and retail trade, financial insurance, real estate, and government.[8] Agricultural employment declined by 0.7 million. In other words, the great increase in employment occurred in the sectors utilizing the least capital. The United States, with a vast market and high wages, must be one of the most capital-intensive countries of the world. Yet, in 1976, the expenditures for producers' durable equipment, farm and nonfarm, but not including structures, were only 6.1 percent of the GNP (a little less than the figure for 1950, 6.9 percent).[9] The expenditures of manufacturing alone on durable equipment *and* plant amounted only to 1.6 percent of the GNP in 1974 and 1.4 percent in 1975 (so machinery alone would be even less).[10] In the totals entering into GNP in 1975 and 1976, the value of "services" exceeded that of "goods."[11]

Thus, on balance, the many hundreds of billions of dollars of investment from 1966 to 1976 in the United States in manufacturing, mining, construction, transport, and public utilities neither "created" jobs nor displaced workers. Clearly, one can have full employment with very little or no capital or with a great deal. The relation of capital to employment is very tenuous indeed.

Another statistic may be of interest in showing the danger of simplification in a dynamic society. From 1953 to 1964 in the United States, total gross nonfarm, nonresidential private capital expenditures amounted to $500 billion. Yet, employment in manufacturing, an important outlet for capital formation, actually declined. Very heavy capital formation did not provide a single additional job in manufacturing; yet, overall employment increased by 11 million at steadily rising real salaries and wages.[12] The ILO Report on Colombia states, however, that capital requirement figures "suggest that to create jobs in manufacturing costs 2 to 10 times as much as settling peasants on new farms."[13] The implication is that the correct policy is to increase the farm population. The basis of the fallacy is the implicit assumption of unchanging factor proportions and, even worse, unchanging composition of output, assumptions proven invalid over time.

Likewise, in the case of disguised unemployment, or labor whose product is worth very little, the issue is not the amount of capital used per worker, but the output per capita and the distribution of the output. To deliberately replace the investment criterion of efficiency or maximum returns by the criterion of providing more employment per unit of capital would be to reduce output per capita. But to bring about a shift of workers from low-paid to higher paying jobs in itself increases output per capita and assures better distribution. To forbid automatic elevators or to require manual operators in all automatically equipped elevators is too costly a form of redistribution of income, as it wastes the potential productive powers of able-bodied workers. (Attitudes are reflected in choice of words. People speak of the inability of cities to "absorb" labor, or of industry to "provide" jobs. We *should* be speaking of taking advantage of the latent productive capacity of human resources currently being wasted.) Policy should have as its objective making unskilled and low-paid labor so scarce that the value of its product rises to approximate the value of the product of currently higher paid labor, allowing it to share in the increased productivity made possible by capital formation, greater specialization, and economies of scale. The ideal is to facilitate mobility and not impede it.[14]

Inequality and Unemployment

Another source of confusion is the idea that inequality in distribution creates unemployment. Inequality can and does create contrasting patterns of consumption that can be extremely repugnant—luxurious homes and shacks, private cars and crowded buses, and so forth. But this is a question of equity and should be treated separately from employment, which depends on aggregate demand and not on the composition of demand.[15] Greater equality following on greater mobility (plus transfer payments) would certainly have the effect of changing the composition of final *consumption*. The fact of inequality in wages must be sharply distinguished, however, from a rise in wages in a particular firm or sector more rapid than productivity increases, so that costs (and prices) rise *before* there has been a growth in aggregate monetary demand. This rise does result in wage or cost-push inflation and unemployment. It is the rise *relative to productivity* rather than the fact of differences in wages that may cause unemployment or force expensive monetary policies.

Applicability of Argument to Countries in Different States of Development

Few economists would explain unemployment in more developed countries in terms of excessive use of capital-intensive techniques or advocate deliberate state intervention to change factor proportions to a more labor-intensive mix in such countries, except occasionally for specific groups of workers. The implication is that conditions are so different in LDCs that both different theories and different policies are called for.[16]

This implies, however, an *absolute* difference between the two groups of countries that does not exist. The difference is one of degree—the degree of poverty, productivity, or, in the distinction used here, the degree of domination of the environment. In LDCs, there may indeed be more very poor people in the countryside, or less mobility, or, in absolute terms, less capital per worker. But these differences of degree provide no basis for a different theory of employment or growth. In its simplest terms, poverty everywhere arises from low output per capita generally exacerbated by poor distribution. No policy that retards growth or that favors less efficient methods can provide the appropriate solution for it. We are brought back to the efficiency versus distribution issue; it would be difficult to make a convincing case that, in a mixed economy, absolute poverty can be relieved by no-growth but by better distribution forcibly obtained. Faced with this dilemma, some advocates have had to argue that better distribution, say of agricultural land, would also raise the rate of growth. But this in turn leads to the necessity of a whole package of measures and can only be sustained if unrealistic, or at least uncharacteristic, assumptions are made on income and price elasticity of demand for agricultural goods. (See detailed discussion of rural poverty in Chapter 9.)

Surely the validity of the concepts of efficiency, output per worker, mobility, and specialization all apply, regardless of the degree of poverty. Indeed, it would appear that the poorer the country, the more good economic theory can contribute, and the less justification there is for the perpetuation of economic fallacies.

Conclusion

The observant reader will probably have noted in this chapter, as well as elsewhere in the study, a certain "unsoundness" on my part on policies relating not only to encouragement of technology, but also to protection, import substitution, and trade according to comparative advantage. If so, I fear I must plead guilty to the extent that I believe that one's attitude on such policies must be influenced by dynamic, increasing returns and disequilibrium assumptions. There seems to be a need for a new "school" that will use cost-benefit analysis and comparative advantage, where appropriate, and dynamic increasing returns assumptions, where applicable, in an analysis that may not appear so "rigorous" but may prove to be appropriate for the attainment of certain objectives over time.

Much of the popular reasoning on "openness," free trade, comparative advantage, and market prices and forces is undoubtedly sound, given the underlying assumptions. What we question here are the validity and relevance of the assumptions. In Colombia, for example, the comparative advantage of coffee was so great that an absence of a differential rate of exchange, or a tax on coffee exports and a free rate of exchange that would have equilibrated imports and exports, would have resulted in conditions tending to discourage the development of other types of exports and to encourage the importation of goods that might otherwise have been produced in the country, which, from a dynamic point of view of the development process, would have been unfortunate.

Colombia has also recently become one of the world's leading exporters of flowers, that is, it possesses a comparative trade advantage in this field. Presumably, the advantage was present throughout the 1950s and 1960s, but it remained latent until the later years of the 1960s when exchange conditions and subsidies and knowledge and growth of the market combined to encourage the initial efforts, which entailed much risk and the overcoming of various technical obstacles. Thus, it is possible to support policies relying on both exogenous stimuli *and* market forces, depending on actual circumstances. Naturally, the argument for intitial protection applies to problems of infancy and not of senility, and export incentives are subject to abuse. In this field, generalizations must be accompanied by studies of specific measures and cases.

In short, as argued throughout, the distinction between more and less developed countries is a qualitative one of relative efficiency or control. As such, it may properly influence the choice of policies but not the validity of economic theory.

On the grounds of feasibility, as distinct from theory, the case against the conscious selection of labor-intensive techniques to promote employment—the less sophisticated advice that has frequently been urged—is also strong. With all its imperfections, it appears that the market generally offers safer criteria for the factor proportions mix than are available to or will be used by public employees. Even if by chance a better mix from the viewpoint of efficiency is set by public policy, the growth of the market and changes in factor prices will promptly call for modifications of the mix. And the less developed the economy, the less likely it is that public policy decisions will be based on considerations of efficiency.

In the case of the distortions arising from specific cases of price fixing, however, it appears more feasible to attempt to modify such cases to permit the market to determine a better mix (especially interest rates, exchange rates set below the market, rent controls, and so forth). In such cases, however, advice would be motivated by considerations of efficiency or growth per capita rather than employment per se.

4
COLOMBIA'S PLAN OF
THE FOUR STRATEGIES,
1971–1974

There were roughly three periods of fairly intense overall macro planning and advising in Colombia, and I played some part in each. The first was from 1949 to 1953; the second from 1960 to 1961; and the third started at the beginning of the 1970s. Since this work is in no sense a history, I am proposing to begin with a discussion of the third period, in which the Plan of the Four Strategies was adopted. This period illustrates perhaps better than the others the possible role of the planning agency in the field of macroeconomic policy and the theme of the preceding chapter.

I propose to preface the discussion of the adoption of the plan with some history that will supplement the theoretical treatment. This will furnish a necessary antidote to the impression of inevitability that the discussion of past events always seems to create and will illustrate the important role played by chance and personalities.

Naturally, I have a personal bias in favor of the plan—a bias, I hasten to add, not shared by all Colombians. Despite my bias, I hope I have drawn some general conclusions that will meet with approval and will illustrate the distinction between selectivity and comprehensiveness and their relation.

The Setting

Colombia had been growing in terms of per capita income since World War II, despite an initially appalling rate of population growth, a period of extreme political instability, and some serious mistakes in policy. The rates of growth, gross and per capita, from 1950 to 1972, were more or less in line with the targets set by the Alliance for Progress, 5 percent and 2.5 percent, respectively, with some tendency to accelerate after 1967. Three basic transformations in the development process were taking place—the country was passing from a predominantly rural to a predominantly urban composition, the birth and population rates of growth in the cities and hence in the country as a whole were beginning to fall, and exports were changing from a reliance on coffee to more diversification. These were gratifying developments, but to this generation, the progress appeared distressingly slow, the gap between per capita income in Colombia and Organization for Economic Cooperation Development (OECD) countries appeared to be growing, and a projection of historic rates would mean a modest per capita income by the year 2000 and a still larger gap in relation to more developed countries.

President Carlos Lleras, whose term had expired in 1970, took measures to continue the pattern of growth. He had fostered the country's Planning Agency and gave it independent powers; in 1969, he had nominated as director Jorge Ruiz Lara, an economist with a doctor's degree, and had taken part in preparing a plan known as the Plan for 1969-1972 (a name later changed to the Plan of 1970-1973); had invited Richard Musgrave of Harvard to make recommendations on tax reform; had invited the ILO to send a mission to study the employment problem; and had negotiated international loans and prepared the national budget for 1970-1971.

At virtually the first meeting of the National Economic and Social Policy Council in August 1970, the director of the Planning Agency (Departamento Nacional de Planeación, DNP) presented the incoming president, Misael Pastrana, with the Plan for 1970-1973. The plan stressed public investment (mostly the programs of the various ministries and centralized agencies), which, after a rather perfunctory review, the president accepted. He could not count on a majority in the Congress (which earlier had rejected the Musgrave tax recommendations), and he was under some obligation to the ex-president, who had supported him. It appeared, therefore, that except for minor changes, the period 1970-1974 would witness a continuation of the policies adopted or followed by the previous administration.

At this point, chance and interpersonal relations played their role (as they so frequently do) and resulted in an unexpected modification of the course of events. Some frictions developed between the president and the director of the Planning Agency, which suddenly flared into the open in December 1970; the director and most of the heads of the main divisions of the Planning Agency resigned. The president accepted the resignations and appointed Roberto Arenas as the new director. Arenas, who had been impressed with my teaching and with whom I had been on cordial terms, promptly asked the president to invite me back to Colombia as adviser to the Planning Agency. (I had been teaching in Canada and Great Britain since 1967, when I had left Colombia, thinking that my advising days were over.) The original request was to advise on the implementation of the ILO recommendations, which I declined. The invitation was then modified to permit me to advise on a plan in general, which was too tempting to refuse. I arrived in Bogotá in June 1971.

At the beginning of 1970, the country had been exposed to the reports of three full-dress missions, in addition to the suggestions of the resident Harvard Mission and an overall plan prepared by the Planning Agency. The resident representative of the World Bank had his office in the Planning Agency. By the middle of 1971, except for a few surviving members of the Harvard Mission, I was the macro adviser in the Planning Agency and was in a position to prepare a draft of a plan and attempt to have it adopted, with three years of a new president's term remaining.

In June and July, I wrote the guidelines of a new plan, the main elements of which were accepted by the director of the Planning Office and by the president and incorporated by the president into his major speech opening the Congress on July 20, 1971.[1] After many conferences within the Planning Agency and with the president and the ministers concerned with economic matters, a final draft was written under the title of the Plan of the Four Strategies. In the first week of December 1971, the president presented the draft to congressional leaders as the government's Plan of National Development, together with the detailed on-going programs and budgets of the individual ministries and decentralized agencies. In winning acceptance of the plan, the director of the Planning Agency played the leading role, and much of my time was spent in supplying him with ammunition and in studying what needed to be done to implement it.

While the plan itself was fairly well received, opposition to it was intense and vociferous both within and outside the government. Had it not been for the happy discovery in the Constitution of a hitherto unused presidential power, the institutional changes could not have been effected. After many meetings, the president decided in favor of the measure and signed the requisite decrees on May 2, 1972, although the system did not actually start until September of that year. To embark on an untried and unpopular course took a great deal of courage on his part.

Elements of the Plan[2]

The objectives of the plan were conventional: an accelerated rate of growth and a better distribution of the benefits thereof. The novel features were to be found in the diagnosis of poverty and a too slow rate of growth, and the strategies proposed to achieve the objectives.

The diagnosis will be reviewed here only briefly. Widespread poverty accompanies low productivity, a rapid growth in population, and poor distribution, which together yield too low a standard of living rising too slowly for most of the people. Techniques and specialization are not adopted more rapidly because of the slow growth in the market. Resources are badly allocated and underutilized. Poor public administration nullifies, to a large extent, efforts to secure better distribution by transfer payments. Many obstacles to mobility—economic, cultural, and political—have to be overcome. Two of the bases for this diagnosis are found in Adam Smith-Allyn Young[3] and in J. B. Say. A third I encountered in an early study by Nancy and Richard Ruggles,[4] now confirmed by many others, of the inverse relation between birth rates on the one hand and incomes and education on the other, the latter two of which are higher in urban areas with consequent lower birth rates. With the addition of my studies of the New Deal period on the motivation for investment and the use of "leading" and "following" sectors, the diagnosis also suggested the elements of the indicated strategy.

In short, the idea was to identify potentially large sectors where unsatisfied latent demand was high and there existed high and continuing income elasticity of demand, or where an addition to supply would not affect prices or price elasticity of demand noticeably. Government intervention to stimulate such "leading" sectors could thus be selective and strategic. The resulting impact would then affect the "following" sectors, varying with varying income elasticities of demand for their products, and the mobility mechanism could be aided. Income per capita could be further raised by the consequent urbanization through the shift to higher incomes and the fall in the fertility rate. The leading sector strategy would supply an element missing from the Young analysis—the mechanism by which the rates of growth, which, once established, tend to be self-perpetuating, can be raised.

It may help to visualize the process by looking at a breakdown of national accounts. (See Table 1 in Chapter 2.) The different rates of growth of the sectors reflect both obstacles to increased output and varying income elasticities of demand. The overall increase in demand (output) is a major determinant of the growth in demand in each sector. But the overall rate of growth is the sum of the (weighted) individual sector growth rates. The overall rate is dependent on sector rates; the sector rates are dependent in large part on the overall rate. The process tends to be self-perpetuating (increasing returns) but at a constant rate unless some impulse or deterrent *exogenous* to the continuing process intervenes. If there is widespread underutilization of both men and machines, as in the Great Depression, a Keynesian increase in simple aggregate money demand may suffice. If factors are fully (even though poorly) employed, the exogenous factor must probably have to take the form of providing a positive incentive to shift factors so that the increase in aggregate money demand reflects and arises out of an increase in real output.

In Colombia, in 1971, there appeared to be two main sectors that could qualify as "leading"—exports and building: exports, because a good base had been established in industry and a modern sector in agriculture (the addition to non-coffee exports would be significant for Colombia but so small as not to affect world prices); and building, because there was reason to believe that a large latent and unsatisfied demand for housing existed in the fast-growing cities. Although the figures are derived only from building licenses, they suggest that urban building amounted to only 1.4, 1.3, and 1.2 percent of the GDP in, respectively, 1970, 1971, and 1972.[5]

Implementation of the Plan

Colombia had been rather long on plans but short on their implementation. Hence, attention was concentrated on this aspect. The diversification of exports by the use of a subsidy and by monetary correction in the exchange rate had been a major policy of the previous government, meeting with considerable success. Conventional programs to stimulate agricultural production were being followed. The weakness of the administration in Congress and the state of finances prevented further large transfer payments to improve distribution. In order to secure the benefits of concentration, therefore, the plan focused on building. The single government mortgage institution was paying and receiving negative rates of interest when account was taken of inflation. The demand was believed to be large, and the supply of funds, small. The institution was rationing credit, and in such rationing it was the most creditworthy, the well-to-do, who naturally received preference. To provide the requisite stimulus in an inflationary situation, new financial institutions were created to pay savers and to charge borrowers modest rates of interest, *but with monetary adjustment (indexation) of the principal of deposits, construction loans, and mortgages.*[6]

Initially, I was assisted by an informal advisory discussion group of businessmen, lawyers, and urban planners, mostly old friends, with whom I tried out ideas and discussed alternatives and who proved of enormous help both in working out details of the implementation and in creating an informal group to support it.

Time was pressing, and the system, to survive a change of governments, had to be established quickly and had to create its own vested interests. For this I advised a system of joint stock savings corporations, permitting the big commercial banks to participate (up to 30 percent of the capital) and even provide staff and space for the first year but with separate boards of directors. These banks had their own savings departments, and we appeared to be putting our little sheep into the lion's den, but we gambled on competition, and fortunately the gamble paid off. When one financial group formed a corporation, others felt compelled to form their own or be left out. After some rather frantic maneuvering, the new corporations began to receive deposits at the end of 1972. Within a year, corporations were functioning with branches throughout the country and with 5,000 million pesos[7] in deposits, which at the time was a sizable figure for Colombia, with applications for loans far in excess of the fast-growing deposits. Although its growth was later deliberately restrained by the succeeding government, the system was able to survive the political campaign and change of governments in 1974, the legal challenge, carried to the Supreme Court, of its constitutionality, and the unsympathetic treatment meted out to it in 1974-1977.

While the original presidential decrees were simple, the change they envisaged was drastic. A system was put into operation designed to correct a discrimination against building caused by inflation, in order to provide the investment stimulus needed to secure greater mobility and hence higher productivity of labor. It was designed to release pent-up demand; it was not in itself a low-cost, popular housing system.

An interesting conclusion that might be drawn from the experience is the growth in the general efficiency of the private sector that has taken place. Within a year, a system of daily indexed savings, construction loans, and mortgages had been established and was running smoothly in ten new corporations with branches throughout the country. Statements separating interest from monetary adjustment were sent to depositors monthly, and information for tax purposes was mailed out at the end of the year. This would have been a remarkable performance even in more developed countries.[8]

What has been lacking since 1974, however, is a regulatory board between the banking superintendent and the monetary authority to safeguard the interests of the depositors and borrowers, promote the system, and integrate it more directly into overall urban design. The subsequent limitation on indexing and the acceptance of fixed interest deposits have both been dangerous, reflecting a lack of discipline in macroeconomic policy and an inclination to accept *ad hoc* measures rather than to adhere to principles.

Difficulty in the Synchronization of Policies

While adoption of the leading sector strategy in the Plan of the Four Strategies did not require a new urban design of growth, it was my hope that the system of financing of building could be linked to the cities-within-cities policy, which had a high social content and an impact on distribution.[9] But that part of the plan was even more radical, or at least novel, than the financial one, and it was thought that it would need the influential backing of a United Nations Development Program (UNDP)-World Bank sponsored study. Actually, and in retrospect, the importance of foreign support was probably exaggerated, as both President Pastrana (in 1972) and President López (in November 1974) accepted and supported the urban plan. In waiting for the results of the Bank's studies, the key moment for marrying the financing system to urban planning passed.

An Appraisal

The Plan of the Four Strategies, with its impulse to the leading sectors of exports and building, was in no sense a "gosplan" or an "indicative plan," but a concentration on a very limited number of what were considered to be strategic factors. Virtually no legislation was possible under the prevailing conditions, and thus the plan of the cities-within-cities was not implemented. In order to improve distribution, reliance was placed on better employment, especially urban, and a more rapid rate of growth in output and the already existing progressivity of the tax system. For increased productivity in agriculture, which could occur without undue hardship for the traditional farmer since there were increasing job alternatives, there was already an on-going and more conventional program, handicapped, however, by several years of very poor weather for crops.

In general, it appeared that the underlying assumptions were valid: insufficient funds for building, unmet latent demands, the ability to increase funds and activity by lessening discrimination against saving in this form, and unutilized slack in the economy, even at a growth rate of 5.8 percent in 1971. The success of the plan should be judged not only by the stimulation it provided in a short period, but also by consideration of what would have happened to building with a rise in inflation but with a continuation of financing under the old system. Instead of a further decline, building permits in the larger cities, in terms of meters, in the second half of 1973 ran 30 percent above the second half of 1972, and another 30 percent in the first half of 1974 over the first half of 1973. Value added in urban building rose by 68 percent from 1972 to 1974 (in constant pesos), but, with a change in policy, declined in 1975 to below its 1972 level.[10]

Note also the high rate of growth that prevailed *before* the adoption of the plan, and the drastic fall that accompanied its abandonment. The rate of growth in 1971 over 1970 was a relatively high 5.8 percent, a rate exceeded in the following three years despite poor harvests. It fell to 3.8 percent in 1975 and 4.6 percent in 1976. Recent data on quarterly movements of the GDP are even more striking. The average annual rate of growth in the nonagricultural portion of the economy fell from 8.1 percent in the first two quarters of 1974 to a low −0.1 percent in the last quarter, only one of two negative quarterly rates in the entire period 1960-1979.[11] Finally, note the impetus to increased employment in the cities at higher rates of remuneration than prevailed generally in the country up to the middle of 1974.[12]

The Plan of the Four Strategies did not halt inflation, and the indexation system has been blamed for this failure. The inflation problem is discussed in Chapter 7. Here it will simply be pointed out that indexation was not designed to stop inflation, but only to avoid one of its harmful effects.

Possibly there is some basis for the criticism that more autonomy should have been provided for the savings/mortgage system by creating something like the Home Loan Bank Board. But a precedent for this did not exist in Colombia and would probably have been unacceptable. I did propose, and the proposal was accepted, that in the exercise of his powers the president seek the advice of a savings and housing board (Junta de Ahorro y Vivienda) created by him and composed, ex-officio, of the ministers of finance and of development, the manager of the central bank, the director of the Planning Agency, and two non-ex-officio "civilian" members and their alternates. The first four were also members of the monetary board (Junta Monetaria). With the change in government, the two "civilian" members and their alternates were simply not appointed, and the monetary board became in effect the adviser to the president in the exercise of his powers over savings.[13] But even a completely autonomous board would have been the creation of the president by decree, and its elimination could have been brought about by another decree. Only a law would have given some promise of continuity and autonomy, and, in the conditions prevailing in 1972, a law was out of the question, especially as it would have required a modification of the Constitution.

Conclusions

It is most encouraging to realize that, even under unfavorable legislative conditions, it is possible, with some luck, ingenuity, and the support of the chief executive, to pull off a coup. However, one must be prepared to seize opportunities when they appear. The difficulties and obstacles are so formidable as to make such occasions very much the exception.

One of the factors contributing to success was that, for the most part, the field in which I worked was special and did not encroach on the work of the various sectors of the Planning Agency, except in urban policy, where I encountered some opposition. I attended none of the weekly meetings of unit heads or of CONPES, so that the agency's regular functioning was not visibly affected by my presence. My low profile was aided by the fact that the agency was physically scattered and my regular meetings with my advisory group occurred after office hours. I led a voluntary discussion group in economic theory, not policy, for younger economists of the agency and aided a number to secure scholarships abroad. However, my influence was strictly dependent on my relations with two successive heads of the agency and their relations, in turn, with the president. In a country where the government changes every four years, assuring the permanence of policy change is very difficult. A president or a minister (or even the head of a planning agency) is inclined to feel that he gains little credit for continuing a policy and that something new and different is expected of him. The number of different but effective policies is unfortunately not all that great. This bias can be offset or neutralized in various ways. One is by the use of semantics. Most of the elements of the Plan of the Four Strategies were familiar, but the title was fresh and new. Another technique is to have a number of people identify their own interests with the new policy. Within a year, in the joint stock savings corporation system, one thousand jobs and sixty thousand depositors had been created, and, in another year, the corporations had set up their own trade association. The construction industry had become dependent on a flow of mortgage money through the system, and behind the construction industry were the building material suppliers. The old mortgage institution, which had fought the system, was now dependent for its future growth on indexed deposits rather than on tax-free, fixed interest-bearing bonds as formerly. The opposition of the powerful financial interests (banks and insurance companies) had been sensibly lessened by their stake in the new system. It was this complex of interests that saved the system from dismantlement by the new government.[14]

Although one of the reasons for the success of the plan was its concentration of effort on one activity selected from all the competing government programs, there was one serious area of conflict deserving more of the agency's attention—monetary, fiscal, and exchange policy. Although the use of indexation was designed to offset the harmful effects of inflation in a sensitive area, it was the growth of inflation and the rise in the monetary rate of correction that nearly wrecked the system in its early stages. The failure to secure a greater measure of stability subjected the plan to heavy attack. In other words, selectivity was necessary, but consistency and compatibility of policies were also highly desirable.

The episode suggests a possible role of a planning agency in advising a chief executive on overall macroeconomic policy. It is highly unlikely that a minister of finance, greatly overburdened and with many executive tasks, could give the time necessary to study an initiative like the Colombian plan; nor would he be likely to sponsor a move so opposed by financial interests. However, the episode was not at all typical, and as control of the new system passed to successive ministers of finance, other considerations came to the fore and the potential of the system was only partially realized. The point is discussed further in Chapter 15.

Finally, the importance of adequate implementation cannot be overstressed. Otherwise "a plan" is liable to remain an exhortation rather than an operative strategy. But the opposition will generally center on the implementation.

5
COMPREHENSIVE REPORTS
OF COUNTRY MISSIONS

For over twenty years, a characteristic form of economic advice-giving was that of short-term comprehensive "country missions," sponsored by international organizations. Their findings and recommendations were incorporated in subsequent reports addressed to the country concerned, the organization, and the world at large. Such reports customarily covered aspects of economic and social life, and gave prescriptions for the attainment of overall high growth, employment, and better distribution. Many such missions and reports were sponsored by the World Bank, and a rash of them in the 1970s by the International Labor Office, with large-scale reports on a number of countries.

In general, despite their distinguished sponsorship, these missions have had little influence on policy, although they have provided scholars with much factual information. There appears now to be a tendency to abandon this type of advice-giving, although the World Bank and other international agencies are continuing with both sector missions for individual countries and intercountry sector analyses for LDCs in general.

The first of such comprehensive study missions—the World Bank Report on Colombia in 1949—seems to have been responsible for much misspent or at least disappointing subsequent effort. As the director of the mission and the editor of its report, I feel that the proper lessons were not drawn from the experience, and I propose to analyze it in some detail in this chapter. I think it is generally conceded that in contrast to subsequent missions, the first had a large measure of success and considerable and continuing impact on the country as well as on the Bank. I shall limit the discussion to those elements bearing upon the influence of the sponsor, the content of the advice and its implementation, the precedents that were made and followed by subsequent missions, and those that were made but not followed.

The First World Bank Mission to Colombia

The mission originated in a most casual way.[1] In 1948, the World Bank was just beginning to turn its attention from the reconstruction of Europe to the problem of its developing members, and Colombia had put out a feeler for a loan. John McCloy, who was president of the Bank, called the executive director for Colombia, Emilio Toro, in for a chat and, probably to be provocative, suggested that the Bank could not be sure that the particular loan at issue would finance the country's most urgent programs. Maybe there were other, more important things to be financed. With great presence of mind, Toro, without hesitation, replied that the Bank should send a study group to Colombia and find out for itself. Somewhat taken aback, McCloy said he would give it some thought. He passed the matter on to the vice-president of the Bank, Robert L. Garner. In May 1949, Garner formally broached the matter of a study mission to Toro, who was able to convey an enthusiastic response from the Colombian president, Mariano Ospina Pérez. The same month, Garner, whom I had known slightly in New York, called me and sounded me out as a possible head of the mission (having first assured himself on my soundness on the matter of private enterprise, as a faint unsound aura of the New Deal still clung to me).

It is almost unbelievable that less than thirty years ago so little precedent existed for such a mission or study.[2] I was given complete discretion over the planning of scope, size, timing, requirements for personnel, and much of the recruitment. Having no very definite ideas of the problems we should encounter, I planned the study to be comprehensive, mostly by sectors but to be tied together in an internally consistent manner and to include noneconomic as well as strictly economic fields. The mission numbered fourteen people in all for periods of time varying from a few weeks to four months. The Bank nominated a few juniors, but for the rest it accepted my suggestions in recruiting people from different fields and borrowing others from other organizations. I even persuaded Garner to let me take on an assistant-surgeon general of the U.S. Public Health Service, Dr. Joseph Mountin, sponsored by the Pan-American Sanitary Bureau. I also persuaded the International Monetary Fund to attach a man to the mission, Roger Anderson.[3]

The first members of the mission arrived in Bogotá in July 1949, and the last left in November of the same year. To give the mission status and prestige, Garner accompanied us, initially for the first few days. He entered into the matter with such enthusiasm, however, that he remained nearly two weeks. After the mission, I returned to the Bank for the trying work of editing and of attempting to make a collection of separate monographs consistent parts of a whole. The first draft was finished by March 1950, and the report was published in August of that year in English and Spanish.[4]

The oversized report went through several editions and was compulsory reading for other country study teams. Its success in influencing policy in Colombia (and in leading to many loans) made it a model and led to a conviction, which was a long time dying, that this type of countrywide study was the appropriate springboard for a development program.

The Nature of the Report

At the time, there was little literature specifically on development, or even on growth.[5] The economic theory was fairly elementary, but upon rereading it appears to be on the whole sound. My own fields of concentration had been monetary, fiscal, and international trade theory. Richard Musgrave was a member of the mission, and I followed his lead on taxation and budget presentation. V. L. Bassie went over all the material we could gather on national accounts. We had an excellent man in transport (Frederick Gill) and an industrial engineer (actually trained as a physicist), Carl Flesher, in whom I had a lot of confidence. Agriculture remained a problem, but Joseph Mountin was a tower of strength in public health. Two strong convictions (or biases) permeated the study. One was a very progressive stance on objectives, which were variously expressed as raising the standard of living, meeting basic human needs, and reducing inequality, especially in consumption. (The report was almost Puritan in its condemnation of ostentatious consumption.) This attitude was shown in the choice of programs, as well, which included wide-ranging reforms and increased expenditures in health, education, and public services of all kinds. This "liberal" stand on objectives was counterbalanced by an equally strong "conservative" stand on the necessity of raising productivity per capita and of relying to the fullest extent feasible on market forces—competition, mobility, and economic incentives, with as much freedom from direct controls, rationing, and subsidies as possible. (Although Colombia had a highly oligarchical governing class at the time, with only as much interest in the masses' standard of living as was politically expedient, the country was passionately devoted to controls and had little faith in the market, so that both biases of the report ran counter to current beliefs.)[6]

Although the recommendations of the report were designed to raise the standards of living, they can be grouped in two main categories: (1) measures to bring about a rise in the growth of income per capita, or productivity, and (2) measures to ensure better distribution directly. The second category included better administration and enlarged expenditures in education, in public health (both preventive medicine and health centers and hospitals), in public services (water, electricity, and so forth) and housing, and in shifting a larger burden of taxation onto a progressive income tax, covering both ordinary income and capital gains.

To increase productivity, emphasis was placed on improving the infrastructure ("social overhead capital") and the economic atmosphere or environment. The mission found that because of topography and neglect, the country could be classified into at least four main economic zones with wretched communication and transport among them. Hence, the small total internal market (11 million people with an average income of US$175) did not even provide, except for a very few goods, a single market where some significant economies of scale could be achieved. The report paid a great deal of attention, therefore, to the necessity of providing a highway network that would connect the main cities and the ports with paved roads built to modern grade and curve specifications, a single-gauge interconnected national railroad system that would replace the existing multi-gauged bits and pieces, improved ports and waterways, and a modern air transport organization. While the main cities were being interconnected, they were to be supplied with larger electric generating systems (mostly hydro), telephones, water, sewers, and intracity transport.

While providing this infrastructure for industrialization and urbanization, the report urged that the state reduce its own industrial and commercial activities, controls, and subsidies and create a more favorable atmosphere for competitive private enterprise, domestic and foreign. The emphasis was on competition, since actually the few large companies in various fields shared many privileges and advantages, which did not always appear on the surface. Thus, the report was critical of a proposed new state-integrated steel plant, but it favored smaller and competitive electric scrap-reducing furnaces for the production of a few standardized products, together with foundries for miscellaneous work. (See Chapter 12.)

The report's position on agriculture puzzled many and aroused considerable opposition. Even at this early date, I favored increased productivity per worker in agriculture, in part to meet the needs of the growing cities and in part for export, but largely to release manpower to produce other things. (Over 60 percent of the work force in 1951 was still in the countryside.) But I was bothered by the fact that there was literally no cultivation on the flat temperate lands near Bogotá and little in the rich valley of the Cauca River, so that corn, cassava, cooking bananas, potatoes, and vegetables were grown mostly in small patches on steep hillsides. I took a dim view of using flatlands for raising dairy and beef cattle on an extensive scale and came up with the idea of a capital tax on land inversely proportional to its yield. (There was some precedent for this idea in similar rates on urban land held off the market.) But the motivation was not so much "agrarian reform" as it was providing an incentive for the more intensive use of good land by the existing owners. The other recommendations for agriculture were conventional and not controversial.

Part of the improved economic atmosphere was to be provided by greater price stability, greater freedom of trade and of capital movements, a neutral and single rate of exchange (the various rates were chronically overvalued for all potential exports except coffee), a more competitive market for credit, and a higher level of governmental efficiency and planning in general.

The setting for this ambitious program was not propitious. The country was torn by political strife. The majority party had abstained from the election of 1949 and was now boycotting the government. The Conservative president, who took office in 1950, was ill as well as unpopular, and the governmental machinery was functioning poorly. It was the furthest possible remove from a popular reformist government one could imagine; when a military dictator assumed office in April 1953, he was actually hailed as a liberator.

Results

Although the country fully merited the description of a less developed country as defined in Chapter 2, which signified a severe restraint on measures, as distinct from objectives, that could be safely recommended, and although many of our specific suggestions were not, or not immediately, implemented, the results were quite remarkable, as the following list will indicate:

Stability. The index of prices of consumer goods, with 1940 as 100, had risen to 182 by 1946, 250 in 1948, and 272 by the end of December 1949.[7] Prices had risen a further 20 percent in the first nine months of 1950. However, monetary expansion was arrested after a determined effort in the later part of 1950, and a relatively long period of stable prices followed. Means of payment expanded by only about 66 percent in the period 1950-1956, and the workers' price index rose by only 31 percent. This was the first real attack on monetary inflation, with a published explanation of causes of changes in the money supply.

Exchange Rate. A devaluation was carried out in 1951 expressly to correct the external overvaluation of the currency and to permit a liberalization in imports and progress toward a uniform rate of exchange. The devaluation was carried through smoothly with no accompanying rise in prices. (See Chapter 7 for more about this devaluation.)

Surface Transport. A host of small bits and pieces of road construction and a completely unrealistic railroad program were replaced by a major road-building program (assisted by a series of loans from the World Bank) to connect the large cities and the ports by a modern, all-weather paved highway system. Virtually all the railroad proposals of the mission were accepted and acted upon, following suggested further study.

Air Transport. A government agency was created to take over the ownership, construction, and management of airports and the provision of air traffic control. The construction of a number of modern airports was recommended.

Agriculture. Tractors and tractor-drawn equipment invaded crop after crop in the flatlands of the Sabana de Bogotá, the Valle del Cauca, Tolima, and the lower Magdalena Valley. The long discussion in the report may have influenced this trend to mechanization.

Taxation. A surprising number of the mission's tax proposals were accepted, but only after a delay and then by a military government.

Public Administration. The Ministry of Agriculture was reorganized, a budget office was created (but in the Treasury), and a planning office was established that was directly responsible to the president. Most of the recommendations, however, were not acted upon.

Intangibles. The report was widely read and studied inside Colombia, and for probably the first time many people grasped the idea of an economy as a functioning organism with interconnecting parts. Much of the advice was not accepted, or accepted much later, but the idea of planning was strongly implanted.

Colombia became a favorite country of the Bank throughout the following decades. By the end of 1974, the country had received in per capita terms the largest volume of loans from the World Bank of any major developing country, despite the two-year interlude of the military dictatorship, when no loans were made. Foreign investment in Colombia increased in the 1950s, and a good deal of import substitution in industrial products occurred. This may also have been related to the favorable publicity on Colombia created by the report and the foreign exchange and monetary policies it recommended. What requires explanation now is the relative success of the mission and its report in such unpropitious circumstances.

It was generally assumed that these gratifying results justified the "country mission" approach to development planning. An essential and generally unrecognized element in the success story, however, was the device used to translate a foreign report into a national program. This device, modeled on the British Royal Commission, took advantage of the latent desire of prominent citizens to serve their country in an influential and prestigious capacity.

Before completion of the Bank report, I had accepted an invitation to organize, on a private basis, another mission to study the reorganization of the executive branch of the Colombian government. I saw, therein, an opportunity to promote the organization of a "Royal Commission"-type committee to study, chapter by chapter, the Bank report. I volunteered to act as its adviser and to make available for this purpose some of the time of members of the public administration study. The World Bank agreed to make the services of other technicians available for varying periods, and the Colombian government undertook to provide a national staff. Finally, as a private person in the summer of 1950, I could, without impropriety, take an active part in securing the nomination of six outstanding citizens to serve on the committee—three Liberal and three Conservative, of whom three would be from the western half of the country and three from the eastern. So far as I know, no one of the members was close to the president.

The idea was to work through the report by subjects, looking at each to derive specific recommendations by an eminent group of Colombians. The Committee on Economic Development, as it was called, met regularly for nine months and always with a technical paper before it. Decisions were almost always unanimous. The strength of the group derived in part from their individual and collective standing (nonpolitical) in the community but more from the assumed support it received from the Bank and the fact that its recommendations, based on the mission's report and the further work of foreign technicians, would be expected to carry much weight with the Bank. Recommendations were submitted to the government as rapidly as they were arrived at, and they were published in a single volume in July 1951.

Unexploited Possibilities

Whatever success the original comprehensive country mission report had was, therefore, owing in large part to the "Royal Commission" instrument and the fortunate accident of an able and aggressive minister of public works.[8] It was my hope, however, that the Bank would be prepared to exploit the situation's full potential. My design was that upon the submission of the committee's report there would be top-level meetings of the government and the Bank, at which the Bank would indicate what parts of the overall program it would be prepared to finance and the government would indicate what it wished financed by the Bank and what parts it was prepared to accept and finance with its own resources.

By placing responsibility for recommendations upon the head of the mission (who in this case was not an employee of the Bank) and by having the recommendations studied by a prestigious group of civic-minded citizens, I felt that the top Bank officials would not need to feel they were responsible for recommendations in the fields of education, health, and public administration. Hence, the idea of top-level meetings and division of tasks did not actually seem so farfetched, even for 1951. One fateful day, however, Garner suddenly realized where I was leading him, and he drew back, saying, "Damn it, Lauch. We can't go messing around with education and health. We're a *bank!*" Rarely can the collapse of a Grand Design be so pinpointed in one remark. The Bank retreated to a procedure that was to become familiar: financing the foreign exchange costs of transport and power projects and using its leverage to assure that these projects would be well planned and executed and that utility rates would be raised to cover operating costs and debt-financing charges. Even monetary, fiscal, and exchange policies and instruments of policy were to become matters in which the Bank would not ordinarily play an active advisory role. A bank was an institution that made loans. Terms and conditions must be related to the loans and to the projects financed by the loans.

The Use of Leverage or Influence

At the time, I felt that the Bank had missed an opportunity to establish a precedent of linking nonbankable with bankable projects in an overall country program by using the device of the "Royal Commission." For example, my ensuing study on public administration—staffed almost entirely by technicians from the U.S. Office of Management and Budget—was in large part stillborn without Bank sponsorship and especially without a Colombian organization prepared to study, adapt, and push its recommendations, as was the case with the mission report. This has been the general story in Colombia ever since. As late as 1970 and 1972, two overall studies of Colombia by the ILO and the World Bank, even though both were published and sponsored by international organizations, had no perceptible influence. A report addressed to the world at large is in effect addressed to nobody.

It may have been proper for a group of technicians to be content to analyze and offer advice and not to advocate or reform. It would also, it seemed, be relatively ineffectual, at least if differences of opinion exist on recommendations. In matters not touching on political or economic differences, more attention would doubtless be paid to purely technical advice. But this consideration brings one back to the content of advice. If one feels strongly that some policy is for "the good of the country," one is tempted to advocate using a lending institution's influence to have the policy accepted or at least taken seriously. But if one feels equally strongly that the policy recommended is inappropriate or even harmful, one's attitude toward the use of leverage is likely to be radically different.[9]

The Bank's use of its influence was fairly indirect in relation to the 1950 report and followup. The Bank, *as a bank*, actually did not advocate any policy. But by sponsoring the mission, publishing its study in English, and making the services of Bank technicians available to the committee, it unquestionably exerted considerable influence. In the background was always the expectation of bountiful loans to come if Bank approval was obtained. And the Bank did do what it thought it could with propriety to build up and maintain the influence of the Committee on Economic Development, even to the extent of not accepting applications for loans until the committee had had an opportunity to express its views on the projects to be financed. On the other hand, once there was an interim report of the committee on the highway program with priorities indicated, the Bank moved rapidly to agree in principle to an initial $16.5 million loan with the minister of public works in advance of the committee's final report. Although this piecemeal approach threatened the hope of Bank participation in an overall country program, it did serve at the time to enhance the prestige of the committee, whose members had to be assured that their work was influential to induce them to serve. They were, after all, expected to devote a good part of their time for nine months, uncompensated in financial terms, and to take positions on topics that were in some cases controversial.

In the end, indirectly (through the committee), the Bank did exert some influence on highly controversial matters such as inflation and exchange policy. It could be argued, however, that this influence was less than it was later to exert, with relatively little complaint, in joining with the International Monetary Fund in direct pressure in exchange and monetary matters on the Colombian government, and in managing the Consortium of Foreign Lending Agencies to Colombia.

Although the Colombian Committee on Economic Development owed its initial inspiration to the Royal Commissions of the British Commonwealth, it was charged with the study of matters that would generally be reserved to the government of the day in Commonwealth countries. The device is often used there to do something about a matter that the government is not as yet prepared to act upon; it is also used to study matters on which public opinion is as yet not sufficiently formed to permit legislation. For this latter purpose, the analogy and the use of the device to secure a study of a country program appear appropriate.

The failure of developing countries to make use of the "Royal Commission" device is due partly to the reluctance of ministers to sacrifice any power, partly to the skepticism of private individuals as to the worthwhileness of the proposed studies, and finally, to the usual shortage of competent technicians to staff such commissions.

Appraisal

To overcome all these handicaps, it appears that the international lending agencies could play a highly significant role and that the failure to study the Colombian experience more carefully was regrettable. In the 1972 evaluation of the Bank's work in Colombia, scant notice is accorded to the committee, and a curious slip was made in stating it had "disintegrated." Actually, it finished its labors with suitable fanfare, the president conferred decorations on the members, and the committee's report was published in Spanish. It received very little attention, however, in the monumental official history of the World Bank.[10] This was a pity, as the connection was sufficiently indirect and remote to diffuse the Bank's responsibility for policies.

In a curious way, less attention was paid to the Colombian experience just because it was the first of its kind, and its relative success was taken as a matter of course. It was felt that there was nothing remarkable about it as this was how the Bank would always operate and be received in developing countries. If it had occurred after a number of failures, it might have received much more attention.[11]

The lapse of the initial show of interest on the Bank's part in Colombia's taxation, public administration, health, and education put the Bank back many years as a development institution. In 1952, for example, it rejected an application to finance the foreign exchange requirements of a water treatment plant for Barranquilla on the grounds that it was for a "social" and not an "economic" purpose.

To restrict loan criteria to creditworthiness, as a commercial bank does, would hardly justify the existence of international or national publicly financed lending institutions for "development." Once one moves beyond this point, however, one enters the realm of advice, and there are no clearcut dividing lines on what is appropriate and what is inappropriate. What can be said for a "Royal Commission," or other such devices, is that it enlists more collective responsibility in the borrowing country itself and reduces the element of individual imposition of will from the outside. As long as lending agencies intend to invoke criteria for loans beyond those of creditworthiness, and terms beyond rates and maturities, they are employing leverage and are assuming responsibility for the national policies of borrowers. The question is solely one of degree, and it certainly appears preferable to further collaboration than to impose conditions.

Experience in Colombia suggests the desirability of some followup mechanism to enhance the chances of acceptance and implementation of recommendations. Without the initial mission and the subsequent study committees, there would still undoubtedly have been World Bank loans, probably for highway construction and power plants. However, the projects would not have been part of an overall plan with carefully chosen priorities, at least initially; they would not have covered all forms of transport and community facilities; and they would not have been accompanied by discussion on the creation of conditions favoring growth. Many of the recommendations in the fields of education, health, public finance, and administration were acted upon in good time. Some, such as placing the office of the budget in the presidency and creating a ministry of urban affairs, have never been adopted. More prompt action on such matters would probably have been less difficult to secure than were the reforms in civil aviation that were achieved in the face of very heavy opposition from entrenched interests.[12]

In the thirty years of development after 1949, only this one country mission made a perceptible impact on policy in Colombia. One cannot say positively that this exception was owing to the content of the study or to its transformation to a national program by a Colombian committee assisted by foreign and domestic technicians and by the show of interest by the Bank. But since other overall studies and plans sponsored by the World Bank and other international agencies did not have this impact, the presumption is that the advice of the mission was appropriate, and in general acceptable, and that the integrating steps to ensure a serious study of the report within the country were effective to a degree.[13]

In general, governments accept advice not because it is good for the country, but because they need it to resolve a technical problem whose solution is necessary to proceed with a desired project, or because of the favors in loans or aid they expect to receive, or because the advice enlists the support of specific key individuals. Rarely can a general mission recommending a comprehensive program fulfill these conditions.

Although emphasis has been laid on the role of a well-staffed "Royal" advisory commission in this episode, this was only an effective means to an end. The end, in the case of overall country advice, was how to convert generalized advice into specific plans and projects that could be translated into terms of budgets, loan applications, and integral parts of a government's program.

The General Plan for Colombia of 1961, prepared by the United Nations Economic Commission for Latin America, had many projections but was short on specific steps for the government to take to realize them. The ILO comprehensive plan of 1968 was long on declarations and exhortations but very short, again, on specific, carefully worked out steps in a program that could be sponsored by a specific agency or minister. The World Bank Report on Colombia of 1970 contained much good generalized advice, but the specific key to growth appeared in a formula that related foreign borrowing to growth, and Colombia needed no particular arguments to borrow as much as it could absorb. Such comprehensive reports, lending themselves to specific national plans and projects, might well have profited from use of the device of well-staffed advisory committees to facilitate the conversion from recommendations to policy formulation.

The device was utilized in 1968 by Richard Musgrave, who persuaded the Colombian government to appoint a tax commission of national and foreign scholars, over which he presided and which sponsored a far-reaching series of tax recommendations. His prestige was such, however, that the commission was promptly labeled the Musgrave Commission and was not thought of as the independent author of its report, even though individual members made some disclaimers in the text. Nevertheless, in the end it was the participation of nationals that later resulted in the adoption, for better or worse, of many of the recommendations.

There is a possibility that a conclusion of doubtful validity may be drawn from the success of the first World Bank mission. It was stressed that in the report and in the work of the advisory committee we were dealing with a comprehensive, integrated, and internally consistent set of recommendations covering a very broad field in economic policy, public administration, and technical assistance, and that a gratifying number of recommendations had been adopted. This would appear to justify a broad-scale attack on many fronts, and this actually became the practice among advice-givers. It is important to keep in mind, however, the very special nature of the experience. It was the first World Bank mission, and expectations were high. The country had had virtually no experience in overall planning, and there were hardly any national economists, which left a vacuum for foreign economists to fill. I was in the unique position of being able to coordinate the work in the fields of economic analysis, public administration, and technical assistance. Finally, the committee and the successor Planning Council (Consejo de Planificación Nacional) provided vehicles for following up recommendations and enjoyed high prestige. This combination of circumstances is very difficult to duplicate. The World Bank backed away from program financing, in the sense of underwriting part of the foreign exchange costs of a comprehensive country plan. Most LDCs now have cadres of national economists. My position at the time would be very difficult indeed to duplicate today in any country. In view of the remote possibility of repeating the experience, I shall in fact argue later that planning (and advising), whether by foreigners or nationals, offers more chance of being effective if it is selective in emphasis rather than comprehensive.

Thus, the important moral to be drawn from this story of the relative success of the first World Bank mission is that it was exceptional rather than typical. It cannot be cited, therefore, as an argument for generalized advice-giving by foreign missions when sponsored by a highly prestigious loaning institution. More is required, and the less developed the country, the more difficult the task of advising and the more necessary are additional and favoring conditions.

6
ADVICE OF RESIDENT MISSIONS: SOME CASE STUDIES

In this chapter, I discuss the work of resident advisers in relation to local planning organizations, focusing on the *process* of advice-giving and the conditions under which it is carried on. The experience of Colombia is particularly rich and varied in this respect, and there were a number of distinct experiences with which I was concerned in one way or another, making various generalizations possible.

Consejo de Planificación Nacional (1951-1953)

This Planning Council, which I helped establish as an outgrowth of the recommendations of the Committee on Economic Development (see Chapter 5), reflected my earlier experience in the U.S. government and with the World Bank mission to Colombia. I had recommended the committee form as I thought it more suitable than a single individual for the formulation of policy advice and the reconciliation of differences. I felt, however, that if it were to be influential, the committee must possess the confidence of the president, and so I made this the only qualification for membership. I still felt at that time that foreign advisers were desirable but that they could function more effectively and appropriately through a lay committee rather than directly. If they could persuade a committee on a course of action, the committee in turn would be in a better position to persuade the president.

Three prominent individuals, all on good terms with the acting president, accepted membership on the Planning Council, and Albert Hirschman was appointed as a foreign adviser. Upon completion of a study mission to a state government, I was also asked to serve as an adviser. This arrangement of equally ranking advisers, albeit giving council members an opportunity to secure different points of view, did not make for easy relations between the advisers.

Originally, the council was supposed to continue with the comprehensive program initiated by the World Bank mission and the Committee on Economic Development, and I drew up a report on the organization and work of the council.[1] As the expected assistance of technical advisers from the World Bank[2] was not forthcoming, however, Hirschman and I remained the chief advisers and could only cover a limited field.

In monetary policy, the committee filled a serious gap, since there was, at that time, no monetary board, and the board of directors of the Banco de la República, which acted as such, was composed mostly of private bankers and other borrowers from the Banco. Consequently, work and interest tended to concentrate in this sector. Curiously enough, the Planning Council played a more prominent role here during these first few years than it was ever to do subsequently. And this was a period of relative price stability aided initially by a fairly valued peso, following on the devaluation of 1951. The council's position in monetary and exchange policy lapsed after General Gustavo Rojas Pinilla assumed power in 1953. Doubtless the council was attempting too much too soon and depended too heavily on the close personal relations that existed between the acting president (Roberto Urdaneta Arbelaez), the members of the council and the minister of finance. When this relationship lapsed, the influence of the council also declined.

Before I left the council in 1953, I was able to use its prestige to prepare urban studies, mostly for public services, among them one of the City of Barranquilla, for which I grouped a plan of infrastructure around the need for expansion of the waterworks. After the project had been rejected by the World Bank as too "social," I secured on behalf of the council and the City of Barranquilla a loan from the Stabilization Fund of the Banco de la

República (whose abolition I had recommended earlier!), with a provision that a "Watchdog Committee" (Comité de Vigilancia) should report monthly to the Banco de la República on the progress of the plan until the loan was repaid. The Comité proved to be a most productive "Royal Commission." Although it had no real authority, the prestige of the members, the fact that it was reporting to the powerful Banco de la República, and the rapid turnover of administrations in city and state, which made the Comité the only stable organization, ensured its life throughout the period of the loan and a 90-percent fulfillment of the plan.

This, however, was in the nature of a tour de force, and I am not sure that it lends itself to generalization, except that when one is confronted with such a loss of dominance of environment, resort to desperate measures and even tricks may be justified. The device of the Comité served to create for three prominent citizens of a politics-ridden city and state a position that they could use for the benefit of the city. The whole episode had similarities to the British grant-in-aid system where the central government in effect paid the local authorities to do what was good for them or at least what the central ministries thought was good for them.

The lesson drawn by the next civilian president (1958) was that the Planning Agency did not have sufficient power in its own right, which he proceeded to give it. In view of a renewed period of disintegration after his administration, the more profound lesson would appear to be the importance of the relation between the advisory Planning Agency and the president. If the latter does not wish to use the former, he cannot very well be forced to do so regardless of its statutory powers.

Operation Colombia (1961) this was not advice by a resident mission, but its subsequent history may justify its inclusion here. I wrote the working paper in December 1960 and presented it some months later. I could not have chosen a worse moment. It was the year of the promised billions under the Alliance for Progress, of the Agrarian Reform, and of the General Ten-Year Plan prepared by UN technicians. Moreover, my suggestions flew in the face of prevailing ideas on development. Not surprisingly, it was rejected by the president in July 1961. However, in the strange way noted in the case of other plans in this study, its basic ideas were revived and adopted ten years later.

Operation Colombia proposed the measure, shocking for the times, of aiding and facilitating the exodus of poor farmers to the cities—a process that had always gone on in countries experiencing growth but that was, nevertheless, almost universally deplored. The project represented a marriage of my views on the inadequate mobility of the lowest paid labor, the conditions that must favor the adoption of technology and more efficient ways of doing things, and the possibility of tapping by exogenous means unexploited real demand in important sectors and so giving a positive stimulus to the mobility process. The study contained considerable detail, with quantitative targets of employment, building, and a system of indexation to boost savings and loans to finance building.

The lesson for advisers in the brief story of Operation Colombia is that to gain a hearing, much more than bright ideas is necessary. The moment must be propitious, and the ideas must have some chance of winning powerful sponsorship. There are vested interests in ideas as well as in property, and they will be clung to and defended if threatened. Ideas, however, are insidious things, and if names are changed and the ideas later fill what is thought to be a real need, they can be revived and acquire a life of their own.

Resident Mission of Technicians of CEPAL (1960–1962)

It is generally forgotten or unknown even in Colombia that the General Ten-Year Plan of Economic and Social Development for Colombia and the Four-Year Plan of Investment of 1961 were almost entirely worked up by a small number of economists assigned to the Colombian Planning Agency by the United Nations Economic Commission for Latin America (headquarters in Santiago, Chile; referred to as ECLA in English and CEPAL in Spanish). The commission maintained a very low profile indeed and received virtually no mention in the press.

Undoubtedly, this self-subordination on the part of CEPAL was a factor in the subsequent official adoption of its proposals by the Planning Agency (Spanish initials DNP) and the government. The price paid, however, was the absence of critical review before its adoption. This was a very high price indeed, as the plan was stillborn and tended to discredit or at least discourage overall planning for a number of years.

As in so many similar efforts, the plan was an offspring of the earlier Harrod-Domar models linking capital formation and growth. It contained a mass of projections that are mathematically consistent. What it lacked was a causal analysis that would stand examination, a positive program to achieve even modest growth targets other than by foreign borrowing, and an exploration of the possibilities for more rapid growth. The key rate assigned to the exchange constraint was not supported, and alternatives for changing factor proportions and the relation of output to imports were not explored. The increase in growth was to be attained by an increase in investment from 15.9 percent of GDP in 1959 to 22 percent in 1964, but how this increase was to be attained and why the private sector should increase its investment were not explained. Most of the postulated net foreign borrowing (US$100 million a year) had already been attained by 1961, and no other source of investment was indicated, other than investments by the government not covered by additional taxes. It was the latest model, but unfortunately, it lacked a motor.

There was no compelling reason why growth should bear a constant relation to capital formation and the GDP. Foreign borrowing had already reached the set target of US$100 million a year net, and there was no discernible reason why "investment" should be further increased to the percentages postulated. (In its subsequent approval of the plan, the World Bank technicians raised the target of foreign borrowing to US$125 million a year[3]—a small increase to power such a big model.)

This, then, was a case of a foreign resident mission taking advantage of an opportunity to have its recommendations adopted as a national plan. Unfortunately, the plan did not lend itself to policy formulation, except possibly in encouraging "public investment" expenditures not covered by additional taxes. Although its ready acceptance appears to reinforce the importance already noted of the maintenance of a low profile by foreign advisers, the fate of the plan also suggests the importance of what was lacking—the enlistment of local advisory groups and the paramount necessity of defensible links between the diagnosis and broad strategies embodied in the advice and appropriate, feasible policies. With a thoroughgoing, critical review, these weaknesses would doubtless have become evident, even, and perhaps especially, to its authors.

The Harvard Resident Mission in Colombia (1963-1971)

Background. The Harvard Mission to Colombia,[4] undoubtedly one of the longest, largest, and costliest resident missions, was organized by the Harvard Development Advisory Service (HDAS) and funded by the Ford Foundation, with help later from the Interamerican Development Bank and with counterpart funds from the government of Colombia. It took the form of a resident staff of advisers under a director, together with short-term consultants, training associates, well-known lecturers, scholarships, and family supplementary allowances to Colombians to study abroad.

The Ford Foundation was doubly involved, as it had made possible the Harvard Advisory Service itself in May 1962, by a grant of $750,000. Although the grant was couched in general terms, its purposes were clear. It was "to permit the University to continue and expand its advisory work in underdeveloped areas, in order to improve the understanding of the development process, to increase the number of experienced foreign advisers available for such work and to increase the capacity of the underdeveloped countries themselves to handle their problems of development."[5] This formalized the work started by the Graduate School of Public Administration in the early 1950s that had been carried on by the Center for International Studies, and stessed the twin objectives of advice-giving and training in development work. Despite this clear statement, uncertainty about the terms of reference played an important role in the Harvard mission's subsequent history in Colombia.

The files of the Ford Foundation contain many letters, interoffice memoranda, and memoranda for the files which again and again stress the training aspects of the project. But it appeared that the basic interest of the service was to advise on policy. Members of the group frequently stressed "institution building;" which straddles training and advising on policy. But there is no point in creating or improving an institution unless its impact on policy makes this worthwhile.

Harvard Mission: Earlier Work, 1963–1966

The mission was contracted in September 1963. Though small, it was given a substantial grant: salaries and fringe benefits, tax free for Americans out of the country a given time, were sufficient to make the posts highly attractive. A contribution was also made to the overhead of the headquarters of the service. Harold Dunkerley had been chosen earlier as head, apparently because of his previous experience in advising in Vietnam, and he arrived in Colombia at the end of May 1963.

The group, while small relative to the magnitude of the job to be done, numbering no more than two or three at a time, was competent and well-trained. It was unfortunately not able to accomplish very much. This finding is that of both Harold Dunkerley and later Gustav Papanek, the latter being head of the Advisory Service at Harvard. Given the sponsorship and the composition of the mission, it is important that the cause of its relative failure in this first period be understood. For this, some brief description of the economic and political framework is indispensable.

When Alberto Lleras Camargo became president of Colombia in 1958, he reconstituted the Planning Council, which had disintegrated, giving it more powers and responsibilities. However, he preserved the council form of organization with four full-time members (two representing him, one the Senate, and one the House of Representatives), and he also gave the head of the Planning Agency staff independent powers, which later created conflict. Apparently, this arrangement did not work too badly as long as President Alberto Lleras took an interest in the work of the council and kept an eye on it. Under his successor, however, things changed rapidly for the worse. Dunkerley reports that, upon his arrival in 1963, he found conflict not only between the members but also between some of them and the administrative and techical head of the staff. It was upon his recommendation that the council was abolished, at the end of 1963, and full power was vested in the head of the Planning Agency. Dunkerley had established close working relations with the head of the agency (Diego Calle) and had played a role in an institutional change that had the hearty support of the sponsor. This was the time described later by Dunkerley as the period of promise.

It is true that a new National Economic and Social Policy Council (CONPES) was substituted for the council. But this was a large, loose group of cabinet and other members, presided over by the president and attended by various ministers, heads of agencies, and advisers. The head of the Planning Agency was a member, while the secretary (really deputy head) of the agency acted as secretary of CONPES.

Thus, the council organization remained in form, but its composition changed radically. Attendance frequently exceeded twenty members, making it difficult for the Planning Agency to thrash out problems in any depth with the president.[6]

When Calle was nominated as minister of finance (February 1964), the office of head of the Planning Agency was left vacant for nearly nine months. The agency promptly deteriorated. Furthermore, on certain key issues, the president was not disposed to follow the advice even of his new minister of finance. If a president does not wish to plan, it is difficult to force him to do so.

The point is that too much weight should not be given to administrative changes by themselves. Moreover, placing all responsibility in the hands of a single individual head of an agency yields satisfactory results only when there is a competent, working head served by a competent agency, and the head enjoys the confidence of a president who is prepared to follow his advice. As it was, Dunkerley, having cast his lot completely with one man, felt he had no choice but to follow him to the Ministry of Finance, where he became a kind of personal adviser until the minister's resignation in April 1965. It appears that other members of the Harvard mission were left more or less to their own devices and did some work with the secretary of the Planning Agency, who was an economist. In the absence of a head of the Planning Agency, the minister of finance assumed some of his functions (in relation to the investment budget and international loans), weakening that institution still further. Since it seems to be a natural tendency in all countries for the power of the finance minister to grow, it could be argued that the process did not require additional help from HDAS and should have been resisted rather than aided. The president never met with the Economic and Social Policy Council (which itself did not meet).

This first effort at institution building could hardly be called successful. Not only did the Planning Agency disintegrate, but even the Superior School of Public Administration (ESAP) proved completely unsuitable as a training agency for the higher ranks of public employees who, in any case, were virtually all political appointees. The Ford Foundation had limited interest in what advice Dunkerley might be offering the minister of finance, and it is difficult to determine the exact nature of this advice from the files of either the Planning Agency or the Foundation.

The mission itself did not have any particular "plan," and its head was skeptical of a "paper plan." He was inclined to place emphasis on monetary and exchange policies, but the Planning Agency had little role to play in these fields and concentrated on the "investment budget" and on projects for possible international loans. While such an approach should have led to an improvement in specific "allocation of the nation's resources" as envisaged in the original Ford Foundation letter of April 1963, it gave no assurance of a more economic overall allocation and did not take into account the degree of utilization of resources and the rapidity of transfer of technology.

The conclusion seems inescapable that if the Harvard mission had ended as originally planned at the end of 1965, it would have had little to show for its labors. It was a period of disillusionment and frustration, especially after the departure of Diego Calle, and it was widely assumed that HDAS would depart when its initial contract expired in 1966. Dunkerley placed the blame pretty squarely on President Guillermo León Valencia, and undoubtedly economic planning reached a nadir during his administration. But in retrospect it might be added that the president's attitude toward planning was already very evident by 1963, and it might be argued that both the Foundation and HDAS would have been well-advised to have delayed their effort. But this may be asking too much.

It should be noted, however, that even in the conditions prevailing in 1963, some opportunity for overall planning did exist. There was widespread discussion at the time of two quite different approaches to the problem of planning—the CEPAL General Plan and my own Operation Colombia (see above discussion). The plans, being so different, would have provided a good basis for entrance into this field, and one of the mission members (John Sheahan) did look at both proposals.[7] It was a moment when the country had no overall plan or policy, and the mission might have performed a highly useful service in filling the gap. I would gladly have cooperated, and no doubt CEPAL would also have done so. However, the opportunity was not seized, and the Planning Agency ceased to work in overall planning.

In any case, as early as the spring of 1964, the local Ford Foundation representative (Robert Wickham) had serious misgivings, had written off ESAP, and was pressing for a review of the project.[8]

Harvard Mission: Second Phase (1966–1970)

By 1965, the Ford Foundation was prepared to wind up the Harvard project when its original term expired at the end of that year. Yet, within a year, HDAS had a new and larger four-year contract with the Foundation and with the Colombian government, and the DNP was again an important cog in the governmental machine, with restored prestige. Why the dramatic change? In this case, it is possible to attribute it without reservation to a single person, the new president, Carlos Lleras, who took office in 1966. Even before he assumed office, he talked to representatives of the Ford Foundation and expressed his determination to build up the Planning Agency, to raise salaries, and to give it more responsibility and prestige. He also expressed the hope that the Harvard mission would remain. HDAS was naturally anxious to wipe out what it felt was a blot on its record; the Foundation was equally anxious to realize something on its previous expenditure of money and effort and was glad to take advantage of the changed circumstances.

CONPES was revitalized, and steps were taken to increase the agency's budget and to upgrade salaries. Edgar Gutiérrez, who had had experience as head of the agency under President Alberto Lleras Camargo and had been a strong promoter of the CEPAL-prepared General Plan of 1961 (see above), was appointed head of the Planning Agency.

HDAS shifted its director of operations in Argentina to head the mission in Colombia (October 1966). He was Richard Mallon, a well-trained economist, fluent in Spanish, diplomatic and "simpático," with a firm grasp of what was required for survival in personal relations of a foreign adviser. He quickly made himself very useful to the new head of the Planning Agency but did so in an unobtrusive manner.[9] He remained until September 1967, and, from Cambridge, he continued to keep in close touch with the mission and prepared the influential evaluation of the project in early 1968 that furnished the basis for the new contract. The mission had two other directors from 1967 to 1970; in the whole seven-year period, the mission had four regular chiefs and three acting chiefs for varying periods.

The president continued to go out of his way to build up the prestige and quality of the agency. The training of the professional staff was steadily raised and the number increased. A prodigious number of anonymous staff "Green Books" were prepared for presentation at the weekly meetings of CONPES. President Lleras was known as a "strong" president who was inclined to make all important decisions himself. Generally, at meetings, he did most of the talking. But in the case of CONPES he would listen patiently to lengthy and usually arid reports, many on relatively minor topics. Perhaps nothing testified more to his determination to create a strong planning agency that would outlast his time.

DNP was established as a highly technical agency during the Carlos Lleras administration. While it was a stormy period with strong feelings aroused on various issues (constitutional, foreign exchange, proposed use of employees' funds, urban and agrarian reform, among others), both the head of DNP and of HDAS cultivated low profiles, taking no active part in any of these issues and letting the president act as the lightning rod for all attacks. People were not sure what DNP was doing, but the impression spread that it was a technically competent group working on important issues. It was in general understood that the president was his own spokesman. Even his minister of finance made few statements, so that the relative silence of DNP was interpreted as being in accordance with the wishes of the president and not as suggesting that it had little to say.

The number of additional responsibilities given to DNP, in fact, also now included many matters that might be considered routine, such as the approval of public utility rates, government guarantees of loan obligations, foreign investments and borrowings, and "public investment." A complete reversal had occurred from the first three and a half years of the Harvard mission. Both agency and mission now occupied a highly favorable, indeed privileged, position. A strong and competent president, impressed with the importance of economic and social planning, had increased their power and prestige to a degree unusual in lesser developed countries. Conditions were favorable for the reception of advice on policy.

Criteria for Evaluation

Before appraising the work of the mission, it must be noted that the confusion on objectives or terms of reference typical of the earlier period remained. Representatives of the Ford Foundation as individuals undoubtedly had their ideas on what should be done, but *as* representatives of the Foundation they were reluctant to urge particular policies on a government. They regarded themselves rather as administrators of trust funds whose contribution to the general welfare must be judged in a long perspective and not be jeopardized by possibly ill-timed crusades that might embroil the Foundation in controversy. Hence, they were inclined to stress training and "institution building."[10] While the successive permanent heads of HDAS were prepared to abide by these terms of reference and to give attention to training, the staff members were in general more or at least equally interested in policy and research. How to build an institution was never made clear. It would be rather pointless to argue that a planning agency may be a well-organized and trained "institution," but unfortunately persistently gives bad advice. In other words, it seems unrealistic to separate the quality of an institution from the quality of its product. The Foundation could legitimately hope that good planning would follow from good training. But this opens up the subject of what constitutes good training in economics. As Albert Berry pointed out in a later evaluation of HDAS,[11] economics is not something one learns by "in-training" or by assisting somebody else in a piece of research. It requires rigorous training in fundamentals, with reading and essay work, tested by carefully chosen questioning.

Until there is a solid core of well-trained national economists in a developing country, able to give graduate training, work in foreign universities is highly desirable and probably indispensable. The small part of the HDAS grant used to finance such training and the small portion of time spent in selecting candidates undoubtedly paid high dividends and will continue to do so over the years. From the Foundation's point of view, funds would probably have yielded still higher returns if they were employed in postgraduate training abroad. My task here is not, however, to evaluate training, but rather to point out that the bulk of the large sums involved and the time of the staff in a planning agency had to be occupied in work bearing on planning. The dichotomy of interest was never satisfactorily resolved.

The influence of the terms of reference on the mission's self-image is very clearly brought out in the evaluation report of the Harvard-Colombia Advisory Group submitted by Richard Mallon in March 1968, on the basis of which the contract with Harvard was renewed for a further term. Despite the fact that in the previous fifteen months, the periodic reports of the mission had listed no less than 120 memoranda by title, many dealing with policies or with matters having policy implications, the evaluation contained *not a word on policy*. This omission does not appear to have been questioned or even noted. The evaluation was exclusively concerned with training, as was a further evaluation report submitted in March 1970. Only one policy recommendation (to curb excessive capital-intensive investment) was included.[12] In short, the question of what the mission was supposed to be doing was not squarely faced.

Evaluation of the Work of the Mission

The output of the Harvard mission is obviously too large to examine in detail. The task must be broken down into segments, and resort must be made to sampling, with some attempt made to assess the impact of the whole.

As pointed out earlier, President Lleras conferred specific administrative, almost routine, tasks on DNP, partly to ensure that it could not be ignored in the future. This "bread and butter work" had, however, technical aspects with which the agency needed help. Hence, some of the time and a number of the memoranda of the mission were taken up with public utility rate-making problems. Similarly, a good deal of work was imposed on the Planning Agency in passing annually on "public investment," requests for foreign loans, and requests for government guarantees on obligations of decentralized agencies. As with most budget work, the task generally narrows down to new additions to expenditures, and very frequently the decision turns on regional or political considerations, so that the decision-making power here appears more impressive than it is in practice. However, the time of one of the members of the mission was largely occupied in such work, and doubtless there was an opportunity to work in benefit-cost analyses and to improve the basis of evaluation.

For a considerable period, a regular member of the mission (Richard Bird) and a consultant (Malcolm Gillis) were occupied with both substantive and administrative aspects of tax proposals. Another member of the mission helped to develop the theoretical basis for guidelines in the allocation of industries within the Andean Pact Group of countries, and another worked full time in the field of primary education.

These various activities were specialized tasks that could have been done by individuals or separate missions and, except possibly for the investment budget, were somewhat apart from what one would think of as the main concern of a mission to a planning agency.

In the case of the first World Bank mission, treated above (Chapter 5), or the successive IMF missions, where there was a group under a director, the aim was specific, and the director assumed responsibility for the division of work and the character of the recommendations. The Harvard mission, as noted repeatedly, had no specific objective or goal in the field of policy and was organized not to diagnose underdevelopment and to elaborate a program to remedy it, but rather to work generally in broad sectors. The director also worked on disparate projects when he was not occupied with administrative tasks. The studies, therefore, reflect in large part the personal inclination and specialties of individual members of the mission, though there is also evident a conscious effort to be useful to the agency in dealing briefly with a number of smaller problems. In the director's trimestral report for January-May 1970, for example, there is appended a revealing list of future work programs as "prepared by the advisers," which includes (1) a dropout study in primary education, (2) credit to small industry, (3) material for Andean Group negotiations, (4) continued work in effective customs protection, (5) macroeconomic studies in employment, (6) causes of inflation, (7) bank interest rates, (8) minor exports, (9) a macroeconomic model for Colombia, (10) agricultural credit and pricing policies and the postwar performance of agriculture, and (11) studies on five topics in the field of technology transfer, patents, trademarks, and royalties.

All or most of these proposed studies dealt with matters bearing on national policy in various fields. They lack, however, a unifying theme. There could be more of the same or less, without impact on real growth or distribution; thus, it is difficult to see what function the mission played in developing a national policy.

This lack of focus and orientation helps to explain what otherwise is puzzling—why President Lleras, with an enlarged and greatly improved central planning agency assisted by a high-powered foreign mission, should have invited the ILO and a large mission to Colombia to study unemployment (1969-1970), and, a little earlier (1968), arrange for a special tax reform mission, or why, at about the same time, the World Bank should also have dispatched a comprehensive mission to Colombia to propose ways and means of accelerating growth. The tax mission under Richard Musgrave may have been somewhat specialized (see Chapter 8), but the other two necessarily dealt with the most important overall economic problems of the country, and tax policy should not be divorced from overall policy. Clearly, neither the president nor the World Bank felt that these problems had been dealt with adequately in the work of the previous six years. This was most certainly not because of lack of ability on the part of the members of the Harvard mission, but because HDAS did not feel it was commissioned to do the jobs that were undertaken by the ILO, Musgrave, and the World Bank—which brings us back again to the original problem of terms of reference.

The government of Colombia might have been expected to insist on work in national programming. That this was not done in 1963 might be attributed to the fact that the head of planning was new and inexperienced and Colombia presumably had a plan (the CEPAL-prepared General Plan of 1961). But it is surprising that President Lleras did not bring the point up in 1966. When the new chief of DNP undertook to prepare an investment plan for the period 1969-1972, which was accepted by President Lleras and highly publicized, he apparently got some help from one or more of the members of the Harvard mission, but relied chiefly on his Colombian staff.

An incident that occurred during the visit of the ILO mission on unemployment throws light on attitudes. The director of the Harvard group, highly cooperative, prepared a paper for circulation among the members of his staff before the meeting with the ILO group and later took some satisfaction from the fact that the latter appeared to accept the views of the paper. All this is doubtless right and proper, but one might have expected some show of feeling that the ILO was in fact encroaching on the field of the Harvard mission and that the ad hoc mission was not really necessary. If there was any such natural resentment, it was well concealed. Within a year there were three reports on development in Colombia—none by the Harvard mission.

Absence of an Adequate Overall Program

The elaboration of an overall program did not occupy much of the Harvard group's time or attention. The first head of the mission was presumably concerned with the prolonged exchange crisis that continued during his incumbency. In any case, he was skeptical of "paper plans." There was then a gap until Richard Mallon assumed the headship toward the end of 1966. In his four memoranda on overall programming, he found the constraints on growth to be the lack of exchange and inadequate capital formation. The former was to be made up by increased foreign borrowing and the latter, by borrowing and restriction of consumption. He took a gloomy view of urban growth and growing unemployment, anticipating the view of the ILO mission of 1970 and concluding that additional employment would have to be found in agriculture. His last memorandum stressed the importance of public investment and the use of labor-intensive methods. Not one of these memoranda, addressed to the head of DNP, was submitted to CONPES, and none had any discernible impact. So, despite the very close and cordial relationship of the directors of the DNP and the Harvard mission—a condition that should have resulted in specific policies—either the advice was too general or the director of the DNP did not have enough influence or confidence to sway the president. Mallon has stated that he refused to attend any of the cabinet committee meetings and did not allow any other adviser to do so;[13] hence his group was rather remote from current overall policymaking.

Fiscal and monetary policy occupies an important place in overall planning in all countries, and in Colombia the head of DNP is a member of the monetary authority. Thus, it might be expected that the mission would be much concerned with this subject. But there is surprisingly little in the files before 1968 (near the end of the mission). (As is noted in Chapter 7 on monetary advice, the position of DNP in this part of the field of planning was weakened, curiously enough, by President Lleras himself in the exchange crisis of 1966-1967, when he shifted discussion and decision making from CONPES to the Junta Monetaria.) The work on taxation by Richard Bird in 1965 and 1967 and by Gillis in 1969 was in general extraneous to the work of the mission and was carried on in the Treasury, where Bird produced numerous memoranda. Some valuable work was done in the elaboration of a series on industrial production but with the departure of the expert, interest lapsed. Work on the problem of the rural poor and on urban and regional policy had a minimal impact.

Overall Appraisal of the Mission and Its Work

It must be emphasized that the above is a treatment of a representative sampling of a flood of memoranda and articles, designed only to give a feeling of the work of the Harvard mission. Of the memoranda submitted by DNP to CONPES and the decisions of that body, only one was written by a Harvard adviser (on education), and the mission itself was only recorded as being mentioned once in the period 1966 to 1971—by President Lleras and in complimentary terms. Whatever influence, therefore, the mission may have exerted on policy must have been through its influence on the anonymous authors of the DNP memoranda, probably more in the underlying analyses and in discussions than in formal recommendations. Many of the views expressed in individual Harvard mission memoranda can also be found in DNP memoranda submitted to CONPES, but they were usually views that were generally held or were "in the air." It is likely that the Harvard group was strongest in the analysis of "micro" questions—specific projects in the investment budget and for foreign financing.[14]

In contrasting the length, size, and sponsorship of the mission with the rather meager results obtained, one is forced to concur with the verdict of the Ford Foundation, the Interamerican Development Bank, and the Colombian Planning Agency itself, that the results hardly justified the effort. For training, money spent in foreign scholarships paid higher dividends. The upgrading of the Planning Agency was in large part due to President Carlos Lleras. For a portion of the period of the mission, the conditions for macro planning were not propitious, certainly, but for other portions it appears that excellent opportunities were not seized, though here it is possible that the ambiguities in the terms of reference may have stood in the way. The views on overall policy were not carefully worked up, were conventional, and acted to block consideration of other approaches in the long period from 1963 to 1970. That opportunities existed is suggested by the fact that President Lleras turned to other groups for suggestions on macro planning.[15]

A number of factors contributed to the relative ineffectiveness of this experience in advising, of which perhaps the most important were the uncertainty in the terms of reference and the accompanying absence of concentration on strategic elements. Efforts were diffused and uncoordinated, and objectives varied with individuals and in any case were multiple. None of the agencies involved—the sponsor, the host country, and the group itself—had a clear or unanimous view on the purpose of the advising group.

In 1970, the Interamerican Development Bank rejected an application for a new loan as its contribution to the cost of the mission, and the Ford Foundation let it be known that, while it would not make up the deficit, it would continue with a reduced contribution to the Planning Agency. An evaluation committee of unit chiefs proposed that the agency negotiate directly with individual advisers. In the meantime, however, HDAS had contemplated phasing out over a longer period and had already contracted advisers whose terms extended well into 1971. Consequently, and unfortunately, the long association ended on a somewhat sour note, with scarcely concealed recriminations and bad feelings.

7
ADVICE ON
MONETARY, EXCHANGE,
AND PRICE POLICIES

In this chapter, I propose to examine the process of advice-giving in that part of macroeconomic policy that comprises the monetary, fiscal, exchange, and international trade fields and that has as its objective stability and growth. The fields cannot, or at least should not, be treated in isolation.

Although there is perhaps no area in which more advice is given, the extent to which governments, even of more developed countries, will accept and act upon such advice has become almost a measure of social discipline, as the recommendations, as distinct from objectives, are almost invariably unpopular. Advice to less developed countries in this general range of subjects, therefore, has difficulty gaining acceptance. Countries rarely *ask* for advice in these areas; it is usually imposed.

Much of the story has to do with advice given by the International Monetary Fund, advice often "tied," in the form of conditions attached to loans (although some is untied and some takes the form of praise or criticism of current policy). Of interest, as a prelude, however, is an almost forgotten devaluation in Colombia, which resulted from foreign advice *not* from the IMF. It is in part, and unavoidably, a personal story.

The Devaluation of 1951

As remarked earlier, an IMF economist, Roger Anderson, covered the foreign exchange field in the World Bank's first mission to Colombia. (See Chapter 5.) He collected a mass of material, part of which I used in the mission's report, tending to show that the peso was overvalued (at 1.95 to a dollar) to the detriment of noncoffee exports, that it was maintained by the licensing or rationing of exchange, and that Colombia enjoyed (or suffered from, depending on one's point of view) a variety of exchange rates, some open and some concealed.

When I returned to Colombia in 1950 and the Committee on Economic Development had been established (see Chapter 5), we quickly got involved in price stability, transport, and a big issue involving a steel works. As recorded in Chapter 11, the battle was lost on this issue, and even the compromise proposal that the committee urged on the government was not accepted. Fearing that the prestige of the committee and its enthusiasm had been damaged, I cast around for some way to restore it. I decided, rather naively, that an objective, valuable in itself, that would also serve this purpose would be correction of the overvaluation of the peso, which in turn would permit the reduction of restrictions on imports. There was no exchange crisis and no pressure for devaluation at the time, but I was fairly confident that once the issue was raised in the committee, a "crisis" would be created and action of some sort would result.

The committee was glad to turn from the unrewarding issue of the steel works to the exchange problem, which would place it in the limelight. On a crude purchasing power parity basis, I calculated that the peso was overvalued by about 40 percent, or that it could be moved with benefit to the country to 2.75 to a dollar. When the subject was broached in the committee, the minister of finance immediately had the Banco de la República suspend all dealings in exchange, thus creating the "crisis" and the need for some action, but at the same time avoiding an outflow of capital, advance purchasing of imports, and loss of reserves.

The president was shocked by my figure, insisting that it would result in an inflationary price rise and proposing instead a devaluation of 10 percent. I had convinced the committee that this figure would be completely inadequate, and we gradually, through the minister of finance, persuaded the president to raise his figure from 2.20 to 2.30 to 2.40 and finally to 2.50. At this point (a 28-percent depreciation), he dug his heels in and refused to consider a higher figure, and we settled for that.

I had blithely[1] calculated that since imports in 1950 were 700 million pesos and the GDP was around 8 billion, the impact on the domestic price level of a 25-percent devaluation should be in the neighborhood of 25 percent of 9 percent, or 2.25 percent. Actually, prices rose hardly at all at the time of the devaluation, and the level of consumer prices in 1952 averaged only about 6 percent above the level of 1951—little more than would probably have occurred in any case. (The volume of money at the end of 1952 was 35 percent above the volume at the end of 1950.) The devaluation was accompanied by a sweeping transfer of goods from the prohibited or licensed to the free list. I recall the banker on the committee, Martín del Corral, looking at me shocked when I suggested that now we could do away with applications for exchange altogether and saying, "No, no. That is out of the question," and my replying, "Well, you can require applications for statistical purposes if you like, but you don't *need* to continue licensing." Needless to say, licensing was continued but on a very liberal basis.

An internal study made much later in the World Bank made an interesting attempt to calculate a "scarcity ratio of exchange" by comparing the rate that could have provided exchange equilibrium without recourse to controls, advance deposits for imports, and tariffs. While necessarily rough, the orders of magnitude and direction of movements are probably not far off for privately imported goods. It suggests that this hypothetical equilibrium rate fell from double the official rate in 1950 to approximately the same as the official rate in 1954, doubled again by 1957 and remained around double through 1963 (despite the devaluations of 1957 and 1962), shot up to treble in 1965, and returned to a little over double in 1966 and 1968.[2]

The committee was highly pleased with its work on this issue and felt that its prestige had been reestablished. Doubtless, the IMF had mixed feelings. The president made no acknowledgment to the committee, but he probably was satisfied, although he may not have felt convinced that the devaluation was necessary. It was doubtless greater than necessary from the point of view of the balance of payments, but this was largely an accident due to the high coffee prices and good harvests. It was not excessive, however, for it permitted some liberation of imports and encouraged non-coffee exports.

Exports rose from US$394 million in 1950 to US$483 million in 1952; imports from $364 to $415 million; and international reserves from $113 million at the end of 1950 to $166 million at the end of 1952.[3]

The limited increase in imports suggests that importers expected the new rate to hold; that the previous restriction had not been as severe as had been thought; and that the desire to import was moderated by the depreciation of 28 percent in the exchange rate. The new rate remained until 1957, by which time it had itself become overvalued.

Lessons

The success of the devaluation, and the absence of adverse price repercussions, the considerable liberalization of trade, and a concurrent strengthening of the reserve position of the central bank were due partly to luck and partly to fortunate timing. For one thing, coffee prices and exports were strengthening at that time, and for another, this was the only devaluation in Colombia, up to and including that of 1966 (discussed below), that was not forced and took place when there was no pressure on exchanges and hence no expectation of a large price rise. In short, the best time to devalue is when nobody expects it!

Monetary and Exchange Advice in the 1960s

Monetary and exchange advice in the 1960s was given almost exclusively by the International Monetary Fund, supported on occasion by the World Bank and the Agency for International Development in the State Department (AID). The IMF's advice-giving activity began with a review of the balance of payments, payments restrictions, and creditworthiness of member countries in granting short-term balance-of-payment loans, in deciding what terms such loans should have under the articles of agreement, and in checking on the extent to which member countries were adhering to the international code of conduct agreed to in this field. Many elements lead up to an exchange crisis, however, so that a staff review of such elements, a sequential analysis, and recommendations both to the government of the country concerned and to the executive board of the IMF in time became a rich source of data and advice.[4] Over the years, an expert staff has been developed that is able routinely to put together a picture in a surprisingly short time.[5] Staff missions were not only dispatched when countries applied for loans, but also continued periodically as long as the loans were outstanding. The IMF kept itself informed on developments in member countries even when no loans were outstanding.

The views of the IMF should be given considerable weight because they are often invoked in a time of emergency or crisis (despite reiterated statements by the IMF that action should be taken well in advance to avoid the emergence of a crisis) and because other and longer term lenders or suppliers of aid frequently follow the IMF's lead in fiscal, monetary, and exchange matters. Hence, a country is likely to find itself confronted with large demands for payments it cannot meet and simultaneously to have further credits denied to it when it needs them most. A country always has the option of declining the "advice" and resorting to severe exchange controls. But few countries can afford to run the risk of finding other sources of credit closed to it or at least restricted.

Underlying Theory

The IMF was not originally created to encourage "development" or growth—that was to be more the positive function of the World Bank—but rather had a more negative role of preventing restrictions on trade and payments, discriminatory practices that might lead to retaliation and further restrictions, and of actively promoting greater freedom. (The IMF was planned in wartime, and it appeared urgent to attempt to remove the host of wartime restrictions.) The theory was that unimpeded exercise of private initiative, economic incentives, competition, and mobility of capital and technology would lead to a highly desirable division of labor on a world scale and to world trade on the basis of comparative advantage, in which each country would specialize in activities it could perform with greatest relative efficiency. The task of the IMF, therefore, was to use its powers to avoid the necessity of restricting imports or, through the use of multiple and discriminatory exchange rates, of securing advantages in exports *not* due to superior efficiency but to subsidies and dumping. Although it is true that the original aim was to avoid resort to exchange rate variations as a means of correcting payments imbalances, by the 1950s the IMF was stressing the desirability of "realism" in this area.

Although the objective was free trade and "neutral" exchange rates and practices, the task of securing reductions in tariff barriers was left to other agencies, and it was envisaged that the IMF's activities would be restricted to exchange practices. Tariffs were so universal that the founders decided not to attempt to deal with such obstacles to trade.

Given the underlying theory, the effectiveness of the IMF's work relating to development or growth is conditioned by the extent to which growth is limited by international trade. When, in the 1950s and 1960s, stress was laid on the volume of imports necessary to sustain certain rates of domestic growth, the IMF promoted exports since they offered a means of acquiring imports. It did not look with approval on exports that led only to a growth in central bank reserves, but it used its influence to ensure that increased exports were balanced by increased imports and lessened restrictions. These imports, in turn, were expected to stimulate internal growth and the ability to export as well as to ease the balance-of-payments problems of other countries. Thus, although the interest of the IMF has broadened in the course of time, the original articles of agreement and the orientation they reflect still play an important role and must be kept in mind in appraising the IMF's "advice."

The idea persists that the IMF is dedicated to fixed exchange rates. Since at least the early 1960s, however, it has urged devaluation on countries whose currencies were obviously overvalued and has accepted floating rates as "temporary" stages to an "eventual" return to fixity.[6]

The IMF founders expected a worldwide bias toward excessive devaluation, but in practice, at least until recently, the contrary was true, and most governments (with the notable exceptions of

West Germany and Japan) tended to maintain overvalued currencies. Governments must always exude confidence to avoid a possible run and tend to believe their own assurances. In time, the IMF
recognized this fact and adjusted its policy accordingly. It was slow
and hesitant, however, to accept the principle of the creeping or
crawling peg (rate of devaluation) or the application of monetary
correction to the exchange rate to compensate for relative inflation
and other relative influences, apparently because it was thought
that this would weaken the incentives to work toward domestic
price stability and to liberalize quantitative restrictions on exchange payments. I will return to this very important point after a
brief review of the IMF's Colombian experience.

The IMF and Other Agencies

Although member countries undertake the responsibility of supplying the information needed by the IMF, periodically dispatching
factfinding teams to such countries became the practice. Initially,
the facts as well as the "advice" were limited to matters bearing on
the balance of payments, but it was soon discovered that such matters touched upon a very substantial part of a country's economic
program.

Hence, there was overlapping of subject matter among the IMF,
the World Bank, and later, other lending or aid-granting agencies.
It will be remembered, for example, that the IMF objected to the inclusion of a recommendation on the exchange rate in the first
World Bank mission report on Colombia. (See Chapter 4.) Later,
however, it did not hestitate to give opinions on general development policies, thus overlapping and on occasion differing with the
praise or censure or advice of the Bank and other development
agencies. That this has not resulted in more confusion than prevails
is partly because some effort is made at critical times to present a
united front of lenders, partly because the IMF's public expressions
of opinion are generally limited to balance-of-payments matters,
and partly because the Bank and other agencies tend to work with
ministries, planning offices, and decentralized agencies. In contrast, the IMF works almost exclusively with central banks and the
ministers of finance. Essential differences remain clear. While the

Bank or AID may proclaim that development has to do with the direct fulfillment of basic human needs, the IMF is more inclined to see development in terms of foreign trade, price stability, and growth in GDP.

Events in Colombia Preceding the Effective Devaluation of 1966

There were three fairly massive devaluations in Colombia leading up to the 1966-1967 episode. All three were characterized by prior excessive monetary expansion, an overvalued exchange rate for imports and for non-coffee exports, and quantitative restrictions on imports.[7] Remedial measures were excessively delayed, giving rise to widespread expectations with consequent efforts by individuals to anticipate events, bringing on "exchange crises." Finally, the liberalization of imports was excessive from the point of view of expectations and the amount of support made available by the IMF. The resulting lack of confidence and cynicism showed themselves in widespread price and wage markups and heavy stocking up of imports, which quickly recreated the conditions that led to the devaluations in the first place. Unfortunately, the conclusion was reached that the devaluations were themselves to blame, and even the severe restrictions on trade were preferable. The creation of a monetary board in 1963 did not noticeably improve the functioning of the system.

This was the background of the situation that confronted President Carlos Lleras when he assumed office in the middle of 1966. A brave attempt to achieve an open economic society in 1965 had ended in dismal failure. With slower growth and rapidly expanding population, the growth in income per capita in the years 1962-1965 had fallen to 1.5 percent per annum. Monetary expansion had been excessive, mainly because of borrowings from the Banco de la República to finance the purchase of the coffee crop from growers at prices above the world market.

The Events of 1966–1967 and the "Confrontation"

With the balance of payments in very bad shape, international reserves negative, and arrears in some payments, the IMF in early

November 1966 was pressing for a devaluation of the most important rate of exchange from 13.5 to 16. Its position was being supported by the World Bank and AID. The president was in a most
difficult position since devaluation had become a dirty word, and
in any case he did not believe that a simple move to another rate
would be sufficient. On November 19, 1966, therefore, he made the
bold move of "rejecting devaluation" by reinstituting strict exchange controls on payments, suspending the free exchange
market, and providing a "capital market" rate of 16.25, which
could be used to make payments for various purposes and which
would provide a breathing spell while the situation could be
studied. In other words, he instituted a partial and *de facto*
devaluation, stopping the drain of reserves, securing a more
realistic external value of the peso, and establishing a basis for
foreign loans. He managed this by having a public difference with
the IMF, while in effect agreeing to terms it would accept.

A series of meetings followed both in Bogotá and in Washington,
D.C., culminating, in March 1967, in a unilateral adoption of
"Decree-Law 444" as an alternative to devaluation, which was
stated to provide for a floating rate of exchange determined by the
"forces of supply and demand." This was followed in a few days by
an application to the IMF for a standby credit of US$60 million.
The government of Colombia proposed various targets and ceilings
to apply to exchange policy for imports and internal credit exten-
sions and substituted a coffee export tax for a special exchange rate,
but provided for quarterly adjustments of the targets as it proved
necessary. It set a new informal target of a 15-percent expansion in
the money supply as well as adjustable ceilings on central bank
assets. These were all targets and ceilings which the IMF had infor-
mally proposed or would be expected to require, and the standby
credit was granted on April 14.[8]

As far as the public was concerned, the president, in the role of
David, appeared to have brought Goliath to his knees and in doing
so converted a dangerous political liability into an asset.[9] However,
the IMF secured the devaluation it had been urging and succeeded
in various undertakings designed to further the objectives of stability
and trade. Thus, another crisis had been weathered.

A consequence of the expert political handling of the exchange
emergency discussed above was that the Colombian government

was able to secure authority to codify the laws and regulations relating to exchange management in Decree-Law 444. Presented as a major transition to an exchange market whose rate would be freely determined by the forces of supply and demand, the Decree-Law did not officially *authorize* the Junta Monetaria or the minister of finance to regulate the supply and the demand and to fix the rates and the types of transactions they governed. But in actuality, the Junta and the minister were *enabled* to do so. *The standby credit was public; the commitments to the IMF were not.*[10] The head of the Harvard mission in Colombia at the time, Richard Mallon, said in a report to the Ford Foundation in February 1967 that the formula had been drafted jointly by the Colombian government and the IMF and "is one of the most unique and flexible ones ever conceived." The president was quoted as saying that he did not favor a condition in which the exchange rate could be varied by direct administrative action of the government,[11] but this is actually what resulted, and no criteria or guides for the determination of the rate are provided by law.

Decree-Law 444 and the effective devaluations of 1966-1967 did not obviate the danger of excessive monetary expansion, an overvalued peso, and quantitative import restrictions. What they did do was open the way for small, continuous "adjustments" to the exchange rate, thus avoiding the possible traumatic effect of massive exchange devaluations. The relatively conservative monetary policy of the Carlos Lleras administration kept expansion within bounds; the "creeping peg" resulted in yearly devaluations in terms of the dollar of 6.9, 5.9, and 6.9 percent, respectively, in 1968, 1969, and 1970, which, after allowance for the rise of prices in the United States, was not far out of line with the rise in prices and costs in Colombia. The rate of economic growth increased to 7 percent by 1970, other measures were taken to encourage non-coffee exports, and the reports of IMF missions in 1969-1971 were complimentary.

Appraisal of IMF Advice

In the events leading up to the 1967 "confrontation," it would appear, in retrospect, that the IMF should have been keeping in closer touch with the situation; should have assisted Colombia in securing larger credits; should not have been initially so favorable to such a large shift to unrestricted entry (by October 1966 almost 80 percent of all imports had been freed from quantitative restriction); should have exerted a lot of pressure to prevent excessive monetary expansion; and should have urged the government to have the Coffee Federation cover its losses and allow coffee to be exported also at world prices by private exporters.

On the other hand, the IMF did urge in 1965 that the devaluation should not be to a fixed, unalterable rate but that the door should be left open for a truly flexible exchange rate "until stability is more firmly established." It urged the same policy in 1967, and such a policy was actually adopted.

There is a popular impression that the IMF favors "massive" devaluations and mistakenly urged those on Colombia. But it seems that the necessary devaluations were "massive" only because they were unduly delayed by the resistance of governments. It was a pity, however, that the IMF did not officially favor the principle of monetary correction or indexation as applied to the rate of exchange. While talking of a "realistic" rate, it left its determination purely arbitrary.

There can be nothing but praise for the IMF's attitude throughout the "confrontation" of 1967 when it settled for the substance of policy and let others take the credit, and indeed let itself be put in an unpopular light in order to facilitate necessary reforms.

IMF Performance in General

On monetary policy, the IMF urged a fundamental reorientation of attitudes which, had it been accepted, might have changed subsequent history. Staff papers throughout the 1960s stated that selective channeling of central bank credit "must be subordinated to the overall quantitative limitations of monetary expansion dictated by the over-riding objective of external and internal/stability." Unfortunately, this good advice disappeared from staff papers after 1970. It can be argued, however, that the IMF placed too much reliance on arbitrary ceilings on central bank credit, which again and again proved ineffective, and not enough on ceilings on the growth in the means of payment, with frequent reports and consultations on whatever ways and means appeared appropriate to enforce them.

The IMF appears to have been unable to make up its mind on what money was and what, therefore, it was trying to control. It acquiesced in the illogical practice of approving an expansion of money in excess of the growth in estimated real output on the grounds that the current rise in prices also required "fuel" to maintain it. Following this course, with a consequent chronic rise in prices, one could never expect to arrive at a parity unless other countries did the same in the same percentage and experienced the same rise in prices.

The analysis of current economic development in Colombia often leaves much to be desired. In 1972, for example, real GDP grew by over 7 percent. With favorable terms of trade and an exceptionally high rate of production of agricultural goods, agricultural exports increased. But prices rose by 14 percent, whereas the central bank credit ceilings and limitations on the short-term foreign liabilities of commercial banks had been set to produce a monetary expansion that was thought consistent with a rate of increase in domestic prices of only 8 percent. The higher inflation rate was blamed on increased velocity of circulation, since bank "credit" to the private sector was declared to have grown by only 6.5 percent. The increased velocity in turn was blamed in part on the growth of savings deposits in commercial banks and in mortgage banks at the expense of demand deposits. But the only way this could happen would be to reduce the reserves available against demand deposits, which, in fact, *increased* considerably. A more obvious explanation of the failure to restrict the rate of inflation to the target of 8 percent was that total money (M_1) expanded 24 percent. At the same time, the income velocity of money rose by 4.6 percent. The Colombian monetary authorities set ceilings for 1973 that were thought to be compatible with a growth in the money supply of 18 percent above the average level of 1972. Apparently, the IMF staff raised no objections to this policy. As it turned out, M_1 rose by 25.2 percent in 1973.

There appears to be no escape from the conclusion that on occasion the monetary analysis and the monetary checks proposed were inadequate. After such a long record of the inadequacy of the ceil-

ing used to check excessive monetary growth, one would have
thought that the IMF would have tried to put the ceiling on the
volume of money itself, spelling out the ways and means of controlling commercial bank reserves through open market operations.
The discussion of the new savings and loan system based on indexation and started at the end of 1972 also left much to be desired.
Unsubstantiated statements were made that funds for housing had
been adequate prior to 1972, that interest rates had been adequate
(actually they were negative and the only buyers of the previous
"bearer" mortgage bonds were people who saw these as a con-
venient way to escape all taxes, especially inheritance), and that a
static volume of savings was diverted from other purposes. While
there was fairly constant concern over the distortions caused by
overvalued exchange rates, there is a strange *absence* of concern
for the distortions resulting from undervalued interest rates. The
introduction of monetary correction in the savings/mortgage
market, where the distortion was most felt, was not hailed as a step
in the right direction. Rather, it was criticized for creating distortions because it raised effective interest rates to a realistic level and
might be followed in other sectors![12]

The IMF, it seems, was too insistent on utilizing all the proceeds
of exports to increase imports, rather than building up more adequate reserves, even if this required prolonging restrictions. Tariffs,
which it condoned, are also a form of restriction on imports, so the
matter is really one of form and degree of restrictive action. While
free trade may be an ideal for the world as a whole, it is difficult to
see how LDCs can industrialize without some form of industrial
protection, such as more developed countries used to protect their
own infant industries.

The degree of pressure which the IMF can exert is admittedly
limited and subject to attacks. For one thing, almost everything it
recommends is unpopular—raising taxes, cutting expenditures,
restrictive monetary policies, devaluation, freer trade, and removal
of subsidies and price controls. And its self-imposed policy of silence
prevents it from making an effective answer to nationalistic attacks. Finally, the penalty of refusing a loan to curb a speculative
flight is so extreme that it can be used only under most excep-
tionable circumstances. It invites the danger that a country will
suspend payments and place highly restrictive controls on all

imports and payments, blaming the consequences on "the international bankers." The problem for the IMF, therefore, is to persuade the member in straits to accept as much advice as it will by the use of a combination of praise and blame, threats and rewards and, for the rest, to tolerate with as good grace as it can muster the continuance "for the time being" of policies of which it strongly disapproves.

Over the years, missions of staff members have visited countries, collected data, listened politely to assurances on the budget, monetary policy, balance of payments, prices, the removal of restrictions, and the realistic adjustments of the exchange rate. In some way, they have conveyed to the member who wishes a new or renewed loan that it would be well advised to include in its application specific quantitative targets for increasing imports by such and such an amount, and placing a ceiling on the accumulation of international reserves and on the volume of central bank internal credit outstanding, all on specific dates, and all subject to certain adjustments if certain eventualities occur. If the ceilings are not observed, the member undertakes not to make further drafts on standby credit without permission of the IMF.[13] This sounds tough. The catch, however, is that *permission appears always to be forthcoming.* There are always explanations and the explanations are accepted, and assurances that new measures being taken will prevent a recurrence are accepted.

Again, domestic pressures *are* very strong, governmental statements of intentions are not publicly known, and little can be done about the basic weakness of the IMF in championing unpopular policies. The IMF could probably maintain with justice that the pressure and persuasion it has been able to exert have contributed to greater stability and fewer restrictions, and hence more growth, than would otherwise have occurred. Whether one would favor a tougher policy on the part of the IMF depends on how one feels about the content of the policy.

Failure to Control Inflation in Colombia (1971-1974)

The Plan of the Four Strategies of 1971-1974 is discussed in Chapter 4 and the underlying theoretical basis for that plan is treated in Chapter 3. The guidelines expounding the plan warned against the danger of inflation but did not make a positive anti-inflation program one of the principal strategies. Even though the DNP was in a weak position in this field, it is clear, in retrospect, that the plan's failure to take a stronger stand against inflation was a serious defect.

The criticisms that the rise in inflation in 1972-1973 was due to indexation, however, can be disposed of easily. The rate of inflation stepped up well before the indexation system was inaugurated. Furthermore, the rapid growth in real savings and their partial sterilization because of initial inability to disburse loaned funds as rapidly as deposits grew were both counterinflationary forces. Nevertheless, the rate of inflation rose from 9.2 percent in 1971 to 13 percent in 1972, 19.1 percent in 1973, and 24 percent in 1974, and clouded the otherwise good economic record of the administration of President Misael Pastrana.

To account for rates of these magnitudes, recourse must be had to expansions in the money supply. Spontaneous change in the income velocity of circulation, a rise in the price of imports, poor harvests, industrial bottlenecks, and cost-push factors—other explanations offered for inflation—cannot generally account for more than a few points rise *unless* accompanied by an expansion of money at a rate higher than the rate of economic growth. In other words, for high and sustained rates of inflation, there must be an expansion of money (cash in the hands of the public plus demand deposits) from whatever cause in excess of the rate of growth. From 1960 to 1973, the demand for money in Colombia remained remarkably constant (equal to 50 to 58 days' value of production—that is, an income velocity of money between 6.3 and 7.3), and the rise in prices bore a very close relation to the growth of money in excess of the growth in output. With the rise of prices experienced from 1971 on, however, it was to be expected that people would seek to economize still more in their real holdings (or that the velocity of circulation would rise), so that the aggregate money income would be fed from both an increase in money and an increase in velocity. This actually occurred, exacerbated to a minor degree by the other factors mentioned above. The means of payment (yearly averages of quarterly figures) in the years

1971-1974 expanded at 12.8, 16.9, 27.5 and 23.1 percent, respectively, and the velocity of circulation, 3.4, 4.5, 2.6, and 9.8 percent, respectively.[14] The monetary base was increased by financing the government's internal cash deficit and by expanding central bank loans to commercial banks and other borrowers to meet "credit needs."

As noted in Chapter 3, monetary policy in Colombia had, by tacit consent, passed from the purview of the National Economic and Social Council to the Junta Monetaria. On fiscal policy, the DNP retained some veto powers over "investment," especially foreign borrowing. But in Colombia, the minister of finance is, practically speaking, the dominant figure in monetary, fiscal, foreign exchange, and borrowing policies. He presides over the Junta Monetaria, which is the equivalent of the Board of Governors of the Federal Reserve System, and politically he far outranks, in power and in status, the head of the Planning Agency.

In the case of the Plan of the Four Strategies, the director of the Planning Agency had taken issue with the minister and the Junta Monetaria on the adoption of a limited degree of indexation to stimulate and protect savings for housing from the effects of inflation, and, with the support of the president, he carried the day. It was very rare indeed for the president to overrule the minister of finance and the top officials of the Banco de la República in a matter of such importance. It was felt that to carry the battle to a second front might mean a loss of both, and monetary correction seemed to offer better possibilities and the long-term stakes appeared greater. The severity of the struggle over the "first front," with the issue remaining in doubt until the final meeting with the president on April 28, 1972, seemed to confirm the wisdom of this political judgment.

By the end of 1973, however, the government's whole program and record were being placed in jeopardy by inflation. Much of the mounting criticism was being directed at the monetary correction system because it stimulated building, because it diverted funds from industry and agriculture, which "forced" an extension of central bank credit, and because it was increasing "quasi money." Under the pressure of this criticism, the basis for calculating the adjustment to principal was extended so that the "correction" was less than the current inflation. Savings deposits were piling up faster than construction loans could be spent, and the excess was deposited in the central bank, exerting a contractionary effect. In 1973, the new director of the DNP, Luis Eduardo Rosas, having urged restrictive monetary policy to the Junta Monetaria without effect, planned to devote the entire issue of the DNP's journal to criticism of current monetary policy. I contributed one of the four articles[15] and in a private talk with the president again urged the need for monetary restraint. Our arguments and charts carried the day, and the president went on television to announce the new policy of monetary restraint, pointing out the incompatibility of the central bank acting both as a monetary authority and as a bank of development. It was very late in the day, unfortunately, for the elections were in March and the change in government in August. Although the president's insistence had its effect in slowing up the expansion of money for the remainder of his tenure, a new government took office in August and the expansion was renewed.

Conclusion

Despite the efforts of the early Kemmerer missions to enforce stability by law, and despite great efforts by the first World Bank mission, the IMF, and the Planning Agency in the 1971-1974 period, it is clear that in the field of monetary and fiscal policy advice failed to win acceptance. The field is admittedly technical, and the belief that the central bank should also or primarily be a development bank is strongly entrenched and has created its own powerful set of vested interests. The accumulated experience abroad has been disregarded, and the controversy in more developed countries on the causes of inflation has weakened the authority of the "expert" in this field. It is a field in which the LDCs are reluctant to ask for foreign expert advice. Thus, it seems that the hope must be in the advanced technical training being received by more and more national economists.

8
ADVICE ON
TAX POLICY

Like monetary, price, and exchange policies, tax policy is a field that is both technically difficult and usually unpopular. Also like the others, it provides a test of a country's degree of development. Generally speaking, the less "developed" a country, the less efficient is its tax administration and the lower its tax tolerance. Conscious of this fact, a government may find it useful, indeed necessary, to place the onus for unpopular proposals on foreign advisers.

A classic case of the characteristics of tax advising can be found in the Musgrave Commission's experience in Colombia. The treatment here is short and is directed largely to illustrating the importance of tempering the ideal with the practical.

In 1968, President Carlos Lleras invited Professor Richard Musgrave to organize and head a commission to recommend tax reform in Colombia. The terms of reference in the decree creating the commission were extremely vague, merely calling for an adequate, fair, and stable regimen. Apparently, it was felt that the need for "tax reform" was self-evident, so that the Musgrave group could write its own terms, which it promptly did. The objectives were to acquire more revenue to finance more public investment and education expenditures, to speed development, and to secure better justice among contributors, a 6-percent rate of growth, and better distribution.

Preliminary estimates[1] indicated that by 1971 there would be a need for from 3,000 to 4,500 million pesos ($) in additional revenue to finance the gap between projected revenues and expenditures (or a rise in revenue of some 15 to 20 percent). Elsewhere in the report, the deficit was estimated at $8,000 million, which, it stated, would raise revenue requirements by 40 percent.[2] The report did not explain why these substantial increases in government spending in agriculture, transport, and electrification would assist in generating the 6-percent growth target it postulated. In any case, a substantial rise in additional revenue was recommended, but a rather disingenuous remark was added, noting that if it did not prove "necessary," rates could be lowered. Considering that the total projected yield of actual taxes by 1971 was expected to be $20,000 million, a proposal to raise an extra $3,000 to $4,500 million was lending a special connotation to the phrase "tax reform." What was really being proposed was a wide series of tax *changes* to yield substantial additional revenues.

As a matter of fact, in the years 1967 to 1970 the national government deficit rose only from $230 million to $1,462 million and was financed entirely by external borrowings.[3] In 1968, the year of the Musgrave Commission, the national government had a deficit of $573 million which was more than offset by borrowings of $1,061 million abroad. The case for increased revenues, therefore, had to rest on the grounds that an increase in "public investment" was necessary to raise the rate of growth. But by 1970, with no change in tax rates, the rate of economic growth had risen to 6.7 percent and was to rise above 7 percent in 1972-1973. The further justification for increased revenues seemed to be a subjective feeling that government expenditures in certain sectors should be larger than they actually were. This may very well have been true, but it is difficult to prove, and one may question whether such advice had really been expected or required.

It is true that the tax revenues of all governmental units were relatively low in the period 1966-1970 (11.95 percent of the GDP), but the elasticity due to various administrative improvements was respectable (increasing from 10.66 percent in the period 1961-1965). The picture was somewhat better for the national government alone (9.55 percent contrasted with 7.31 percent) and for the income tax yield alone (from 4.1 percent to 4.7 percent).[4] This does not dispose of the case for greater equity and uniformity of treatment, but it raises some question about the need for such a large addition to revenues as recommended. However, the sizable assumption of the burden of increasing popular education (1968 and again in 1971), which constituted an important step toward better distribution, was to place a heavy financial load on the national government as time passed.

If the Musgrave Commission had stuck to tax "reform" in the narrower sense of the term, by reducing some items to offset the abolition of certain tax exemptions and by lessening evasion in other items, its proposals would have had a better reception and the president might have allied the favored groups to help push through the reforms in equity and uniformity of treatment. The commission did recognize that the Colombian system bore heavily and unfairly on salaried income and that the burden was increasing yearly with chronic inflation. By proposing little relief and many additional changes, however, they lost, for the time being, the opportunity to introduce some badly needed reforms both in ending exemptions and in lowering or at least pegging the burden on salaried workers. The argument given for not recommending indexation of the tax brackets was the very tired one of "lessening people's will to fight inflation."[5]

It is possible that, had he been asked, President Lleras would have agreed to a modification of the terms of reference to include a discussion of the desirability and the source of more revenues. There is no indication in the record, however, that he had been asked. Even if he had agreed, the question still remains whether such brusque changes in rates as were recommended, despite the terms of reference, are indicated when the tax administration is at a relatively low level and tax tolerance is low. Although the point was recognized in the report,[6] there is no evidence that it was accorded any weight.

In any event, implementation of the report was not immediately forthcoming. President Lleras, who contracted the commission, was due to leave office shortly after its report was published. His successor, President Misael Pastrana, had much less influence over Congress, and such sweeping changes were unattainable by ordinary legislative procedure during his administration. Thus, for the most part, the report remained a dead letter until President Alfonso López assumed office in August 1974 with a big majority in Congress.

Subsequent Events and the Tax Reform of 1974

In the years 1970-1974, despite rising levels of real growth and growing inflation, governmental revenues displayed an inadequate elasticity. As the nominal tax burden increased and some tax rates rose, the inducement and the ingenuity to evade and avoid taxes appeared to grow with them. Revenues did rise with inflation but not sufficiently to meet growing needs and to avoid a domestic deficit. Thus, the yields of taxes of the national government remained, on an average annual basis, a constant percentage of the GDP in relation to the period 1966-1970, and departmental and municipal revenues, as a percentage of the GDP, declined. The yield from the real estate tax was especially disappointing (0.34 percent of the GDP).[7]

Although these were disquieting trends, the growth in the national government deficit from $1,305 million in 1970 to $3,664 million in 1973 (or from 9.8 percent of total expenditures to 15.4 percent) was largely covered by foreign borrowing and was not an important part of the explanation of the expansion of the monetary base. (Except for the year 1971: in 1970-1973, it accounted for 2.1, 49.4, 3.8, and 12.3 percent, respectively, of the expansion of central bank credit.)[8] However, mostly for other reasons, the means of payment (not including official deposits in the Banco de la República) expanded by 11 percent in 1971, 24.4 percent in 1972, and 29.2 percent in 1973. This was far in excess of the growth in real production, and the workers' cost-of-living index rose by 11.4, 13.5, and 20.8 percent, respectively, in the same years. The year 1974 started off badly with rises in the first four months of 3.0, 2.6, 3.4, and 2.9 percent. By the end of February, the president had taken a personal hand in monetary policy, insisting that expansion be curbed; he had the Banco de la República ask the Federal Reserve Bank of New York for an expert in open market operations.[9] The following months saw a slackening in both the growth of means of payment and, a little later, in the rise of prices; the rise in the index fell to 1.2 percent in May, 0.9 percent in June, 0.7 percent in July, and 0.2 percent in August when the government changed.

The Constitution of 1968 had included an article that permitted the president to find that an economic emergency existed and to take remedial action by legislative decree, subject to subsequent ratification by Congress. Under this provision, the new president declared that inflation constituted an economic emergency. By implication, he found that the cause was a cash deficit arising from insufficient revenue, and he enacted by decree (Reforma Tributaria of 1974) tax changes that were closely modeled on the Musgrave Commission recommendations. But Musgrave had taken no position on monetary correction (except on capital gains where he favored correction of either 100 or 50 percent). The framers of the Reforma ignored the subject, except to allow a fixed and arbitrary number of percentage points of inflation (8 points) to be deducted from the rise in the value of property when they introduced a new tax on capital gains equal to income tax rates less a small deduction. Sales tax rates were raised to a maximum of 35 percent. The real estate tax rate was not raised, although the commission had recommended a tripling of the rate.

While the government continued with the system of monetary correction for savings for mortgages and construction loans, it placed a limit on the correction (which was well below actual inflation). The 8 percentage points allowed for deduction from the monetary correction for tax purposes amounted to about 40 percent of the limit placed on correction and much less as a proportion of actual inflation. So, for tax purposes, the government was putting itself in the position of declaring as true income subject to taxation a substantial part of what, for purposes of saving, it was labeling as not true income but the result of a "correction" for inflation.

As the tax package was unexpected and became known only toward the end of 1974, the taxpayers were caught off balance, and revenues in both real and nominal terms bounded upward in 1975. In that year, however, the results of weak administration and the well-known ingenuity of Colombian taxpayers reasserted their influence. In 1976, the receipts from the payers of income tax (in 1970 pesos), despite high inflation, fell 17 percent from the 1975 level and in 1977 fell another 14 percent from the 1976 level.[10] Between 1974 and 1977, the number of outstanding appeals against personal income tax assessments rose from 139,388 to 152,401,[11] which implied a significant increase in unpaid taxes pending the processing of this backlog. It is an indication of the increased administrative burden associated with the reform. The settlements made by the Ministry of Finance fell from 19 percent of the claims in 1973 to 14 percent in 1976.[12]

The results of the sales taxes continued positive. The big rise, however, was in the government's share of coffee receipts, which could hardly have been foreseen in 1974, since the coffee price rose only in the second half of 1975.

After 1974, inflation actually accelerated. Between October 1974 and early 1978, the cost of living index had already doubled; yet there had been no changes in the rate structure for personal income taxes.[13] From published calculations,[14] it can be inferred that a nominal income of, for example, $105,000 (about US$4,000) in 1974 was equivalent to $210,000 in early 1978. Yet, by 1978 this same real income was subject to an average tax rate of 29.5 percent instead of 19.8 percent.

One authority later found that the elasticity of the tax system had been reduced, that the proportion of indirect taxes was higher, and that taxpayers whose incomes were from work were paying a higher percentage of their income than were others.[15] Another writer found that the elasticity of the yield from the income tax had been considerably reduced by the "Reform." Indeed, a projection of trends in the absence of the reform would have resulted in a much higher stated tax obligation in pesos of 1970 ($8,112 million in 1977 in place of the actual $5,932 million).[16]

In a subsequent seminar—a form of postmortem—by Musgrave and various of the authors and critics of the reform of 1974, one of the authors blamed the disappointing results on exemptions ceded by the government, as well as on increased evasion.[17] All were in agreement that tax evasion had become more widespread. The daily press covering the seminar (July 1978) reported that Musgrave himself attributed the results to a failure to utilize monetary correction and to poor tax enforcement. But his own somewhat casual attitude to monetary correction noted above will be recalled, and a critic might point out that the state of the tax administration was one of the conditions that should have been given much more weight in framing recommendations. His recommendation for a threefold increase in real estate tax rates, for example, would have encountered the same poor administration. If the annual real yield of the real estate tax (in pesos of 1970) increased in the period 1961-1965 to 1966-1970 from $457 million to only $553 million, the remedy, in view of the rapid growth in the commercial value of real estate in the cities, would appear to have been better assessment and tax enforcement rather than a threefold increase in rates. As an ex-director of national taxes very wisely observed, "There is a considerable gap between the sophistication of tax objectives and the capacity of the Office of Taxes." He pointed out that of 2,274,835 tax returns in 1974, only 22,673, or 1 percent, were investigated.[18]

In Musgrave's paper prepared for the seminar, however, there was almost no reference to the 1974 changes. He had shifted to other issues: insisting that, in developing countries, the tax structure should take into account the necessity of increasing saving, which should then be used especially to create labor-intensive employment,[19] and that, above all, successful tax reform requires political support, which the commission proposals of 1968 obviously did not have.

There was little criticism, in the seminar, of the manner in which the changes had been achieved (the declaration of an "economic emergency" for stated reasons that entailed, to say the least, a lack of candor), nor was notice taken of the somewhat traumatic initial impact on business activity. The public investment budget had to be cut drastically in 1977-1978, tax elasticity had suffered, and the tax system in general appeared to be less equitable than previously. The indexed saving system became less attractive (though borrowing was made more attractive), and the tax treatment of monetary correction was one of the factors contributing to a sharp decline in saving and building in 1975-1977. As for the ostensible reason for the reform—inflation—it may be noted that the average rise in prices in 1975-1977 was 26 percent compared to 16 percent in the years 1971-1973.

In fairness to Professor Musgrave, it should be pointed out that he had no opportunity to review his recommendations of 1968 in the light of the conditions prevailing in 1974. In view of his remarks in the subsequent seminar and the rise in prices from 1968 to 1974, it appears likely that, had he been consulted, he would have recommended greater resort to monetary correction. Quite apart from the merits of the recommendations, however, Rodrigo Manrique's study of tax "reforms" since 1886 in Colombia[20] suggests that this is a field in which much care must be taken before sweeping reforms are made, and that unglamorous improvements in administration may very frequently yield more positive results than changes in rates. In short, my previous remark that this is a field where use may be made of a prestigious foreigner to propose unpopular measures must be supplemented: it is also peculiarly a field in which intimate knowledge of local conditions is necessary. Furthermore, it is a field in which personal values play a very prominent role, and it is particularly incumbent upon a visiting scholar to make it very clear when he is expressing personal views based on such values.

What doubtless happened is that Professor Musgrave fell victim to an occupational hazard of advisers that makes one unable to resist suggesting sweeping reforms. No academician, and I would not exclude myself, is free from this hazard, especially if he leads a mission or is responsible for a report. The good strategy of accomplishing a smaller but very worthwhile reform is lost sight of in the desire to indicate what a really thoroughgoing reform would look like, regardless of whether it is feasible or requested. If one thinks a broad change is desirable, it is not difficult to persuade oneself that it is also feasible. Even commercial firms like to leave monuments to which they can point with pride. Hence, if the contractor of advice wants the minimum of change to accomplish his objective (assuming he has one) and is genuinely desirous of improving the functioning of some aspect of the government or economic machinery, he would be well advised to seek informal advice and avoid "final reports" (the monuments). When the expert is anonymous, he will be less likely to advocate sweeping reforms and will acquire a better sense of what is feasible *in the circumstances*.

So much for appraisal of the *content* of the advice. In this case, its *acceptability*, even though delayed, was very much a matter of chance and arose partly from the fact that young nationals, who had worked on the initial report, later arrived at a position to have the advice adopted.

PART 3
SECTOR AND
PROJECT ADVICE

9
RURAL POVERTY

Poverty is the reason underlying the widespread concern with the less developed countries, especially what has been called "absolute" poverty, in which the basic physical needs of man are not met. Since the bulk of poverty can be found in the rural sector, that sector has received more advice than any other. For most writers and agencies, abolishing or ameliorating rural poverty is the first and major problem of underdevelopment. Another reason for concern with the rural poor is the almost universally excessively high birth rates concentrated in rural areas. A third is that the poorer the country, the larger the number of people in agriculture; the impulse is to attempt to do or to promise to do what the spokesmen for farmers demand. Finally, in terms of the definition of development adopted in this book, no country the bulk of whose people are poverty-stricken peasants can be said to possess any effective control over its environment.

The subject is highly charged emotionally. Few things arouse as much compassion as hunger, in few sectors is inequality more repugnant, and the growing of food is universally considered "basic." Hence, it is unusually difficult to treat advice in this field objectively. Counterproductive measures may be defended for distributive reasons. Criticisms of such measures may in turn be criticized as indicating a lack of sympathy with laudable objectives, and some alternative proposals have been attacked on the same grounds. For example, writers and advisers on this area have on the whole shown little interest in or patience with market forces and have not hesitated to recommend and urge "direct action," "assaults," and "attacks" on poverty. So it may be well at the outset to insist that the basic disagreements are not on objectives—we can assume that no one would defend the continuance of rural poverty or be opposed to its elimination—but on ways and means to accomplish this highly desirable goal.

Owing to the enormous amount of advice-giving in this sector, and consequent repetition, the treatment here is general in nature. The basic economic theory applicable to the rural problem is set forth, and the general pattern of agricultural development is traced briefly, with examples drawn from the more developed countries, especially the United States.

Applicable Economic Theory

A theme central to the argument of this chapter is that the tools of economic analysis as well as the analysis itself are as applicable to the LDCs as to the more affluent countries. The concepts of price and income elasticity of demand are not different in the two groups of countries, although the precise degree of elasticity of demand may differ. However, the tendency for the income elasticity of demand per capita for foodstuffs to be relatively low and to fall as income rises applies to all countries, rich and poor. It is the basis of Engels' Law, one of the few "laws" in economics.[1]

That one's real income is not what one actually produces (except in pure subsistence conditions) but rather the value of what one produces in terms of all other goods is as true in agriculture as in other sectors. It is likewise true in all countries where the agricultural product is marketed, whether that product is large or small in relation to the total output. Hence, putting aside transfers of purchasing power by the government, the real income of the agricultural sector, as of other sectors, is the value of the gross output minus the value of purchased inputs. The net value of the output, divided by the number of farm workers, yields the average income per farm worker. The income or net returns per farm may be unequally divided, but this is as true in rich as in poor countries, the difference being one of degree. The smaller the number of farmers producing a given crop at a given price and cost, the larger must be the gross income per farm. The point has been obscured by shifting back and forth from value to physical productivity in agriculture. For example, the assertion is often made that small farms are more "productive" than large ones. It is assumed that here the term is used in a physical sense per unit of land.

That income depends on the value of output (less purchased inputs) explains why a very large harvest may yield less return than a smaller one. Since consumption or demand is unresponsive to price variation for most staple foodstuffs, prices must fall substantially to induce an increase in consumption, while prices must rise equally substantially to lead to a reduction in demand. This is true in all countries.

When, in many industrial sectors, there are few producers (little competition), a fall in demand is likely to be met by an immediate decline in production and the maintenance of price. When the sector is highly competitive, the reduction in supply may only follow from intolerably low incomes and migration. Agriculture is highly competitive, so it is difficult to control supply. This is true in all countries with market or mixed economies. A marked difference in degree, however, is the greater mobility of labor in more technically advanced countries.

Production in agriculture, as in industry, is the end product of a combination of factors. The most economic combination, or the one that gives the highest returns—the factor proportion mix—depends a great deal on the relative prices or costs of the respective factors. The lower the cost of labor (its income), the larger is likely to be the proportion of labor in the mix of factors. The higher the cost of labor, the more it pays to mechanize. I will have occasion to return to the paradox that the lower the returns in agriculture the less the incentive to adopt more efficient techniques.

In short, the difference between less and more developed countries lies not in economic theory but in the conditions to which it is applied. In LDCs, agriculturalists comprise a larger portion of the population and, as a class, are poorer both in absolute and relative terms. Whether these differences of degree in the environment justify different policies is the real issue.

The Pattern of Agricultural Development

Originally, the bulk of the labor force was engaged in agriculture, and the value of agricultural production formed a large percentage of the total of all production. Where growth in output per capita occurred, both the percentage of the work force in agriculture and the value of its output fell steadily relative to the total work force and national product and per capita income.[2] This was as true in Colombia in the past thirty years as in the United States since the time of the American Revolution, or in the OECD countries in general. Even in city-states like Singapore, the consumption of food per capita, as a percentage of total consumption, declined. The only exceptions are a few unfortunate countries where population outran agricultural productivity and income per capita did not rise. In general and in the absence of large agricultural exports (where agricultural output remains a high percentage of total output), per capita income is low and grows slowly, if at all.

This process has gone so far that in the United States only 3 to 4 percent of the work force produce all the foods and fibers, and the United States is also a major exporter. Even this small percentage includes many small nontechnical farmers, so that to produce the great bulk of the crop probably requires no more than 2 percent of the work force. The fact that agricultural prices have not risen over a long period in relation to the prices of nonagricultural goods or only slightly (depending on the base year chosen) is owing to two factors: first, people spend less and less of their growing income on calories and nutrients (as distinct from packaging, elaboration, and restaurant services), and second, farm output in physical terms per worker (which, of course, includes farm owners) has grown spectacularly over the past two hundred years. In 1976, net income received from farming, which approximates value added on the farm, amounted to the astonishingly low figure of 2 percent of total national income. Such results would be possible only if demand had increased slowly and output per worker had increased greatly. Both occurred. The income elasticity of demand in the United States in terms of calories (i.e., the growth in the expenditures on foodstuffs in terms of calories in relation to income per capita) has been zero for some time, so that demand has come only from the growth in population. An index of farm output per hour of farm work rose from 16 in 1929 to 140 in 1976. Despite a fall in farm population in absolute terms from 30.6 million in 1929 to 8.3 million in 1976 (while the total population rose from 122 million to 215 million), and despite the tremendous increase in productivity, the net income per farm in constant 1967 dollars between these dates rose only modestly, from $1,969 to $5,482.[3] (It averaged $4,100 in 1969-1976.)

In Japan, with a small agricultural land area in relation to its population, agricultural employment declined from 35.6 percent of the total work force in 1953 to 14.6 percent in 1971. (Nearly half of the latter percentage were part time.) The contribution to the yearly growth of Japan resulting from the reallocation of human resources from agriculture to nonagricultural occupations was calculated to be 0.78 percentage points for the period 1953-1971.[4] As a percentage of gross national product, the value of agricultural output declined from 17 percent to 4 percent.[5] Since agricultural employment declined by nearly 50 percent while gross agricultural product increased, productivity per worker more than doubled. Yujiro Hayami tells the same story of a decline in the agricultural work force index in Japan from 1955 to 1970 from 96 to 57 and an increase in the index of capital inputs from 186 to 554, with the labor productivity index rising from 280 to 738.[6] Changes in the same directions have been occurring in Colombia.

It is vitally important to understand the interaction of economic forces that gives rise to this type of development, compressing into a few years the process that normally would have taken much longer. Elsewhere I have discussed the revolution in cotton growing in the United States during World War II. It is particularly pertinent because it took place in a "less developed" sector in a technically advanced country, and it illustrates how exogenous factors can accelerate normal processes. The war was the exogenous factor, creating virtually unlimited job opportunities for the most backward and least technical and most poverty-stricken sector of American agriculture. There was a mass exodus of labor from cotton growing, and its cost rose.[7] This provided the incentive and opportunity to replace mules by tractors, hand labor by tractor-drawn machines, and small hillside farms in the traditional "Cotton South" by large farms in the flatlands of Louisiana, Texas, and California. In a few years, cotton growing became one of the most technically advanced sectors of American agriculture, capable of competing in exports with cotton produced by very low-paid labor in developing countries.

The Contribution of a Sector to General Growth

It is the essence of an increase in efficiency that fewer workers can produce the same quantity or that the cost of production per unit falls. If the relative fall in price occurs for a product for which the price elasticity of demand is less than unity, that is, if less is spent on the product than formerly, fewer workers will be required in its production than formerly. The consuming public will reap the major part of the benefit because it will be able to spend more of its income on other things. Labor to produce these other things will be supplied by the release of workers from the production of the first product. If the price elasticity of demand is greater than unity so that more money is spent on its purchase, and more units are sold, the community will still gain in the larger consumption at a lower price, and workers will be attracted, presumably by higher wages from other industries to satisfy the additional demand.

An outstanding example of the first case is offered by agriculture in more developed countries, where the community at large benefited from the astounding increases in productivity created by the release of manpower for the production of a host of other things but with little, if any, increase in consumption of food per capita in terms of calories. An example of the latter case is offered by the automobile industry in the period following the great reduction in costs and prices realized by Henry Ford in economies of scale. The community could buy more cars more cheaply, and both employment and wages in the industry rose.

The idea that the rest of the economy is peculiarly dependent on a prosperous, dynamic agriculture capable of producing a surplus which, when saved, becomes a "wages fund," and that the demand of agriculture is in some way peculiarly necessary to the growth of industry appears at bottom to be based on the fact that food is necessary for life. What this really means, however, is that demand for food is constant, not that it possesses infinite elasticity. But as just said, the "surplus" of food, as of other things, emerges as a result of growing demand and improving efficiency. A common error is to identify a large and growing demand for the final products of industry, which is essential to growth, with final demand from farmers. A prosperous agriculture, unfortunately, does not appear to be essential to growth if "prosperous" is understood in the sense of value rather than physical productivity. Net income from farming in the United States in 1977 was only 1.5 percent of the total GNP and 2.3 percent of total personal consumption.[8] Shifting barter terms of trade may affect the sources of demand, but should not change the total except as they affect the release of manpower to increase overall production.

Agricultural incomes in general have persistently lagged behind the growth in nonrural income in the United States. The abolition of the Corn Laws in the United Kingdom ushered in a long period of low agricultural incomes while industry was flourishing. Indeed, in most countries farm incomes have lagged, though they differ widely in the growth in physical productivity. Thus, unpalatable as the idea may be, industry and services can grow and prosper while agriculture is depressed and agricultural incomes remain very low.

In short, the demand or purchasing power of any one sector has no particular mystical power different from an equal demand from another sector. The strategy of "leading sectors" is not based on such a mystical power, but on tapping a large latent demand for a good for which there is also a high income elasticity of demand at a price profitable to the producers. *Agriculture does not fall in this category.* It is important for it as a sector to improve physical productivity and release labor rather than to increase production and employment.

The implication of this bit of theorizing is that, taking a longer point of view, the emergence of a more or less permanent "agricultural surplus" for city dwellers or for export is not a result of high productivity or bumper crops, but rather the growth of demand which ensures prices that will pay for increased productivity. The United States and Canada produce wheat for export not because they happen to have a "surplus"; they have a surplus because there is a demand abroad for wheat at a profitable price. The same is true of the coffee "surpluses" in Colombia and Brazil.

The Constraint on Agricultural Production

There is a widespread impression that the constraint on agricultural production in LDCs, unlike that on many other sectors, arises from inadequate physical factors—land, labor, capital, and inefficient technological practices. In this respect, it is felt that it differs markedly from the constraint on agricultural production in more developed countries where, clearly, it can be found on the side of demand and in the profitability of production. Despite increases in population and large exports, the value of agricultural output in the United States has increased very slowly. The low income elasticity of demand and the tremendous growth in physical productivity per man-hour of work have combined to enable fewer and fewer people to meet the demand, forcing a very large migration from farming. The capacity of American agriculture to increase output is tremendous, *if and when it pays*. An increase in demand, say, from poor harvests abroad, that has the effect of bettering the terms of trade, is quickly followed by an increase in output, which in turn tends to restore the previous terms of trade (relation of agricultural to nonagricultural prices). Higher relative prices make it profitable to use more fertilizers, more herbicides and pesticides, more irrigation, and more machinery—all of which tend to increase production. Thus, the explanation of the low growth rate can be found in low average incomes per farm, and these in turn on the combination of technical advances, availability of credit, a slow increase in demand, and low price elasticity of demand. While, in the United States from 1947 to 1976, the index of farm output per man-hour rose 5.7 percent per year, production increased only 1.6 percent per year, and value added in 1972 dollars (and including forestry and fisheries) increased only 1.4 percent per year.[9]

The agricultural history, then, of all the more developed and of most developing countries is that increasing productivity permitted labor to be released from agriculture for the production of other things. The essential economic mechanism comprised innovations, competition, low elasticity of demand, and mobility. These motivations were economic. The greater the mobility, the greater the incentive to adopt known but hitherto unprofitable techniques. The more rapid the growth in productivity, the greater the "surplus" labor, the greater the gap between farm incomes and urban incomes, the greater the incentive to migrate if jobs could be found. The system proceeded ratchetwise. An improvement in the terms of trade for agriculture provided an incentive for the larger and better placed farmers to introduce improvements, which increased production, which tended to worsen the terms of trade, which put pressure on the marginal or subsistence farmers (subsistence in the sense that the value of the output provided only a bare subsistence) to seek a better income elsewhere. With fewer farmers, there was a tendency for terms of trade to improve again and for the process to be repeated. Hence, it is not an accident that the higher the standard of living (or the cost of labor), the more technical and capital-intensive became the agriculture. Contrariwise, the greatest obstacle to increased agricultural productivity can be found in low agricultural wages.[10]

Advice in the Agricultural Sector

Advice in this field to LDCs has in general not recommended following the pattern of development of the more developed countries. Even general advice to improve "productivity" has interpreted that term in a physical rather than in a value sense. Generally, a low income elasticity of demand for foodstuffs has been ignored or denied, and advice to increase physical output per hectare and per farm has been applied to all farmers.

Since, however, the ultimate objective was to alleviate rural poverty, it was recognized that higher output per hectare would not yield a satisfactory result if the individual farms were very small, or if laborers had no farms. Thus, most foreign advisers have been in favor of land redistribution, or "agrarian reform" as it is generally called. The ideal became to make all small farmers, or farmers with low incomes, more "productive" with larger farms (or assured titles), more credit, more irrigation, and more advice and aid in cultural practices, marketing, and support prices.

Note that emphasis was placed not so much on agricultural efficiency in general as on distribution and improving the lot of the very small and most poverty-stricken farmers and rural laborers. Measures were proposed not only in land redistribution but also in special terms for agricultural credit and in the direction of agricultural research, and special programs were recommended for rural infrastructure, education, and health. The "right to land" had a mystique not applicable to other forms of capital, and the belief that a rural worker could not make a decent living unless he possessed land was widespread. There was also constant insistence that the growth of industry was limited by the generation of an agricultural surplus and by a prosperous agriculture.

While one can heartily applaud the desire to abolish or ameliorate poverty, especially in rural regions, this does not free an economist from the obligation to follow through the ramifications of price theory, to use his economic tools of analysis, and to study experience in more developed countries.

The concern with poverty may also explain why mention of the fallacy of composition almost never appears in the literature. It is considered perfectly feasible that not only can one farmer increase his output and income without affecting price, but that *all* farmers can, even where they number millions. This point of view probably is traceable again to the implicit feeling that in a poor country the demand for food is unlimited. If need be, country people, it is sometimes maintained, can eat what they themselves grow. This feeling, in turn, may help to explain why research programs to improve seeds and varieties are often oriented not toward the most profitable commercial crops but toward the starchy foods of the very poor.

Perhaps the customary working out of economic forces in more developed countries, noted above, is often felt to be too slow and entails too much suffering. People who have written on the subject generally distinguish between the two forces making for rural-urban migration—the "push" from low rural incomes and the "pull" to higher urban possibilities. Advisers who reject mobility as a solution apparently feel that there is too much "push" and not enough "pull." This is made even more explicit by the constant reiteration of the statements that "the cities cannot absorb the migrants," that "industry cannot provide the requisite amount of work," that migration is only exchanging poverty in one spot for poverty in another, even that urban poverty is worse than rural, and it is often stated that open and disguised unemployment is increasing in the cities. The explanation for this can be found in the misleading calculations of the amount of capital "necessary" to put one person to work. (See discussion in Chapter 3.) There are others who feel that migrants only add to the existing problems of urban life, and still others who tend to romanticize country life. So, for these reasons, it is widely felt that the solution to the problem of rural poverty must be found in the countryside itself and that solutions such as parcelization or limitation on size of holdings, hardly appropriate for more technically advanced countries, are perfectly justified in LDCs.

The Issues

Although the problem of the rural poor has many ramifications, the principal issues can be stated quite simply. On the one hand, in many of the poorest countries, such a large proportion of the population is growing food for themselves that the standard of living necessarily must be very low. Moreover, the level of incomes and wealth is so low that it literally does not pay to make expensive permanent improvements or to use much equipment. Given the low level of effective demand, what is the way out for rural people in such countries? Growing more food for themselves means a continuously low standard of living; producing for export, if possible, makes it difficult for very poor countries to meet quality standards. So the decisive point becomes: if it were possible to increase significantly the output of *all* farmers, would it lead to an increase in their incomes? We come back once more to the elasticity of demand for agricultural goods. Presumably a program for the rural poor cannot be for only a few of the poor but for at least the majority. It has already been pointed out that the farmers of the United States, even after a tremendous diminution of their numbers and the use of much capital, land, and technique, have, on the average, incomes per farm much below the average family income in the United States. This phenomenon must be taken to heart by all who would attempt to resolve the problem of the rural poor by increasing physical production.

The usual answer is that income elasticity figures *must* be very high where there is hunger and malnutrition. If they are not, the policy indicated is to cultivate and give the food away. But obviously, except for a country in desperate circumstances, this must be a minor program beset by a thousand administrative difficulties. In a country like Colombia, for example, probably only a few are chronically hungry, and malnutrition may be partly a matter of ignorance as well as poverty.

From 1950 to 1972, despite growing exports and a very high rate of growth in population, agricultural production in the national accounts in Colombia increased at a rate only slightly in excess of population. Was the constraint on the side of supply or demand? Most people who have written on the subject feel strongly that it is a matter of supply. But the relatively long period of relative constancy in the barter terms of trade in the prices of agricultural and nonagricultural goods may be cited on the side of demand. (There was a marked relative rise in agricultural prices in 1975-1977, but this was associated more with poor weather and harvests than with an increase in demand.)

Annual figures of agricultural production in Colombia, although not too reliable, are available, and the consumption per capita in grams by broad categories can be calculated and compared with what have been set as targets as well as by calories. This is done in Tables 4 and 5.

While these figures are only approximate, they suggest that the calorie intake in Colombia in 1974 was fairly close to that recommended, but that protein intake was somewhat deficient. The subject has been recently studied by Jorge García, who concludes that malnutrition is a matter of inequality rather than of aggregate deficiency and that the long-run solution lies in a permanent increase in the income of the poor through a sustained and continued process of general growth in the Colombian economy.[11] There is nothing here that would suggest a high, unmet latent demand for foodstuffs in general, especially as it appears that the main source of demand— the increase in population—is slackening.

It remains to establish the link between rural poverty and technology. Does the use of technology displace manpower and so

Table 4
NUTRITIONAL VALUE OF FOOD CONSUMPTION
PER PERSON PER DAY

	Actual (1974) Colombian Intake*	Recommended Colombian Intake*	I as a Percentage of II
	I	II	III
Energy (calories)	2,157.0	1,970.0	109
Protein (gs)	43.7	54.2	81
Calcium (mgs)	446.8	526.0	85
Iron (mgs)	12.7	11.0	115
Vitamin A (I.V.)	2,814.0	4,185.0	67
Thiamin (mgs)	0.7	0.8	88
Niacin (mgs)	10.9	12.4	88
Vitamin C (mgs)	84.6	36.0	235
Ribloflavin (mgs)	0.6	1.0	60
Vitamin D	—	—	—

*Instituto Colombiano de Bienestar Familiar, "Hoja de Balance de Alimentos 1972-73-74."

heighten rural poverty, or does the pressure of abundant manpower and low efficiency encourage the use of more advanced technology?

The use of more advanced technology—whether it be seeds, fertilizers, machinery, or improved techniques—"displaces" men, that is, it enables fewer people to produce as much as before. In any given time, there is a large technological gap between the most efficient commercial producer and the average, or between the best experimental work and the best commercial producer. It is a simple matter, then, to calculate what the production and what the manpower requirements would be if all traditional agriculture were as efficient as modern commercial agriculture but under the more conservative assumption that all the *growth* takes place in the modern sector. This was calculated in a recent study for Colombia.[12] On this basis, and assuming no new "green revolutions," the physical production per worker in some eighteen crops was calculated for the year 1972 and projected for the year 2000. The result (expressed in

Table 5
CONSUMPTION OF SELECTED FOODSTUFFS,
UNITED KINGDOM, 1974, AND COLOMBIA, 1975

(kg per person per year)

	United Kingdom	Colombia
Meat products	59.4	31.4
Cereals*	84.6	93.7
Starch foods (with plantain)	67.3	97.1
Tea, coffee, chocolate	4.7	3.5
Sugar, others	22.8	48.4

*The U.K. figure refers to processed cereals, while the Colombian one refers to unprocessed cereals.

Source: Currie et al., Resources, Population and Growth: Colombia 1950-2000 (Bogotá: Instituto de Estudios Colombianos, 1977), Table VII-17. Study conducted for Resources for the Future, Inc., Washington, D.C. and UN-ILPES, Santiago, Chile. Available for reference at the offices of the RFF in Washington, D.C. under the revised title, "Population, Resources and the Environment in Colombia's Future."

1970 pesos) was that the production increased from $17,238 million to $39,545 million, the number of workers declined from 1,308,000 to 589,000, and, naturally, the output per worker per year increased from $13,179 to $67,140. Thus, a generalized increase in production in a sector is compatible with unchanged employment only if demand at a profitable price increases pari passu or more with the production, and we return to the elementary bit of economic theory with which we started.

The example is a bit misleading insofar as it implies that the workers remaining in agriculture would receive the greatly increased value of output per worker. Actually, this output must also cover all the costs of improvements and machinery, profits, and interest. Workers would actually receive more only if they became "scarce" as in the United States, Canada, Britain, and other countries. With the high birth rates and the youthful composition of the rural population, the danger is that labor will tend to remain abundant for many years to come. But in this case, one of the powerful incentives to modernize and mechanize ceases to operate, and we are back to our vicious circle: the lower the wage (and productivity) the less incentive there is to substitute machines and improvements for manpower. Advisers who push technology in the poorest sections are really doing it the hard way.

Others have reacted against technology and have actually glorified labor-intensive methods in agriculture as a means of spreading work which, combined with land redistribution, may also be expected to spread wealth and, it is hoped, higher income. It may be conceded that redistribution, without compensation, carried out once, will benefit recipients of free land, if the land is tillable. If compensation is paid at commercial rates, the benefits are highly dubious. If, as was the case in Mexico and Japan, low limits are set on holdings and sales are forbidden, even the benefits of free land will be lost in inadequate incomes for many years for the recipients and their children.

Hence, much advice tendered LDCs to resolve the problem of their rural poor turns its back on both economic theory and the experience in this sector in all more developed countries, and proposes a policy of restraining migration and spreading unremunerative work, thus generalizing poverty, discouraging more efficient techniques, and perpetuating low output per capita.

In the course of time, economic forces will work themselves out willy-nilly, of course, and provide sufficient mobility to lighten suffering. But the numbers are so great that it may take many years to arrive at a point where agricultural labor actually becomes scarce and its wage comparable with that of urban labor. Policies that tend to arrest rather than promote mobility only tend to prolong the agony. It is indeed ironic that the truly basic solution for rural poverty can only be found outside rural areas and that economic advisers, who might be expected to promote mobility, actually deplore it and, if anything, seek to restrain it.[13]

Conclusions

The conclusion seems inescapable that, in the growth of productivity of Colombian agriculture and in the massive transition from a predominantly rural and agricultural society to a predominantly urban one with an accompanying decline in the birth rate, neither deliberate government policy (with the exception of a brief period in 1972-1974) nor foreign advice can claim much credit. These basic and necessary steps in the process of development were made despite, rather than because of, advice and policy, and indeed much government policy was designed to slow the transition.

In casting about for explanations of why economists persistently disregard not only the economic history of all the developed and the successfully developing countries but even the basic concepts of their discipline, the main answer seems to be that the repugnance to poverty and the indignation over inequality make for impatience with the slowness and the effectiveness of economic forces, hence an emotionally clouded viewpoint.

A related source of the lack of rigor in treating of agricultural problems may be found in the personal values of writers on the relative merits of urban and rural living. That "agriculture is a way of life," and hence worth saving for itself, underlies many arguments. It is highly debatable, however, that farm life is particularly agreeable for a Colombian small holder, with no mechanized power, subject to all the ills of the tropics, with no reserves for emergencies, and at the mercy of uncertain weather. In the highland village near my farm in Colombia, for example, life was grim, and the main aspiration of the younger people was to escape.

Another explanation can be found in the intense specialization that has occurred in economics. Few of us are any longer just economists; rather we are transport, labor or agricultural, or other kinds of economists. The nearest approach we now have to former generalists is offered by "macro" economists working in monetary-fiscal-exchange price level problems, and even they are becoming specialists in the separate fields, are monetarists or Keynesians, or experts in foreign exchange and balance-of-payment problems. But some problems can only be treated adequately as parts of a whole. The complex interaction of technology, factor proportions, elasticities of demand, prices, numbers, mobility, and allocation of resources must be treated together if the treatment of rural poverty in the mass is to be realistic.

The reliability of the factual material in the flood of development literature is questionable. There is a totally unwarranted but understandable assumption that the latest statistics must be the best; hence, we choose the most recent data or even select from the pool those facts that support our previously held convictions. One can affirm that urban unemployment is steadily increasing, that real wages are steadily falling, that thirty years of reported rises in per capita income have not in any way benefited the bulk of the people, and so forth,[14] with little fear that one's statement will be disproved or even challenged. Furthermore, suppositions and hypotheses are fast becoming "facts" in their own right. That the cities cannot "absorb" the growing work force has ceased to be a statistic, if it ever was one; it has become an article of faith that is not open to question.

The Dilemma of Rural Poverty

For a poor country, a principal objective in agricultural as in all other economic sectors is high and rising productivity (income) *per worker* of crops *that pay*. This requires a mix of factors—manpower, land with certain characteristics, capital, technique, and ready access to markets. The most profitable mix will change with the relative abundance and prices of factors, inputs, output, and the availability of techniques.

The less abundant and accessible good land is and the cheaper labor is the more it will pay to use labor and to economize on machinery, capital improvements, and fertilizers. This will be the characteristic of the indicated or "appropriate" mix. But, and this is the dilemma, it is a mix that yields a low output in value terms per man or man-hour. Applied in all sectors, it would yield a very low return per worker and a very low standard of living.

If land is relatively abundant and credit is available, the highest income yields per farm will require a mix of factors, which, though it varies with crops, soils, topography, markets, and weather, will indicate a much higher proportion of land, capital, and fertilizer to labor—the pattern in the more developed countries. But an agriculture organized along these lines would require very few workers to produce the crops for the slowly growing market. If there are no other jobs, the value of labor is driven down in the competition with machinery. More technique, more use of machinery, more capital improvements are restrained by the low price of labor—and the use of these factors tends to reduce still further the price of labor.

In short, much of the current analysis, with an increasing labor force and a slow increase in demand, suggests that the "appropriate" mix is one that would yield a low income per worker in agriculture, a high birth rate, a continuously depressed agricultural sector, and, if it is a large sector, a depressed country.

The only escapes appear to be (1) large reductions in cost, (2) large and increasing demand for agricultural goods, or (3) a rising cost of labor. Escape (1) is limited by the confrontation of increasing productivity with a slow increase in demand and (2) by worldwide competition in the sale of agricultural goods. The only sure answer seems to lie in (3), a rapid increase in the demand for agricultural labor outside of agriculture that raises its value or cost to agriculturalists.

It appears highly improbable, therefore, that advice designed to retain either the percentage of the total work force as farmers or even to maintain their absolute numbers, while attempting to make them all efficient and all more productive on small parcels of land, can be appropriate or in the best interests of developing countries. Explicit or implicit assumptions of growth rates in agricultural production of 5 or 6 percent are highly at variance with historical growth patterns.

A "direct assault" on the problem of mass rural poverty that attempts to accomplish a generalized increase in physical productivity not only rests on faulty theory, but also runs counter to the argument that the less developed an economy, the less likely it will be able to execute effectively programs requiring a high degree of administrative expertise, as would programs dealing directly with millions of small farmers. What appears to be more needed is not a direct attack but the thoughtful framing and testing of the few—very few—key hypotheses set forth above and the incorporation of agriculture and rural poverty into an overall and internally consistent national economic program which will draw on theory, on economic history, and on the current experience of a large number of countries.

10
ADVICE ON
HOUSING AND
URBAN POLICY

In developing countries, it is customarily calculated that rent (or debt service for an owned dwelling unit, or the opportunity cost of an unmortgaged dwelling unit) amounts to around 20 to 25 percent of income. When furnishings, maintenance, water, electric power, heating, cooking, and garbage disposal are added, the figure becomes much higher. Even in high-income countries like the United States and Canada, some 28 to 30 percent of disposable income is spent on these various items lumped together under the category "housing and home operation." Hence, the provision of housing and furnishings and the accompanying services and the shops and commercial buildings that accompany housing make up a very substantial part of the final demand for the products of industry as well as for many services.

The importance of housing is customarily understated due to the fragmentation of national accounts, so that "industry" is treated as being quite distinct from "construction," although a significant portion of the cost of a new building is the purchase of the products of industry, and there are grounds for believing that fluctuations in building frequently initiate corresponding and magnified movements in economic activity as a whole. For one thing, construction activity, housing operation, and getting to and from a home make up a substantial part of the "energy problem." Furthermore, under the customary "sector" approach, housing is treated separately from urban transport and from urban design, and yet, quite obviously, home-to-work trips make up a substantial part of urban transport and the "urban transport problem."

It is equally obvious that housing is much more than a matter of covered space per person. Distance from work, the character and expense of public or private transport, the character of the neighborhood, personal and property security, the adequacy of services, nearness of good schools, shops, and diversion facilities are all intimately related to housing. In few areas are the external economies and diseconomies so pronounced, and in few fields are the feelings of deprivation arising from differences in space and neighborhoods so pronounced or inequality felt so keenly.

The Operation of Market Forces

Despite its paramount importance for many aspects of economic and social life, housing in LDCs has been neglected, except for subsidized or popular housing, on which much has been written but not much done, and which is only a small part of the field. For the most part, where and how people live are left to the operation of market forces, with planning restricted to zoning and norms on such matters as height, air space, width of streets, and protection of property values. The overall design of almost all cities has never been planned and is the result of thousands of individual decisions on land use, influenced by private economic forces.

While in general, and especially for countries with a low level of public administration, there is much to be said for decentralizing decisions and trusting to market forces for the allocation of resources, in this particular case sole reliance on such forces would be excessive because of the limited supply and relative inelasticity of the factor of space or location, a major determinant of rents. As population and incomes rise, the fixed spatial area becomes more valuable, especially in certain favored locations. It is often said that a building of many floors multiplies the space, and in a sense this is true—but only at a cost. It is economic to construct a building of twenty or thirty floors with banks of elevators only when the location is valuable. This is the main reason why a housing unit in a metropolis costs more to buy or rent than in a small town. Land is the scarce and costly element.

Since land in a city of, say, 5 million is scarce, it should be efficiently used. This is the justification for the rise in its value; it is a means of ensuring that a single family house is not built on Park Avenue. However, justification for a rise in land values as part of the mechanism for efficient resource allocation, defensible economically, does not mean that the rise in value must necessarily belong to individual owners. This is a case of monopoly gains, and economic theory has always recognized that where there is monopoly and inelasticity of supply, the market or price mechanism may yield bad distribution results and the state may be justified in intervention in the interests of better distribution.

Many of the characteristics of large cities are attributable to the scarcity of land in relation to the growing numbers and wealth of residents. The segregation of people by income groups, for example, is attributable in most cases to the existence of high-priced and low-priced land in the center or the peripheries. The urban transport problem arises largely from the flight of people to lower density suburbs. Sprawling suburbs contribute to the higher cost of services and to feelings of deprivation. They lead to personal transport, and this requires a large allocation of resources for roads, cars, and gasoline. Rising land values make it difficult to provide adequate open space and playgrounds. They may make it economic to replace buildings long before they have served a normally useful life.

If we probe a little more deeply, it becomes clear that the rise in existing land values is the mechanism by which a portion of the undoubted economies of scale of a large city are transferred from workers to landowners so that the latter (and their children) can exercise a claim on the increasing productivity of the economy. Workers who opt for cheap land in the suburbs (or, in the United States, for blighted or deteriorated center sectors) pay a price in the greater expenses that arise from greater distance from work opportunities (or, again in the United States, greater need for municipal services) and the society in allocation of more resources for transport and services. The mismatch of residences and jobs, as well as many other problems attributable to land scarcity, is common to both developed and developing countries, to both mixed and socialist societies. Land scarcity is thus an essential element of the framework in which a housing policy must be fitted.

Another element is the magnitude of the cost of housing accommodation in relation to income. Even if land were costless, building a housing unit would still be a major expenditure; it would be out of the question for most unless long-term credit were available. Hence, it is useful to break the cost of new housing down into three major elements—the actual cost of materials and work, the cost of land, and the cost of financing. For housing accommodation (as distinct from merely a new house or apartment), the elements are the value of land (which affects its opportunity cost), the age or state of the housing unit, and the value of the unit (or the opportunity cost to the owner; that is, what he could realize by selling and investing in something else). The value of land and of the unit itself is the outcome of a complex of forces—the supply of existing units, the annual net addition to the supply, the desirability of the site, and the number of new family units being formed (or families and individuals desiring a separate housing unit).

The Problem

The problem is to combine good urban policy with housing that is well built, serviced, and located, and provides sufficient space per person at a reasonable cost in relation to incomes, especially of the lowest income receivers. "Good urban policy" means a city whose design does not encourage segregation by income classes or a disproportionate diversion of resources to urban transport and costly services, and of time, money, and effort of the residents for transport. These considerations are particularly important in LDCs, where the North American pattern of deteriorating inner cities and extensive low density suburbs, requiring the use of one or two automobiles per family, is particularly inappropriate.

Typical Advice to Less Developed Countries

In general, the advice tendered LDCs by international agencies and visiting experts involves a "direct attack," including (1) the extension of public, subsidized housing and (2) the encouragement of auto-construction on sites provided by public bodies, with materials provided directly or through loans and with services (water, sewage, electricity, and streets) provided by the state on a free or subsidized basis. Frequently, this is accompanied by suggestions that new housing over a certain value (or loans for such housing) be prohibited and that savings available for mortgages be directed to low-cost housing. Usually, straight mortgages with fixed interest rates are urged, regardless of the degree of inflation that prevails.[1]

This advice is subject to various objections. A very large element of subsidy is involved, and since there are many calls on the limited funds of the state, planners seek cheap land. But such land is usually cheap because it has obvious undesirable features. It is on steep hillsides or swampy sites, or it is located at considerable distances from job opportunities. Another problem is that if private funds are used to further a policy, there will probably be an effort to fix interest rates at negative levels (i.e., below the rise in prices) or below current commercial rates. This naturally results in a smaller amount of savings or funds available.

The direct approach to the problem of inadequate urban housing for low-income groups, then, is likely to lead to poor urban design—extreme segregation by income groups and homes far distant from work, shops, schools, and diversions. In public housing, where the emphasis is on the number of units provided, the temptation again is to locate in the peripheries in dormitory suburbs. If an effort is made to provide better located housing with ample space per person, the subsidy must be large, or the contribution required from the occupants may be so large as to limit the applicants to higher ranges of the lower income groups. The same problem applies to auto-construction: well-located land would not be efficiently used by building single family buildings, which most readily lend themselves to auto-construction. Hence, almost of necessity, the solution is confined to "cheap" land, which, again, is cheap for a reason.

In the case of lower income housing and loans provided at rates below the market, the general taxpayers are being asked to subsidize people who may be better off than they are. This situation actually occurred in Colombia in cases where fortunate owners of publicly built housing for middle- and low-income groups secured them with mortgages at fixed, low rates of interest, which were not adjusted for subsequent inflation. Finally, public service companies that are expected to provide free or below-cost services and facilities in turn experience difficulties in securing adequate financing to expand services in line with demand.

These objections are not unknown to those who give this standard advice. Their answer takes various forms. In the first place, they are inclined to accept, even welcome, the fact that the supply of funds available for heavily subsidized housing (or indeed for housing in general) is strictly limited. This places its possible increase beyond their terms of reference—a familiar consequence of the sectoral approach to problems of underdevelopment—and by this assumption, implicit or simply asserted, they greatly strengthen the case for their advice.

In fact, placing most difficulties "outside the terms of reference" seems to be a favorite response to criticism of subsidized housing and auto-construction. It is usually assumed, for example, that the lowest income people must be provided with *new* housing, no matter how unsuitable this may be. It is frequently noted that the majority of the very poor live in existing housing either as owners or renters; in the worst cases, families occupy a single or two rented rooms and share facilities. In such cases, the basic difficulty is not so much the cost of housing as the absence of decent paying jobs, or the existence of a large "dependent" population for which the social security system makes no provision. Thus, the problem is again placed neatly out of the sphere of the housing adviser. The fact that even in the neighborhoods aided by site and services the owners will let single rooms to as poor or even poorer families is known and deplored, but the solution to this problem appears merely to be to build more houses. There appears to be an extreme reluctance to admit that a renter or owner of existing housing may ever be in a better position than the owner or renter of new housing. A policy designed to make more existing housing available on better terms is usually dismissed contemptuously as an example of the "discredited trickle-down theory" or of providing "cast-off housing."

True, the deteriorated or blighted areas of large cities that can provide conventionally built housing reasonably close to work, shops, and schools often leave much to be desired (Harlem is an often cited example), but even here the conditions could be much improved at less expense than building new homes. The rehabilitation program in Brooklyn is providing good accommodation at much less cost than would new building. The problem here is rather the absence of sufficient job opportunities due to the migration of industry, which in turn arises from well-known causes. (But this, again, is "outside the terms of reference.")

Perhaps the argument that carries most conviction is that income data and housing costs in various large cities in LDCs indicate that the cost of conventionally built new housing units is beyond the capacity of 50 percent or more of the families. This statement appears to have as corollaries, without further discussion, the hopelessness of employing market forces, the indication that the problem is not one of availability of funds for building but of incapacity to meet costs, and the magnitude and hence extreme urgency of the problem. All these implications, in turn, appear to justify resort to the second- or third-best solutions of autoconstruction and site and services in peripheries, regrettable as such resort may be. These conclusions indicate a failure to think in incremental terms and to understand the functioning of the market or price mechanism.

In the first place, the relevant variables for comparison are not the incomes of half the residents and the cost of new and adequate housing. The housing market, on the side of supply, is made up of a great number of housing units of a great variety of kinds and locations. On the side of demand, the source is from the highest to the lowest incomes for many different classes and locations of buildings. All of the people are housed, though some very badly in shanty towns or crowded in single rooms. Just as, throughout this study, I have stressed the importance of mobility in the work force as a means of increasing income and lessening inequality, so here I would stress mobility in housing as a means of adding to and upgrading the entire stock of housing.

If it is assumed that in the larger LDC cities the formation of new family units is proceeding at a rate of 5 percent of the population per annum, an addition to the housing stock of 5 percent of conventionally well-built, well-located, and serviced housing units would represent an upgrading of the entire stock and would obviate the need for more shanty towns and additional overcrowding.

If the addition could be 6 or 7 percent, real rents on the existing stock of housing, as a whole, would have a tendency to fall and would permit the lower income people to acquire more space or better location and reduce the housing "deficit" (degree of over-crowding or unacceptable units). This likelihood that mobility can contribute to a solution of the problem thus depends on the volume of building on relation to new family units.

The role of mobility can perhaps be better grasped by comparing the housing market with the market for automobiles in the United States. A great number of people could not afford new cars, especially if it were difficult to secure financing, and without mobility and financing the overall total demand for cars would be very much lower than it is today. Although a car two or three years old is not as "good" as a new one of the same make and type, it provides transportation and has a value. The same is true, to a lesser degree, of a car five or six years old and so forth. Financing is available for all makes and types. Hence, the *demand* for cars is made up of many types and ages, from the newest, largest, and most luxurious to the smallest and oldest. The existence of a highly organized used car market makes possible a large annual demand for new cars. As long as the output of new cars exceeds scrappage, the entire stock is being upgraded. As incomes rise, cars are scrapped earlier. To describe this highly organized market, "escalation" conveys a more accurate or less prejudicial connotation than "trickle down."

There appears to be no good reason why the housing unit market cannot be as well organized as the North American automobile market, with transfer of ownership and financing made just as sim-ple and as efficient. Both are durable consumer goods, and much the same economic reasoning is applicable to both.

The point of the theory introduced above and the analogy to the automobile market is to emphasize that in dealing with the demand and supply of housing, the whole market and stock of housing must be kept in mind. It may be quite true (although data on incomes are highly suspect in most LDCs) that there would be no demand by a significant proportion of the population for new, con-ventionally built, and well-located unsubsidized housing, but this does not mean that there would be insufficient overall demand to match and exceed the growth of new family units and that it would not be possible to upgrade the stock. It may be necessary, however, to improve the terms of supply of financing and give direct aid to meet the housing needs of the very poorest by providing services and direct subsidies. Moreover, sole reliance on the market mechanism would not in itself provide an economical urban design or the diversion to public uses of an unearned increment to the owners of scarce land rapidly appreciating in value.

An Alternative Solution

This is another case where sector analysis appears inadequate. The solution of the urban housing problem must be fitted into a much larger framework of urban and national employment, distribution, urban design, and the overall allocation of resources.[2] Here we are touching on a number of objectives—a high and sustained rate of growth per capita, a falling birth and population growth rate, a lessening of differences in consumption standards, full employment, and a more economical design for larger cities, which lessens segregation by income groups. Although better use may be made of the market mechanism, defects and imperfections in that mechanism may require direct state intervention.

Part of the solution is a change in the traditional urban design, which attempts to tie an ever-sprawling residential area to a single center, to a cluster of more or less self-contained cities within a metropolitan area—the cities-within-cities approach. These planned cities would be built by private contractors for public urban corporations and would be owned and rented by the latter, with savings protected by monetary correction. This would permit internal cross-subsidization of the lower income residents, with overall nonsubsidization and ability to earn sufficient to supply the requisite rate of interest to increase savings. It would do this if urban corporations continued to own the land and were able to raise the rents on commercial and industrial properties and on higher income units as the sites became more profitable and valuable while restraining the rise in rents on the lower income homes. The rise in profitability and hence rents, which is the source of the problem of low-income housing, could be captured and used for services benefiting the whole community, particularly the lower income groups.

This could also be done in small part if the land and buildings were sold, as in the five cities within the Paris metropolitan area, and if prices, in relation to costs, were varied. But in this case, the original buyers will secure the bulk of the land increment value for an indefinite time in the future, just as now. In the earlier years of the housing estate program in Singapore, probably the largest in the world in relation to population, the economies realized by building and renting were such that rents averaged only 15 percent of incomes, and yet the overall subsidy of the housing estates was relatively low. In more recent years, however, problems have arisen in connection with the resale of flats with large capital gains to the original buyers. The same has occurred to housing units in Colombia with high and chronic inflation. The values of rents rise, and the monthly servicing of mortgages remains constant.

A third alternative would be to take measures ensuring a large amount of multifamily building (as now, only increased), which would do little to resolve the problems of traffic or segregation but would ease the pressure of scarcity and rising rents for the poorest. This might be accompanied by measures to restrict spatial expansion. Probably the worst alternate solution is the one most frequently resorted to—rent control, which leads to a decline in private building and a less rapid addition to the total housing stock and eventually to much higher rents and lower growth and employment. The direct benefit to some renters (including the well-to-do) is at the expense of owners and the poor who cannot find quarters to rent.

The cities-within-cities approach, however, does not attack directly the problem of the very poor in shanty towns and overcrowded quarters. But some of these may in time secure work in the new cities and qualify for the cheap flats. Others will benefit from the release of pressure on housing in general if the net new addition to the housing stock exceeds the number of new family units. If a family can move to two rooms instead of one, it has bettered its housing situation. The same is true if it can move from a ramshackle shack into a habitation built of durable materials. Even more important, funds would be released from building new subsidized housing in distant suburbs to improving and upgrading existing slums. A still more effective outcome would be that real income would increase following a rapid rise in income per capita and more or less full employment.

These arguments will probably not persuade those who believe in the efficacy of the "direct attack." Nevertheless, they rest on the use of the mechanism, improved and accelerated, that has served to improve housing conditions in the United States and other more developed countries over long periods. When the amount of new units greatly exceeds the number of new families, slums may be demolished and removed and the population rehoused, as in Singapore, where a few years ago some of the worst slums in the world abounded and are now (1979) fast disappearing.

We have noted the disadvantages of auto-construction in terms of site and services. Must, then, the low opportunity cost of a very poor worker, especially in his off-hours, be sacrificed? Not at all. If there are large numbers of poorly or underemployed workers, the same argument that justifies resort to an individual owner's work justifies the use of thousands of workers to build a planned community. A building is simply an assembly of materials. When labor is cheap and the raw material of building is limestone, sand, gravel, and wood, the remaining elements of cost are the elaboration of building materials, transport, planning, and supervision. The poorer the country, the lower should be the cost of building. Although the value of land cannot ordinarily be reduced, it can be planned around. For those areas within cities where the planned city-within-city is able to count on higher rents, especially on commercial buildings, to meet the financing costs incurred in acquiring the land (also on a monetary correction basis), a somewhat higher income mix of residents may be justifiable to avoid an overall subsidy. But the basic concept can also be applied to low-priced land in the periphery, without the current disadvantages, by planning to ensure that all the features and amenities of a true city of 300,000 to 400,000 can be secured, and without the loss of the important economies of scale provided by location within a metropolitan area.

The main weakness of a cluster of cities within a metropolitan area may be the unwillingness of some tenants to pay rising rents to a public corporation as the profitability of the site rises. (This is probably less likely with commercial and industrial tenants.) This was not the case in Singapore, however, possibly because of the relative stability of prices, the rapid rise in individual incomes, and the existence of a strong government. In a country where these elements do not exist, the sale of apartments to the lowest income groups and the transfer of mortgages on them to private lenders may be unavoidable, but efforts to collect rising rents from commercial interests and well-to-do renters should be feasible.

A further advantage of the cities-within-cities alternative is that it affords a means and a justification for measures increasing personal saving and channeling it directly into investment. In other words, it does not rely on the efficacy of the mobility and economic incentive motives alone, but does use "direct action" to the extent necessary to ensure that the motives are effective and will work to the public interest. In this way, it forms an integral part of an overall or macroeconomic approach.

A critical question is, of course, whether it is financially feasible for less developed countries to think of providing such conventionally built, well-located, and well-serviced housing for future additions to their urban populations, and to replace, in time, existing slums by such housing.

One recent study indicates the share of GDP accounted for by residential construction in a sample of thirty-nine countries. The poorest third of these countries allocated 2.75 percent to residential construction, the middle third 4.42 percent, and the richest third 6.48 percent, but there were considerable variations within each group. In two of the fastest growing countries studied, Japan and Israel, residential construction accounted for 6.3 percent and 7.3 percent of GDP, respectively.[3]

In Colombia, official estimates of expenditures on urban building have been pathetically low for a number of years. According to the national accounts, the value added on the site amounted to between 1 and 1.5 percent of the GDP for the years 1970-1977. The price tag for Colombia was recently calculated for the six largest cities.[4] If we assume that projections follow historic trends in Colombia (a 5-percent growth rate in GDP and a falling population growth rate), conventionally built housing in a suitable mix to a number equal to the formation of new families in these cities would require some 5.2 percent of GDP; with social facilities, 5.5 percent; with accompanying commercial and office building, 6.8 percent; and with all those plus electric power, water, and sewage, 8.8 percent, rising to 10.8 percent by the year 2000. (Most of the latter expenditures would have to be undertaken in any case.) However, such a program would in itself be expected to lead to a higher rate of economic growth and a lower rate of population growth, as in Singapore. If, therefore, an average GDP growth rate of 8 percent is postulated, the percentage for the total would fall to 6 percent of the GDP. This percentage is so low that it would permit a higher rate of building and expenditures in order to raise space standards and to replace existing slums.

While these percentages may appear high relative to the percentages that personal savings bear to GNP in many LDCs, there has generally been little effort to provide adequate incentives to such savings. In fact, the opposite has been true, with most outlets for personal savings providing a *negative* rate of interest. In Brazil, more or less steadily, and in Colombia, intermittently, savings for mortgages (and mortgages themselves) have been indexed, and the result has been a greatly increased flow of money to building. Most commercial and industrial building is financed from business savings, and the addition to public utility services from other sources. Hence, the addition to housing in terms of the mobilization of financial sources and in terms of the necessary volume of units to permit the mobility mechanism to function need not be ruled out for lack of funds.

A supplementary measure in financing and balancing the benefits of this activity would be a tax or taxes on the existing privately built and owned metropolitan area designed to capture the rise in land values over and above the general rise in prices. Efforts to do this have generally failed. First, they have not distinguished between a real rise in values and purely inflationary rises, treating the latter as real income subject to income tax (or capital gains tax). It is axiomatic that any tax which is manifestly inequitable will, in one form or another, be evaded. Second, policymakers have delayed the application of the tax or recapture until the gain is actually realized. But there is no good reason why the rise in real value, which rarely exceeds 2 to 3 percent of the value of land in a year, should not be assessed every year or two years regardless of the transfer of property. Furthermore, small owner-occupants could be completely exempted from such taxes without much loss of revenue but with a great reduction in opposition, and finally, the proceeds could be earmarked for better public health, educational, and recreational facilities, and the purchase of land for future cities-within-cities.

Conclusion

The advice generally tendered LDCs on urban housing indicates the danger of the sector apprch. By divorcing urban housing from urban design and urban transport and by treating the subject without reference to an overall program of production, employment, and income and without considering the possibility of greatly augmenting the flow of financial and physical resources to the sector, "advisers" can offer only second- and third-best solutions. The failure to come to grips with rising urban land values is especially regrettable.

11
ON THE PROCESS
OF ADVISING:
A CASE HISTORY

On entering the Colombian Planning Agency in 1971, I found that a large study—"Phase II"—on Bogotá was about to be financed by the United Nations Development Program and administered by the World Bank, under comprehensive terms of reference drawn up by the Bogotá Planning Office and the World Bank. These terms of reference stressed transport problems, which seemed redundant, as urban transport had already been covered in a "Phase I" study. I felt that in any case transport programming should follow and not precede urban design and that the new study should be oriented toward securing support for the cities-within-cities design then under consideration by the Colombian government. I had had considerable experience, however, with studies contracted with foreign firms and realized that once a fixed sum contract is signed, the client can exert little further influence. So I persuaded the National Planning Agency to attemnpt to modify the terms of reference, change the form of the contract, and secure a place in the study group's steering committee.

The Bank and the Bogotá Planning Office agreed to a greater selectivity in the terms of reference and to greater flexibility to modify the study as it proceeded. The Bank insisted on a lump-sum contract, however, proposing in exchange to strengthen the steering committee's authority "to review and approve the results of each step before action on the next step is taken so that the conclu-

sions and recommendations of each phase of the study are acceptable to the Government and are consistent with its objectives and
policies."[1] The Bank agreed that the study should be oriented
toward projects that could be started before the conclusion of the
study. Five firms were invited to present proposals. We agreed on a
firm of urban planners, and a contract was signed with this firm in
July 1972. Work began in August.

The first progress report (October 9, 1972) confirmed all my
earlier misgivings. The consultants saw no difference between a
socioeconomic study of a city facing a tremendous period of
growth and the building of, say, a dam or a bridge. After two in-
troductory chapters in which soothing words were inserted on the
change of emphasis to an "action-oriented approach" and a perfunctory discussion of the "cities-within-cities" alternative, mostly
negative, the report laid out the work of 48 staff members and consultants in 78 different "tasks" requiring 305 man-months, with
flow diagrams indicating precisely the dates on which the various
tasks would be started and finished. Any real possibility that the
study could be significantly modified in its course was an illusion.
Staff and consultants were already hired, and work was subcontracted. (A total of 114 man-months were assigned to a firm of
transport specialists to start immediately.)

In the second progress report, in January 1973, well after the
president had endorsed the metropolitan design of a cluster of cities
(September 1972), the consultants accepted the design. Thereupon
the steering committee, with the concurrence of representatives of
the Bank, urged that further work should be concentrated on planning the new centers. But by that time, most of the work had been
subcontracted in accordance with what the consultants believed to
be the original terms of reference. The third progress report (May
1973) and the final report (October 1973) advanced the study of
cities-within-cities very little.

The final report—"The Future of Bogotá"—was an impressive
document of statistics, studies, and alternatives with numerous
charts, tables, and diagnoses covering many aspects of urban life. It
concluded that future growth should be concentrated in a number
of "centers" in still relatively open spaces to the west, north, and
south of the existing city and that the growth of the existing center
or core should be limited. The study, in preparation and actual

time of work, had consumed four years, cost over $1 million, and had utilized the services, for varying periods, of some fifty professionals. It had resulted in an impressive stock of individual and unrelated studies, calculations, projections, and just data. Apart from some useful suggestions for improving the handling of actual traffic, and much general advice, no specific projects appeared, although the necessity for further studies was stressed.

The Bank awarded a further contract of US$250,000 to the original consultants for further studies. The Planning Agency, however, wanted some different points of view and arranged with AID for a series of rapid, strictly defined site studies with suggested mockups. Thus, in the end, there were rival studies. In the meantime, there was a change of personnel in the Bank, and the new staff did not accept the proposed basic design. A number of site studies were made, but it was late in the president's term, disagreement among the technicians hurt the plan, and jurisdictional difficulties arose. The next president accepted the urban design (November 1974), but it was not implemented.

There is a profound difference between engineering and socioeconomic projects; it is dangerous to apply the same study formula to both. In the case of engineering projects, the parameters can be made precise, and it is possible to determine in advance the talents required for the specific periods to do the specialized tasks into which the completed structure can be broken down. In the case of socioeconomic projects, there is an inescapably large element of uncertainty, and room must be left for false starts, blocks, and changing emphasis. The objective may be defined, but room must be left to feel one's way toward attaining it.

This calls for not only flexible terms of reference but a different type of contract, or working relationship. Before signing, the client should either have quite precise ideas on the terms of reference or should consider a series of shorter term contracts, which permit changes in emphasis as one proceeds. In addition, the system of awarding the study contract gives a premium to presentation, since "competitive bidding" cannot be in terms of price and has to take the form of rival proposals. But possession of this special talent need not correspond with the inventiveness, imagination, and ingenuity that the socioeconomic study calls for.

The Colombian experience has shown that timing is vital. The United Nations and the World Bank are large, complex organizations. Compelled over time to develop routines that protect them against capriciousness and abuse of influence, they have lost a certain flexibility. The machine has become ponderous and slow-moving. This is perhaps not so important in financing and preparing plans for a hydroelectric project, which can proceed regardless of individuals and governments. But in projects more in the social-economic-political fields, timing can make the difference between success and failure. When the Phase II study was originally being planned, a new government was about to assume power. When the final report was presented, that government was completing its term and was not in a position to launch a large new program.

The then AID system of financing shorter term studies by specific individuals for specific purposes—the block grant system of technical assistance—proved infinitely more flexible and effective and far less costly. The special expertise of a particular individual or firm, when approved by the AID resident director, could be used to fill a particular gap. If day-to-day discussions on specific points were what was needed, emphasis could be placed on that form of collaboration rather than on a final report.

The case study of this chapter may also serve to illustrate the danger of compartmentalism. It is obviously necessary to delimit a field of study. Yet, the delimitation may cause one to overlook something happening in an allied field that vitally affects one's conclusions. The urban policy of Bogotá would, it was believed, affect the urban policy of the country, which in turn was linked to the process of growth and to the national plan—the Plan of the Four Strategies—being pursued by the government. Failure to grasp the full nature and implications of this resulted in serious differences between the national and local planning agencies, between the steering committee and the consultants, and, at the beginning and at the end, between the National Planning Agency and the World Bank, which had awarded the study contract and expected to finance resulting projects. This source of confusion and difference might have been avoided or at least lessened if the national plan had been clearly spelled out at the beginning, which, in this case, was not possible.

12
PROJECT ADVICE:
A CASE STUDY OF
THE PAZ DEL RIO STEEL
PLANT DECISION

A single project can hardly be considered representative, but the Paz del Rio Steel Plant Decision was so important and involved advice from so many different sources that it was decided to include it in this study.[1] It brings out the difficulties of applying cost-benefit analysis and the criterion of efficiency, and permits making some generalizations on advice that cannot be made from a consideration of only macro or sectoral advice.

When the World Bank mission arrived in Colombia in 1949 (see Chapter 5), a promoting company had already been formed for an integrated steel plant that would utilize national raw materials in Paz del Rio, which was then a rather remote section of the country. The promoting company was sponsored by a public agency created to promote industrialization, which had authority to issue bonds. The agency was later given authority to divert a portion of personal income tax payments into a forced investment (a portion of an existing forced investment in low-income housing). Thus, there was already a vested interest in the construction of a steel plant at a specific location even before a serious study had been made.[2]

The original argument for the plant was the geographical juxtaposition of ore, coal, and limestone, the implication being that this would permit economical fabrication of steel and saving of foreign exchange, the advantages of national autarchy in this sector, and the employment and the subsidiary industries that would

154

SECTOR AND PROJECT ADVICE

be created and promoted in the vicinity, which was a depressed agricultural area. To achieve these advantages, a period of support and protection would doubtless be necessary, but, it was argued, it would be temporary and a small price to pay.

A study was contracted with Koppers Company in 1948, and its report in January 1949 recommended a fully integrated steel plant with an initial capacity of 193,530 tons, to cost US$95 million. For some reason, perhaps because of criticisms already being made by the World Bank mission, this was reduced to a plant with a capacity of 104,600 tons at a cost of US$41 million. The mission report, published in August 1950 but known to the government earlier, was highly critical of the Koppers report. It placed the cost at nearer US$140 million, cited factors making for high unit cost production both in balance sheet and social terms, and suggested that even by 1956 there would be insufficient demand for the few products that could be made by the proposed plant. In its place were recommended a smaller plant on the coast (at Barranquilla), initially for the reduction of scrap, and the enlargement of an existing and profitable electric furnace plant and foundry at Medellin.

This was a highly unpopular finding. The Committee on Economic Development was under tremendous pressure from the press and the government on regional and patriotic grounds to approve the Koppers report. A debate was staged before the committee (and recorded) between its foreign staff and experts of the Koppers Company. Under these pressures, the committee shelved the coastal plant for the time being and accepted a compromise suggested by its staff of a quick study for a small, simple, beehive coke oven plant in the interior to make a limited tonnage of a few products from native ore, requiring an investment of US$15 million. The promoting company "rejected" this proposal, even though it was addressed not to the company but to the government; the government remained silent, letting the company proceed with its proposal by default. The result was hailed as a great triumph for regional and national interests, and a construction contract was awarded to the Arthur G. McKee Company. A small, short-term suppliers' credit was obtained in France. By 1955, not US$41 million but US$160 million had been invested, and by 1959, the cost was approaching US$200 million with total aggregate profits to that date of US$2 million, although the output was still around 100,000 tons of finished products.[3]

This investment in the first ten years was premature and represented a very costly error. The investment almost equaled the net amount borrowed for all purposes in the 1950s by Colombia from public agencies abroad, the earnings were nil, and Colombian industry was handicapped by high-cost steel of inferior quality. Eventually, the shares given taxpayers in exchange for the forced investment permitted a private group to gain control, but the company continued to rely on government support.

It is worth inquiring a little more closely into the causes of the decision to proceed in 1950 with a costly integrated steel plant, despite the existence of much more economical alternatives. How could a difference in investment cost estimates of US$41 million and US$140 million remain unstudied? Why were estimates and proposals of independent technicians sponsored by the World Bank completely discarded in favor of proposals of an obviously strongly biased group?

In the first place, as in the case of the Concorde Supersonic Aircraft and the British Reactor Program, the decision was made on noneconomic grounds.[4] Both regional and national political considerations and national pride were involved. The word "scrap" in Spanish has a connotation of "junk," which carried over to the scrap-metal plant suggested by the mission report. It was argued that half of the steel produced in the United States came from scrap. Echoing the famous *New York* cartoon, Colombians to a man said, "I say it is junk and I say to hell with it." Our cost-benefit studies made the committee members most unhappy, but it was asking a lot to suggest opposing the aspirations of one of the poorest areas of the country, which were, moreover, supported by a high-powered press campaign. The powerful Society of Colombian Engineers met and solemnly declared that steel *could* be made from Colombian raw materials (which had never been questioned) but was silent on costs and markets.

In the second place, in dealing with public investments, the noneconomist rarely thinks in terms of alternatives or opportunity cost. A national steel mill, utilizing national raw materials, can be visualized. The things that cannot or will not be built if the steel plant is built are unknown and hypothetical. It requires some imagination and understanding of the functioning of an economy and aggregate figures to be convinced that a public investment has a cost and that if it is uneconomic or inefficient, the cost must be borne by the community.[5] This lack of a sense of opportunity cost is the most powerful argument for a rigorous and searching cost-benefit analysis for every public investment where such an analysis is feasible. The absence of the check imposed in a market economy by the risk of the complete loss of an investor's money must never be overlooked in considering public investments. In such cases, it seems, nobody feels that he has anything to lose.

In the third place, in explaining why decisions were taken in the past, the element of chance and accident should not be ignored; in this particular case, it was a very near thing. The head of the promoting company maneuvered with great skill and a fine sense of public relations. A less able person in this respect might have lost his case. The head of the Salem Engineering Company, who was to present the proposal for a small, nonintegrated mill, was delayed a week in the United States by a December snowstorm, so that he arrived just as the committee was breaking up for a month's Christmas vacation. That week would have given time for the drafting and signing of a study contract. The vice-president of the World Bank was on the point of permitting the World Bank mission to intimate that the Bank would look favorably on an application to finance the foreign exchange costs of the smaller alternative, even though it was located at a remote spot and would use all national raw materials—but he arrived at this point just a shade too late. One member of the committee broke its unanimity by insisting on adding a note that if the study for a small nonintegrated plant was unfavorable, he favored going ahead with the Koppers proposal. At the time, there was no countervailing private group to promote the plant on the coast. (This was formed later, but only after the plant at Paz del Rio was well under way.)

Not one of these circumstances affected the cost-benefit analysis, but any one of them, slightly altered, might have been sufficient to have changed the decision. Once the decision was made, a new and powerful argument for further investment was the fact that a sizable investment had already been made and a still larger plant

would secure the illusive economies of scale of a "balanced" operation. The use of this argument naturally grew with time and
investment.[6]

Postscript

The subsequent history of the plant is tortuous. In 1956, the
World Bank recommended private operation and an expansion of
facilities. But by 1960, the output was only 102,000, and the
accounting profit was 1 percent.[7] The Koppers Company submitted
a report in 1961 critical of actual operations but optimistic on future
markets. An appraisal by the World Bank in 1972 was critical of
the record to that date. Further studies were made by Arthur G.
McKee in 1972 (contracted by the company) and Dastur in 1975
(contracted by the government via UNIDO), which later greatly
overestimated the market. The World Bank General Report on Colombia of 1972 recommended that the whole steel fabricating problem be reexamined on a national basis. Despite all these studies and
varying recommendations either to "balance operations" at Paz del
Rio or return to the early idea of a plant on the coast, no basic
change in policy had been made up to 1979.

The "infant industry" has remained an infant, dependent on
government protection and support. Production has remained
small, and as much must be spent on steel imports as formerly. It is
one of the smallest integrated steel plants in the world. Colombian
industry and consumption have been handicapped by having to
pay more for a product that enters into the fabrication of many
more finished products, and this has also handicapped the growth
of exports except where imported steel and a customs rebate on
such steel are permitted. Throughout most of its history, the
product has been inferior to the foreign product in quality. While
eventually becoming "private," the plant was in large part paid for
by forced "investment" added to the income tax and proportional
to it. For foreign credits it was and is dependent on government
guarantees. Thus, it receives benefits that other private companies
do not receive. Despite protection and subsidies paid customers by
the government in the form of tax remission, it has not been able to
generate sufficient internal cash flow to provide for expansion.

Conclusion

On the whole, in this case, it would appear that economists took a somewhat broader view of what a national steel policy might be than did the steel-making specialists, who were more concerned with achieving a better balance in operations in a single plant. The initial decision was critical in creating a vested interest that naturally continued to press for its survival and expansion. In a government-sponsored investment of this nature, it is impossible to place responsibility on any individual. Public opinion may be aroused by a scandal but not by a poor public investment. Those who argue for "public participation" in all issues might bear in mind that the public is neither competent nor interested in deciding on the most efficient allocation of scarce resources. This is perhaps the strongest argument for leaving investment in commercial projects to the market.

With reference to the duties and responsibilities of a foreign adviser, the episode raises various difficult questions. Having made economic objections and suggested alternatives, and having encountered such strong opposition, should I have continued to urge the committee to take an adverse stand? Should I have urged the Bank to be a bit bolder in the matter? Should I have looked for a less costly second-best alternative or persisted in the compromise suggested in the report? Did I jeopardize the influence of the committee to accomplish other worthwhile things by opposing the Koppers proposal unsuccessfully? If a government is determined on a course of action on noneconomic grounds, there are obviously limits on what an economic adviser, especially a foreigner, can or should attempt to do to stop it. On the other hand, just to write and present a general economic study is of extremely limited usefulness indeed. There appear to be no clear answers to these questions.

PART 4
A GENERAL
APPRAISAL

13
MARKET FORCES VERSUS SPECIFIC POLICIES

To what extent does growth occur in response to underlying and pervasive forces in mixed economies and to what extent does it reflect the result of specific policies?

The basic economic theory of the growth process sketched in Chapter 3 would in itself lead one to stress the naturally cumulative and self-perpetuating nature of growth. Division of labor, in the widest sense of the term, begets division of labor. Every increase in the size of the market sets in motion a far-reaching series of changes tending to increase the size of the market. In this broad perspective, specific policies appear relatively unimportant—as surface phenomena not really affecting the underlying current of events. Governments and advisers, on the other hand, are naturally inclined to stress the key role played by specific policy measures.

In Colombia, growth has proceeded in periods of violence and military dictatorship as well as in times of national union and adherence to democratic institutions, through presidencies characterized by a virtual absence of anything that might be called a plan as well as presidencies dedicated to economic planning, in periods when priority was given agrarian reform and in periods when emphasis was placed on urban employment, in times of strict exchange rationing and in times of liberal access to imports. During the past thirty years, the administrative level of government was low, as was personal and property security; the exchange rate was overvalued for exports other than coffee; local industry was in general highly protected; the rate of population increase was high; little effort was made to attract foreign firms or to adopt foreign technology. Yet, despite this combination of unfavorable circumstances, the country made giant strides in its transformation to a more developed status.

The proportion of the population living in rural regions declined from 69 percent to 31 percent; an increasing proportion of agriculture became mechanized and modern; the country became a single economic entity; exports became diversified; by and large, the growing urban population was supplied with jobs and with services—electricity, water, sewage, transport, health, and education; the birth rate declined while life expectancy rose. As a result of these various transformations, the growth of income per capita rose from around 2 percent per annum in the 1960s to 5.3 percent in 1972. This was a remarkable advance.

How far it was the result of conscious policy measures on the part of government is another matter. The big transport program of the 1950s tended to create a national market and enabled the country to secure the economies of scale, although the motivation of the program was hardly so sophisticated. In general, the official view throughout the thirty years deplored the relative growth of the cities and did not look upon the process as tending to improve distribution, although its effect was to significantly raise the incomes of lower wage groups. Commercial agriculture received only sporadic support, chiefly in credit facilities. The notable fall in the birth and population rates in the 1960s and 1970s doubtless owes something to the rather grudging support of the lay authorities in the dissemination of birth control information, but probably reflects more the influence of urbanization.

Protectionism by tariffs, especially import licensing, encouraged import substitution, just as subsidies encouraged exports. But these policies were responses more to pressures arising from chronically overvalued exchange rates than to macroeconomic reasoning. The provision of an infrastructure of services made the rural-urban transformation workable, although, again, such a transformation was not intended. The increase in efficiency in the private sector owed little to conscious public policy, except for the indirect influence of educational assistance. In short, while the basic transformations were at times aided by government action, they appeared to have proceeded more as a result of a self-generating momentum. Is there, then, any need for special policies to accelerate growth?

The case for such policies has been argued at two levels: (1) the success, real or alleged, of individual policies at a project or sectoral level; and (2) the overall fluctuations in the rate of growth that have accompanied or followed macroeconomic policies. Clearly, a successful project or sectoral policy may have offsetting consequences in other fields, and, in macroeconomic policy, the causal linking may be only a case of *post hoc ergo propter hoc.*

Wide variations in growth rates by individual years, however (from 3.8 percent in 1967 and 1975 up to 7.8 percent in 1972), suggest the presence in the flow of either extraneous elements such as weather, harvest, and oil crises or the impact on investment of specific policies. (The range is even greater in the case of income per capita.) Such variations do not disprove the existence of underlying growth trends, but they do suggest that events and policies have more than a superficial influence, and it is usually possible to find explanations for oscillations in terms of them.

Another bit of evidence tending to support this hypothesis can be found in the very high rates of growth attained by a few non-oil producing countries (8 percent to 12 percent) and sustained for a number of years.

Still the question remains whether these deviations from the trend are of sufficient importance to justify the great concentration of effort required to attain the positive spurts and to avoid the negative spurts. An affirmative answer may be found in the nature of the growth process and in the phenomenon of compound interest.

The earlier discussion of demand-induced, self-perpetuating economic growth is not intended to imply that growth proceeds at any specific rate. *Any* rate of growth tends to perpetuate itself; there is no economic force that automatically calls into being a period of high growth to compensate for a period of low growth, or vice versa. Every increase in the rate of growth calls into action forces tending to sustain that rate. The higher the rate attained in a given period, the higher the base on which further rates can be computed so that, say, in a period of ten years and through compound interest, the absolute and per capita income can greatly differ from what would prevail in the absence of the original increase. Some calculations on this score were made for Colombia. The growth in income per capita in the period 1950-1972 was adjusted to take account of the falling birth rate of the late 1960s and early 1970s and projected to yield a rising rate from 2 percent to 3.6 percent for the period 1975-2000. This is a relatively optimistic projection based on the continuance of favorable trends that existed in the period up to 1972. It yielded a growth in per capita income in constant 1974 pesos from $7,429 in 1975 to $15,993 in the year 2000.

Another calculation was made of an initial rate of growth of 10 percent in the GDP for the decade 1980-1990, followed by a decline to 6 percent for the decade 1990-2000. These rates yielded a per capita growth rate of 7.9 percent for the years 1980-1991 and 4.5 percent for the period 1990-2000. The income per capita in 1970 pesos would arrive at $28,000 in the year 2000 (without allowing for the probably greater negative impact on population growth rates of the higher rate of growth).[1]

Thus, an accelerated initial period of growth would have resulted in at least a doubling of the per capita income of Colombians by the end of the century over the rate resulting from a mere continuance of favorable trends. (Moreover, the danger of relying on "natural" growth forces is that their tendency to perpetuate a very large proportion of the population in rural subsistence farming may prevent the decline in the birth rate required to offset the exhaustion of resources.) Insofar as an acceleration can be achieved by conscious policy, it appears to be worth the effort.

Another simple calculation is that at the rate at which income per capita grew in the 1960s (2 percent), it would have required forty-four years for it to double; at the rate of 5.3 percent in 1972, fourteen years. Clearly, the fall in the birth rate played an important role in this result, but there is ample evidence that this is not an independent variable but is linked to the growth in income, education, and urbanization, which in turn is linked to the great transformations in the pattern of development discussed previously.

While there are deep and pervasive forces favoring the perpetuation of growth, these can be aided or impeded by specific policies. The implication of this conclusion is that advice to adopt policies accelerating growth will be more appropriate than policies impeding growth. While this may sound obvious, it is worth recalling the UN questionnaire of 116 developing countries in which only three expressed a desire to accelerate rates of rural-urban migrations while ninety wished to slow or reverse them, or, in other words, to *impede* mobility. It has even been argued that the relative decline in the rural population in Colombia since 1961 "proved" that measures to accelerate this process by ensuring urban jobs were unnecessary! With still greater mobility, however, induced by policies that went with rather than against the trend, the lot of the lowest income classes, both those who migrated and those who remained in the countryside, could have been greatly improved.[2]

14
LEARNING FROM THE EXPERIENCE OF OTHERS

The growing literature on patterns of growth serves a highly useful purpose in lessening the emphasis on the conditions peculiar to an individual economy that implies that policies must also be peculiar to a given economy. Quite unwittingly, however, directing attention to the average rather than to the exceptional performances may have created a tendency for policy formulators, judging their own country's performance in relation to that average, to overlook valuable lessons to be learned from the experience of the most successful countries, especially in terms of the potential for high and sustained growth. Similarly, the understandable preoccupation of the international and national agencies with development in the most desperate cases, where frequently the issue appears as bare survival, has led to conclusions and policies that do not appear applicable to countries developing more rapidly.

The tendency is particularly noticeable in what might be called the "average" LDCs. Each "average" country repeats again and again the mistakes made by other "average" countries. At the same time, policy formulators in each country stress the peculiarities of their country and point out the precise combination of social, economic, political, and physical factors that exist nowhere else, and thus make it impossible to follow the example of the "nontypical" successful countries. If a country's growth program has been in the 5- to 7-percent range (or 2 to 3 percent per capita), this has been considered satisfactory. Higher rates are considered as probably unattainable.

The purpose of this chapter is to examine briefly the experience of a number of countries that *have* achieved sustained rates of growth of 10 percent or more: South Korea, Hong Kong, Singapore, Taiwan, and Brazil. Two of these countries are city-states, one of which permitted heavy immigration while the other limited it. Four of the five are in the Far East. None is an oil producer. Their development policies ranged from heavy reliance on the market mechanism (Hong Kong) to considerable resort to direct action by the state (Taiwan and Brazil).

Some Country Experiences

Despite colossal immigration from Mainland China, by 1977 the per capita income of Hong Kong had risen to US$1,430. Primary education was free and universal, and a program was under way to provide some secondary education to all who desired it. Forty-six percent of the people had been rehoused in low-income units. In general, the government's policy was to create an environment favorable to growth and to supplement this by transfers to promote activities in the social field. The engines of growth were exports and export services; the island served as an entrepôt between Communist China and the rest of the world.

Singapore experienced a remarkable period of growth from 1966 to 1973 (11 to 14 percent per annum in the GNP) and another, at a slightly slower rate, following the world recession of 1974. Per capita income rose from about US$480 in 1965 to US$2,450 in 1975. Consumption expenditures in real terms grew at the rate of 7 percent a year; over half the population was rehoused; educational and work participation rates were very high; and the birth rate fell to 1.3 percent. The driving forces in growth were, as in the case of Hong Kong, manufactured exports with growing value added, supplemented by an enormous building program (relative to the size and income of the city), financial services, and tourism (mostly businessmen).

In South Korea, the rate of growth in the GNP accelerated, rising from 7.7 percent in the period 1961-1966 to 11 percent in

1971-1976. Incomes per capita rose from US$102 in 1962 to an estimated US$864 in 1977, accompanied by a falling birth rate and rate of population growth. Although the engine of growth has again been exports, the domestic market has been more significant in making possible economies of scale than has the domestic market in, say, Singapore. More recently, exports and manufacturing for domestic consumption have been supplemented by heavy construction contracts from various oil-producing countries. Growth has occurred in the cities, with the rural population remaining stationary.

A similar demonstration is offered by Taiwan, with a somewhat larger percentage of people still rural. The rate of population growth declined to 2.2 percent in 1976. Income per capita in 1975 was US$930, up from $372 in 1960, or a 6.3-percent annual rate of real growth per capita.[1] The shift to an urban society and to technical processes in manufacturing and for exports followed the general pattern for successfully developing countries. According to World Bank studies, distribution improved considerably. There is consensus that the sustained growth was largely export-led. The government has also sponsored projects requiring heavy capital investment.

In Brazil, while many economists may have reservations on the package of policies employed, the rate of growth was exceptionally high following 1966. Despite a high rate of population growth, the rate of growth in per capita income in 1965-1973 was a high 6 percent, returning to this figure again in 1976. Again, an engine of growth was exports, though here more attention was paid to the creation of a large and growing domestic market to secure economies of scale than in some of the other countries. The familiar pattern of increasing urbanization and industrialization was followed. Through a system of indexation, a sizable proportion of savings was channeled to building, which was a contributing factor in the growth, as in Singapore and Hong Kong. Unlike some of the other cases, foreign borrowing was exceptionally heavy.

Although there were very great differences among these five cases in environment, resources, size, and culture, there were also significant similarities. In the three countries that started the accelerated growth process with a large low-income agricultural population, agricultural incomes lagged behind urban incomes, agricultural values declined relative to nonagricultural production, cities grew relative to total population, and birth rates fell. In the city-states, too, the rate of growth in consumption of agricultural goods lagged behind the rates of growth of consumption of nonagricultural products and services. Most of the cases followed Japan's example, using exports as the economy's "engine"—the sector with the most rapid rate of growth. In Japan there was also the common tendency, as wages rose, for the exports to become increasingly sophisticated and the production methods more capital-intensive.

In fact, for some of the Far East success stories, it appears that more attention was paid to the example of Japan than to foreign advice. Foreign borrowing and debt service were kept low, and the monetary and fiscal policies followed were relatively conservative. While expert opinion differs on the causes of growth in Japan, especially as to whether or not the growth was export-led, it is a fact that manufactured exports were large enough to make an impact and grew faster in the postwar period than did the larger domestic market.[2]

Lessons

From the point of view of the growth process espoused herein, it is important to note not that in most cases growth was apparently export-led but that exports represented leading sectors whose more rapid growth could stimulate the overall rate. It is relatively immaterial whether the high final demand arose from possessing a favorable competitive position to tap world markets or whether it arose from a high-income elasticity of demand for household appliances, automobiles, or building. The important thing is the existence of the leading sectors.

The significance of the fact that most of the countries had "strong" governments while growth was high lies in the resultant relative continuity of policy, which provided a basis for the creation of expectations for continuous growth. The lesson is to provide such favorable expectations rather than to adopt any particular form of government.

Rapid domestic growth requires, in many cases, the import of energy-creating facilities, raw materials, and, initially, capital goods. Our cases suggest that these may be secured either through exports or, for a period, through borrowings. The more secure pattern appears to be by exports.

In none of the cases was agriculture a leading sector in the sense that its growth rate exceeded the national overall rate. The benefits of growing agricultural productivity were reaped in the release of manpower to produce other things together with sufficient mobility to ensure jobs.

Perhaps the outstanding lesson is that it has proved *possible* to attain and sustain rates of growth of 8 to 10 percent or more with or without very large internal markets or great natural resources. In all five countries, rapid growth facilitated the great transformation I have described as a necessary accompaniment to development—relative urban growth, growth of industry and services relative to agriculture, growth of literacy, falling birth rates, diversified exports, and more capital in the factor mix. Underlying this strong growth pattern was a dedication to the importance of growth that gave it top priority among the multiple economic objectives of government policy. Specific policies differed widely but a common characteristic was this dedication.

Events are too recent to permit saying that the growth in these five countries has allowed them to dominate or control the environment in all its aspects and to adopt appropriate policies to meet new problems. But the documented advances *have* been outstanding, and in general the countries have succeeded in meeting the difficult problems posed by world inflation, recessions, and oil crises.

Lessons may also be learned from countries listed in the more developed category. They have all followed the basic pattern of development as outlined here, although they, too, have differed widely in natural resources and size of domestic market. Again, outstanding growth experiences among these countries appear to be related more to the degree of dedication to growth as an objective than to the existence of natural resources or specific policies.

Something of value can even be learned from wartime experience. Given an overriding objective to which everything else is subordinated, the production possibilities are almost unbelievable. In World War II, the United States, without much more infrastructure or industrial equipment than it had in the late 1930s, and with 12 million people serving in the armed forces instead of being formally listed as unemployed, produced a prodigious amount of goods, not only arming, feeding, and clothing itself but also contributing substantially to the needs of its allies.

This was accomplished, not only by rationing consumer goods and discontinuing the production of luxuries (chiefly motor cars), but also by cutting back all investment that could not be expected to make a marked contribution to the war effort. Unskilled people (especially housewives) were quickly trained for industrial work, and key equipment was utilized on a twenty-four-hour-a-day, seven-day-a-week basis. The same economy that a few years earlier could not provide a decent standard of living for its people now did precisely that and in addition waged a tremendous war on many fronts. In 1942, 1943, and 1944, respectively, 36 percent, 45 percent, and 47 percent of total output in the United States went into the war effort. The GNP, in 1954 prices, rose from $186 billion in 1938 to over $320 billion in 1944. Despite rationing, per capita consumption rose throughout the war.

Although it is probably impossible to duplicate the patriotism and priorities acceptable in wartime, war experience does suggest that the fewer the objectives of policy, the more effort is likely to be concentrated. It also suggests that in most economies, for most of the time, there exists considerable slack or unrealized potential.

The rich mine of experience of both the developed and the more successful developing countries has not been as fully exploited by the bulk of the advisers to LDCs as one might expect. Emphasis continues to be placed on differences rather than similarities. "Development economics" is considered to be different from economics. Specialists have evolved for particular countries. It would never occur to anyone to describe himself as a specialist on the United States, but this is done continually for individual developing countries. Part of the price of this intensive specialization has been a relative disregard for what might be learned from the experience of others. The relative success of West Germany in combating inflation is not, it is held, because certain policies have been followed, but because of peculiar characteristics of West Germany. The remarkable success of Singapore is not because of policy, but because the bulk of the citizens are Chinese in origin! More mundane obstacles to a broader understanding are abundant. The literature on any one country is enormous; the local commentators disagree; to obtain a feel for the reliability of the data requires tedious work; factual information is difficult to publish and quickly becomes outdated. It is obviously a field for multinational organizations, but they have not achieved agreement in comparative analysis. There has been a noticeable lack of enthusiasm for evaluations either of the agencies' own activities or of the work of others. Within a country, governments change and ministers come and go with great rapidity. There is little time for study, and policy will generally reflect the views and beliefs that policy formulators had in assuming office. The facilities for knowing with any degree of certainty the success or failure of a particular policy in a particular foreign country are extremely limited.

15
THE ORGANIZATIONAL
FRAMEWORK FOR ADVISING

This chapter focuses on the experiences of different countries with varied types of advising organizations. Although a definite pattern of this particular form of technology has yet to emerge, the sum of experience has taught some useful lessons and permits certain generalizations.

Planning, Advising, and Administrating

Macroeconomic government planning comprises two broad categories. One includes flexible, continuing efforts to achieve such broad goals as faster growth, greater stability, and better distribution; they can be embodied in a series of policy statements and measures. This is the type of planning favored by most of the OECD countries. The other type of planning, probably originally inspired by the Soviet five-year plans, is incorporated in a document with a special title, covers a stated period, and usually attempts to make quantitative projections of growth, overall and by sectors. It is favored by most LDCs.

There exists another distinction between the "plans" of socialist and market or mixed economies. In a centrally planned economy like the Soviet Union, the allocation of all resources and the distribution of all income are incorporated in the national government's budget. The plan and the budget are identical. In mixed economies, the plan attempts to cover the budgets of all public bodies, which presumably are under control, and, in addition, monetary, fiscal, and exchange policies and the economic activities of the larger private sector. These are by their nature subject to varying degrees of influence, and the outcomes of their activities are unknown and uncertain. Plans and objectives relating to them must therefore be regarded as projections. In any case, they are not subject to the same degree of control as are the government's revenues and expenditures.

The latter mixture, often called "indicative planning," was popularized by the French government. It has been defended as affording guidelines to industrialists on the one hand and explicit targets for activities in the public sector on the other. Most developed countries, however, have not engaged in this type of planning (for example, the United States), have tried and abandoned it (as in Great Britain), or have successive "plans" to which little attention is paid and which are subject to constant revision (as in Japan).

Critics of such planning maintain that businessmen are little influenced by government projections, that the only certainty is uncertainty, and that if plans are taken seriously, they may deprive the government of the flexibility necessary to meet the unpredictable course of events. A plan that exposes the government to charges of being mistaken or failing to achieve its objectives and that must therefore be constantly revised is of dubious utility. A further disadvantage of formal plans is that they endanger the necessary continuity of policy. Each incoming government feels compelled to come up with a new plan and to discard its predecessor's plan. This must have a jarring effect on the economy of a country. Furthermore, the alternatives are not many. Politicians generally, and probably wisely, seek to avoid as far as possible specific promises and commitments. Conditions change, and presumably candidates do learn and should feel free to adopt new policies.

On the other hand, a plan does have the merit of forcing a new government to clarify its thinking and to make up its mind as to which alternatives it will stress. For example, the written Plan of the Four Strategies of Colombia (see Chapter 4) contained a relatively short section called "Guidelines," which indicated the main lines of policy: objectives, diagnoses, and the choice of available strategies, with stress on theory and a minimum of quantitative projections. It was accompanied by a bulky collection of documents and statistics on sectoral programs that had been prepared in connection with the national budget, which had already been presented to the Congress. The guidelines focused attention on key points of theory and furnished material for a national debate on these points.

Note that the budget, although it may be said to reflect macro policies such as defense and education, is not in itself a tool of policy. In very large part it represents inertia or, rather bureaucratic momentum and Parkinsonian forces. The freedom of action of any government to vary the relative size of its appropriations is strictly limited. Somewhat more freedom, though not much more, may prevail in the expenditures, though here again inertia and vested interests play a predominant role. In Colombia, tacking the budget and ongoing programs onto the somewhat novel guidelines of the Plan of the Four Strategies did not raise questions. In the United States, while a major new economic issue may arise occasionally, the bulk of current discussion divides itself into changes in the budget at the margin on the one hand and macroeconomic policies of employment, stability, and growth on the other. Even the energy issue is sufficiently large and far-reaching in its impact to be classified as a macro problem.

The 1968 Constitution of Colombia had a novel provision that the administration should present its plan to a large committee of both congressional houses in the form of a bill to be enacted into law. (If taken literally, this provision would create impossible difficulties, but in practice it would probably be satisfied by a very general expression of agreement with the objectives of a given plan.) Although it has proved impossible to institute this machinery, it may perhaps in time be converted into something similar to the practice in the United States, where the Council of Economic Advisers proposes an economic report that, if adopted by the president, is presented to Congress and is referred for study to the Joint Economic Committee of both houses. The successive annual reports of the president and of the committee have provided excellent educational exercises without unduly impeding the desirable flexibility of government policymaking.

The Plan of the Four Strategies in Colombia was followed by another general plan in 1975, called To Close the Gap (between the rich and the poor, between sectors, and between regions). The new plan carried over some of the programs of the previous government but indicated a marked change of emphasis from growth to better distribution as a goal. By the end of the administration, however, the president had reconstituted growth as an objective, setting as a target a rate of 7 percent per annum. This, in turn, was followed, in 1978, by a Plan of National Integration, which placed emphasis on decentralization and on bettering the infrastructure of transport and power.

If Colombia seeks an overall plan in the future, perhaps government spokesmen will continue the precedent set by the Plan of the Four Strategies, setting general guidelines or indications of orientation rather than the more rigid quantitative "year plans" of many LDCs. The objective of a plan should be to clarify issues and to maintain continuity in the pursuit of objectives, but not at the expense of flexibility.

The task of a macroadviser should presumably be to concentrate on this aspect of planning. While attention may have to be paid to sector programs and specific projects, the macroeconomist's special field remains the overall objectives and general approaches to their attainment.

The Organization for Macroeconomic Planning and Advising

Since the level of administrative efficiency is generally low, a characteristic of most LDCs is the multiplicity of urgent problems in all fields. The person finally held responsible for results is the head of state. There is virtually no limit to the number of decisions a president is expected to make, but there is, of course, a very definite limit to the time and energy he can devote to the study and implementation of policy. One solution to this problem is to restrict the range of activities of the public sector and the number of decisions it must take, concentrating on the indispensable activities and policies and delegating as much as possible to the private sector. But partly for ideological reasons and partly because the matter has not been thought out carefully, the contrary has generally been the case. The pattern has been for a state to take on more and more activities, or activities of a nature that require a mass of detailed regulation (such as price controls, the location of plants, import licensing, and tax regulations). Moreover, instead of concentrating a small expert staff on the problem of maintaining overall stability, serious inflation is allowed to develop, "requiring" a great deal of time and energy to make painful price adjustments. This work now appears to be urgent and necessary, but it is only so because of the diffusion of effort in the first place.

Just as there is a temptation for the head of state to spread himself too thinly, so there is a temptation to look to the planning or advisory agency to concern itself with a similar multitude of policies—macro, sectoral, and micro. The proponents of any new activity either wish to place it in an agency created for the purpose, or look to the Planning Agency for advice, regulation, or supervision.

In Colombia, the Planning Agency has been charged with various operating duties, and even in its primary function of advice-giving, its organization was spelled out in the Constitution to cover the sectoral fields of a wide range of ministries. Many of the specific responsibilities of the National Council of Economic and Social Policy (CONPES) are specified in law, and since the Planning Agency is primarily responsible for the agenda and technical papers for that council, a major part of its responsibilities is the result of this relationship. Much can be said for this linkage, as it ensures that technical attention will be given to all matters brought before the council. But these matters include such subjects as granting individual (tourist) subsidies to specific hotels, guaranteeing supplier debts incurred by decentralized agencies, and approving foreign credits.

This, then, is the dilemma. To ensure that some actions receive adequate technical attention, a large part of the time of the head of state, various ministers, and the National Planning Agency is taken up with a number of things which, in a more technically developed country, would be left to operating agencies or to the private sector. As a consequence, less time is available for the consideration of much more important policies. But to relieve the Planning Agency and the top economic council of these "minor" tasks may incur running the risk that macroeconomic decisions will be taken elsewhere, the Planning Agency will not be consulted by the president, its prestige and status will fall, and its raison d'être will disappear. This happened in two administrations in Colombia (1953-1957 and 1962-1966), and the experience helped bring about the present complex allocation of duties.

The larger the staff and the more diversified its activities, the greater the danger that the head of the Planning Agency will perforce become an administrator rather than an adviser, relying on the judgment of subordinates who are further removed from the inner corridors of power. Documents prepared within the Planning Agency in Colombia in recent years were frequently presented at the weekly meetings of CONPES attended by some twenty officials, most of whom have specialized administrative responsibilities. This may be contrasted with meetings in the early 1950s of the three-man Comité de Planificación advised by Albert Hirschman and me, where the discussions on short policy memoranda were vigorous and probing, preparing the members of the committee for their meetings with the president.

It is very doubtful that advice can be forced on a president if he is not disposed to seek it and that a planning agency can play an important role apart from its relationship to the head of state. I would therefore lay more emphasis on a small planning agency whose head (or heads) may not only possess the confidence of the president, but also have time and ability to concentrate on and coordinate macroeconomic policies. The preparation of an annual economic report by such a group would give focus to its contribution and would also contribute to raising the level of public debate and enhance the prestige of the planning agency. (Too frequent reports tend to be routinized and become an end in themselves.)

The dilemma of concentration versus broad coverage exists in all mixed economies; attempts to resolve it have ranged over a wide field. In the United States, a semi-independent monetary authority was created in 1913, the Budget Bureau (now the Office of Management and Budget) was transferred from the Treasury to the

Executive Office of the President in 1939, and the president's Council of Economic Advisers was formed in 1946. The president is thus assured of access to alternative points of view.

The British, however, have opted for a different allocation of responsibility in which virtually all macroeconomic policy is concentrated in the Treasury, although in theory the prime minister and the cabinet as a whole have joint responsibility. In practice, policy in this field is so difficult and technical that the minister primarily in charge, to whom the technical staff is responsible, has an overwhelming voice. The prime minister may challenge this, but he is dependent on the chancellor of the exchequer for the presentation of all facts and alternative policies of a technical nature. Although the prime minister has on occasion intervened, the record suggests that the predominant voice in monetary and exchange policy, the framing of the budget, and fiscal policy has been that of the chancellor.

The organization for policy formulation is intimately concerned with the question of the relation of technicians to administrators and of both to the formulators of policy. A good economic adviser has enough of the academic virus to be a bit bored by administrative work, while an administrator tends to enjoy action and be impatient with "words." The formulator of policy must necessarily take an active interest in politics, the feasibility of policy, the reaction of the public, and the defense and support a policy can rally.

From the point of view of the organization for advice-giving, Sir Alec Cairncross's account of the subordination and anonymity of the distinguished economists who advise in the British Treasury is particularly disturbing.[1] Alan Peacock likewise remarks that "only in rare cases will a senior economist be influential enough to change a minister's mind on a major issue of policy and even then he will be able to do so [only] with the firm backing of senior administrators, and particularly that of the Permanent Secretary."[2] A tremendous amount of discretionary authority appears to be vested in the permanent head ("secretary") of a department, who decides what is to be presented to the minister. Issues may not be raised and debated in public, and in any case the British sense of decorum seems to stand in the way of taking a strong stand on issues either in public or in internal debates. Similarly, P. D. Henderson, in his fascinating story of two major British errors which cost thousands of millions of pounds, points out that the really critical decisions never reached the stage of public discussion until it was too late. In the rowdier Washington scene, however, public opinion was quickly rallied against proceeding with the supersonic plane program. In the great exchange crisis in Great Britain leading up to the acceptance of "hard" conditions for a major loan from the IMF in late 1976, it appears that not only policy formulation but also economic analysis was overwhelmingly in the hands of noneconomists—permanent and deputy secretaries of the Treasury and Ministers. I do not know whether better decisions would have been taken earlier if economists had been closer to decision-makers. The subject bristled with political as well as technical aspects. However, economists specifically trained on the technical side appeared to have played a relatively small role in the really important conferences. Incidentally, the decisive voices on the American side were also those of noneconomists.[3]

The question of organization for policy formulation is thus one confronting all countries, the more as well as the less developed. The case for a certain diffusion of authority and responsibility for major macroeconomic policymaking is that otherwise the head of state is too dependent on the advice of a single minister and may not have the means to explore alternatives. The case for a separate department of government management and the budget directly responsible to the head of state is that one minister should be neither permitted nor required to pass on the appropriations for others or to appraise or evaluate their work. The case for a semi-independent monetary authority under the broad supervision of the head of state is that the control of the money supply should be divorced from the making of loans, and policy must be in the interests of the nation and not of particular sectors. The case for a planning office responsible to the head of state is that it gives him access to sufficient elements of judgment to coordinate all macroeconomic policies of the government. The case against a ministry of planning, which some LDCs have adopted, is that it puts macroeconomic planning on a level with other ministries. If authority really accompanied responsibility, the minister of planning, like the chancellor of the exchequer in Britain, would take over the major economic tasks of the administration. Differences of opinion may legitimately exist on what constitutes a proper distribution of authority for policy formulation and on whether a developing country should follow the model of the United States or of Great Britain, to cite only two possibilities. My view is that since the head of state is held responsible for the current record in economic growth, employment, output, and prices, he should diffuse authority under him but take final responsibility for the coordination of policy. As a general rule, he cannot afford to rely on a single source of data and recommendations but should encourage the presentation of different points of view. In these highly technical fields he would be well advised, however, to have a small technical staff responsible solely to him for the purpose of analyzing data and proposals and of presenting recommendations on a technical basis. In the composition of the expenditure budget and appraisal of its results, he also needs to be assured that the officials charged with these tasks are responsible to him. (In practice, this means a concentration on yearly changes at the margin where some room for maneuver exists.) It seems clear that the monetary authority, wherever placed, should be composed of people who have no official interest in the allocation of central or commercial bank credit. Above all, the chief task of a central bank should be to create or extinguish money and not to assume the tasks of a "development bank."

Developments in the fiscal, monetary, foreign trade, and exchange fields must be coordinated, so that their net impact on current economic activity (output, employment, and prices) is favorable to the stated objectives of the government. The necessary distribution of authority for activities involving spending and political power makes conflicts of interests unavoidable. The head of the government must therefore, necessarily and unavoidably, be the final arbiter. The organization for overall economic planning must be arranged to give maximum assistance to the head of state in the task of coordination and maximum assurance that his broader objectives of policy, for the attainment of which he is uniquely responsible, will not be lost in the swift passage of time, the conflict of personal aims, the overload, and the unceasing struggle for power.

The Germans have located at least some of their economic ex-

perts outside the regular governmental machine in the Sachverständigenrat.[4] The goals of the "SR" are "high" rates of employment, "steady and adequate" rates of growth, price level stability,
and external equilibrium. Naturally, some compromise and interpretation have been necessary, but at least up to 1968 the five
members of SR were unanimous in their recommendations, sought
to be objective, and were often fairly critical of current government
policy. Henry Wallich, in comparing its work as an "outside"
advisory agency with that of the American Council of Economic
Advisers (CEA), an "inside" agency, makes the point that an inside
agency must generally expect to adapt its views at least in part to
the political necessities of the president, as far as this can be done
with propriety. An outside agency seeks to exert its influence more
on the public at large and possibly the political opposition. Because
of the latter possibility, Wallich observes dryly, "It is hard to
believe that another government in its right mind would again
establish a similar institution."[5] In any case, in democratic countries, outside critical agencies will continue to exist, even though
they are not established by the government, and it is probable that
their advice will continue to be more uncompromising than that of
inside experts.[6]

A further example of the diffusion of authority may be found in
the recent Full Employment and Balanced Growth Act of 1978,
wherein the U.S. Congress not only asserted its right to set goals
and targets in the macroeconomic field, including monetary policy,
but also extended the concept of targets to include the rate of
monetary expansion. This legislation amended the Federal Reserve
Act and called for full biannual reports to Congress by the Board of
Governors and Federal Open Market Committee on their objectives and plans and the relation of these to the short-term goals set
forth in the Economic Report to the President. The first such report
was approved on March 12, 1979. The wisdom of setting rates of
expansion by legislation may be questioned, but not the obligation
to discuss and defend policy. Such discussion at a relatively high
technical level in the more developed countries is a far cry from the
state of the art in many developing countries.

To change the thinking of a country on vital economic policies is
no light task, and it is perhaps a good thing that it is so. However,

the inability to distinguish between an improvised policy on the one hand and a carefully thought-out policy on the other and the refusal to make the effort can be most frustrating to an adviser. The only organizational suggestion that comes to mind here is to keep open various channels for the presentation of different points of view, such as the use of the committee or council device in matters that pertain more to theory and policy than to administration. (See Chapter 5.)

Organization cannot guarantee good planning or the implementation of policy. It can, however, improve the setting of priorities, better allocate the time and interest of top policymakers, ensure that policy alternatives are studied before action is taken, and allow economists to make their contribution. The better the framework in which advice is given, the greater the likelihood that it may be appropriate and effective. But a head of state cannot be forced to accept advice, and organization cannot substitute for good judgment on his part in the choice of assistants and policies.

Microeconomic Advising

Although not emphasized in this study, this type of advice is the more usual, and in the period under consideration there were literally thousands of microeconomic studies.

The main portion of the work of the National Planning Agency in Colombia in the microeconomic field is associated with the "national investment budget," advising on loan applications submitted to foreign and international lending agencies and financing studies. The National Planning Agency and other agencies have financed a library of some eleven thousand studies.

All of this activity has undoubtedly contributed to a better allocation of resources. This is not less true even if they do not result in projects.

Tied Advice

Tied advice refers to the conditions attached to loans by national and international aid agencies. It differs considerably from the conditions attached to loans in, say, the Eurodollar market, which are concerned with interest rates and maturities and the general credit-worthiness of the borrowing countries. The loans of the aid agencies, whether or not concessionary, have principally to do with the *purposes* of borrowing. If the purpose is to finance a program which is in favor with the lender, a loan is likely to be forthcoming whether or not the country needs the foreign exchange. Even if some other need has higher priority, it is the loan for the aid agency's "pet" project that is granted. Most ministers or heads of decentralized agencies are anxious to show as much achievement as possible during their relatively short terms in office. Thus, if it is shown that an international agency favors a loan for such and such a purpose, an application for such a type of loan will undoubtedly be forthcoming.

Perhaps the strongest argument for borrowing is the probable continuance of inflation, so that the real burden of the debt is thereby reduced. The cost is the sacrifice of a certain degree of autonomy in the management of the borrowing country's affairs. Furthermore, the debt service mounts rapidly, and the country may be forced later to adopt austerity measures that impede growth. And there is little to prevent uncontrolled borrowing. Lending agencies, of course, are in the business of making loans, and without loans the reason for their existence disappears. Far more damaging than the agencies' self-promotion, however, is the fact that governments, unlike individuals, are inclined to borrow to the limit. The main restraint in the past, in fact, has been imposed not by lending agencies but by the borrowing country's "absorptive capacity," a euphemism for the delays imposed by red tape in meeting loan requirements and getting projects under way.

Some of the most successful LDCs have been very prudent borrowers. Tied advice and matching requirements may not be, as writers on the left often maintain, a modern form of imperialism, but they most certainly entail a large element of tutelage or paternalism, which may or may not be to the benefit of borrowing countries. The question has recently become more urgent with the emphasis on loans for a direct attack on poverty, whose productivity is questionable and which add to the external debt service for years to come. One of the criticisms that can be made against the direct attack is its tendency to substitute subjective criteria for efficiency or creditworthiness. The conditions favored or imposed may embody a large element of subjective judgment, as in the case of a forcible expropriation of land and a limitation on the size of holdings imposed on Japan by the occupation forces after World War II. A more recent case in Colombia was the restriction of urban loans by AID to intermediate cities, housing sites and services, and small farmers. Matching requirements, which insist as a condition that the recipient country match or double the loan or grant without regard to the overall allocation of resources, furnish a particularly questionable case of paternalism.

Terms of Reference and the Contract

Foreign advisers may be contracted for general purposes for a period or for a specific task. In either case, it is important that the sponsor have a fairly specific idea of what he expects from the adviser. If the adviser is left to his own devices and is expected to create his own job, it is unlikely that his work will be very helpful. Or he may find that he is put in competition with national advisers or administrators, and friction can arise. If a sponsor is uncertain about what he should do, the relation with a foreign adviser should be a very close and personal one.

As a general rule, the terms of reference should be both specific and flexible: specific in the sense that both sponsor and adviser know what the adviser was contracted to do; and flexible in permitting a shift of duties or of emphasis as the situation changes or more is learned of the nature of the problem.

The content and terms of a contract with consultants should vary with the nature of the work. The more technical and specific the contract, the safer it may be to spell out the terms and conditions of the work. The more intangible and generalized the subject, the less safe. Once a contract is signed, the host government will probably lose control over the study, and little more can be done to orient it until the final report is submitted.

To contract for a "final report" is more suitable for a bridge or a dam than for an economic or public administration topic, where it is generally advisable either to have a close working and advising arrangement or to make a series of shorter, sequential studies so that the digestion and implementation of previous and current studies can proceed together. In the Phase II Bogotá study discussed in Chapter 11, despite strenuous efforts to provide guidance and an express commitment by the World Bank that orientation would be subject to change as it proceeded, the steering committee had little control over the follow-up study. In the first World Bank mission to Colombia, it was not the final report that led to a number of projects but rather the follow-up study and the modifications and endorsement by the advisory committee working closely with a technical staff. (See Chapter 5.)

One of the advantages of having available a fund for short consultations with a minimum of procedural requirements is that it offers an opportunity to a national economist to check his own understanding of theory against that of a well-known foreign economist. Even if nothing much results from a few days' consultation, the assurance that the theory involved in a proposed action appears to be valid is certainly worth the small sum involved. A foreign expert can also give assurance to the formulator of policy.

It is useful to bear in mind that there is no necessary connection between the cost of a study and the usefulness of its findings. The larger the sum requested or made available, the more diffuse and irrelevant may be the reports. Furthermore, all curriculum vitae are impressive, references are uniformly favorable, and the presentation of the proposal (and the form of the final report) has become a fine art. The "Big Names" listed will likely not be those of people who will do the bulk of the work. For the developing country and the national sponsor directly concerned, large sums of money and elaborate presentations are no substitute for personal acquaintance with the consultant. In the absence of this, efforts might be made to arrange for initial short and specific studies of phases of the work, largely for the purpose of getting acquainted and learning whether further relationships are likely to be worthwhile.

Again, working out a feasible social security system is not at all like planning a hydroelectric works, and the organization of the studies should be quite different. A proposal for a macroeconomic topic in terms of man-months of work tailored to fit a detailed outline and flow charts illustrating the timing should automatically disqualify the consultant for this type of work. If the sponsor knows the consultants and expects to work closely with them, a cost-plus contract may give much better results than a lump-sum contract. If, for some reason, such an arrangement is not feasible, a series of short, specific contracts may be preferable to a long study covered by a lump sum.

Resort to "pilot studies" and "demonstration projects" in the socioeconomic field appears to reflect another faulty analogy to engineering and technical studies and should be avoided. The history of the past thirty years of advice-giving is strewn with pilot studies that remained as pilots and demonstration projects that had no visible demonstrable effects.

The Art of Advising

Advisers work under difficult conditions; if they are personal advisers, they face difficulties that academic economists or institutional advisers do not encounter. Personal advisers must generally present a recommendation in a short, simply worded memorandum prepared under pressure of time and must sacrifice much of relevance for the sake of brevity, speed, and clarity. But in a matter of policies, values, and judgments, the real arguments for a brief recommendation remain mostly assumed or only hinted at or stated dogmatically.

If the adviser has access to the formulator of policy or to a presidential adviser, he can in time acquire a sense of what is likely to prove acceptable or can be made so and of what will undoubtedly be rejected out of hand. If he occupies a lower position in the hierarchy, it is more difficult to acquire this sense as he must first persuade or convince his immediate chief. The longer the chain, the more difficult it becomes for the adviser to know how to present a proposal and the more likely that the argument will become more impersonal and colorless.

If the adviser is conscientious, all this will bother him. If, however, he is overly conscientious, he will not be read. An academic economist can write for his peers, a privilege denied an adviser in his everyday work. The person to whom an adviser is addressing a memorandum will assuredly have his own "iceberg," which probably will be of a very different nature. There is generally no time, even if there is inclination, "to thrash things out." The adviser is often forced to rely on creating a basis of trust or confidence and have his ideas accepted on this score rather than as a result of exhaustive considerations of alternatives. An advisory committee may help to give the policy formulator additional trust in the advice. But generally the committee likewise must be prepared to accept a low profile. An almost irreplaceable advantage of a year's academic course is that there is time for the lecturer to explore the interrelationships of things in a disciplined fashion and build up a more or less tight, logical structure of consistent theory. An adviser, on the other hand, neither has the time nor can he impose the desirable degree of discipline, and finally he must be cognizant of many relevant elements in advice about which he must realize he has no particular competence. Finally, he can rarely claim credit for policies because many people have collaborated in the final outcome and because, in any case, the administrator or the chief executive expects to accept the credit as well as to take the blame for policy.

In economics, all persons have opinions, and often very positive ones. But the chances are that uninformed opinions will be mistaken and counterproductive. Again and again, it has been noted that growth and progress occur despite policy. For various reasons, sound economic advice is likely to be unpopular, while conventional wisdom is likely to be unsound. Hence, a well-trained adviser who conscientiously attempts to use his tools of analysis will generally find himself on the unpopular side of issues. Just as good economic theory is rarely popular, so a good adviser must expect to encounter much opposition and criticism. If he would be popular, he must generally suppress his scruples. One escape is to maintain a low profile, and it is an escape that the people he is advising will generally favor. His release can come on his return to academic life if he has been wise enough to have kept this avenue open, and he can then express his views more freely, if more obscurely.

It early became apparent to me that there were too many people trying to make a living out of agriculture in Colombia and presumably in other LDCs. It was 1961—ten years later—however, that I built a plan around the promotion of mobility and the creation of nonagricultural jobs. This plan was violently unpopular, and I again had the uncomfortable experience of being correct prematurely. Although such a plan was placed in operation for a brief period, it did not absolve me for my sin of proposing the plan ten years earlier. Some eight years still later, when the proportion of the rural population had declined to some 30 percent (still too high), it was gravely pointed out that specific measures to promote mobility had not proved necessary since in any case it had occurred by itself. I was still wrong. So far as I know, not one of the numerous groups of writers who deplored the relative growth of the cities has ever stated that they might possibly have been mistaken in opposing that growth much earlier. The satisfaction for an adviser is not likely to be justification from history but the work itself—and the inner knowledge that one may have altered the course of events constructively, even if just a tiny bit.

Training Advisers

Great diversity makes it difficult to classify advisers or to fit them into neat categories. Training economists who may become advisers poses its own difficulties. The difficulties of training on the job in a field like economic theory are noted in Chapter 6.

In the 1960s, an ambitious training program for economists was launched in a leading private university in Colombia with a distinguished group of professors from the University of Minnesota and the Massachusetts Institute of Technology. The discrepancy in salary scales and workloads between foreign and local professors was so great, however, that the effect was demoralizing. After four unfruitful years, the dean (Eduardo Wiesner) proposed that the money should instead be made available for fellowships abroad and for maintaining a first-class economics library. When this very reasonable alternative was rejected, he took the unprecedented action of terminating the arrangement. General experience tends to support his position that a developing country should, as soon as possible, build up its seed stock of national economists who are well trained abroad. Foreign lecturers can serve as a stopgap but cannot really replace an initial corps of teachers who have received the best training available.

Even the "best training available," however, is not always suited to the purpose. Exhortations to graduate schools in more developed countries to lay more stress on basic concepts, critical readings, and case studies will most probably fall on deaf ears. Basic concepts are often considered to have been taught in undergraduate courses. In the large graduate schools, the professors have an ingrained bias toward formal lecturing and an understandable disinclination to read handwritten essays. To many, the combination of critical reading and the Socratic method of teaching by questioning appears to be too slow and incapable of covering sufficient ground with sufficient rapidity. But the alternative combination of cramming and fragmentation is hardly good training for an adviser. (Even for faculty members, the growing size and specialization militate against the type of general discussion that used to play a highly useful role. Because it is impossible to keep up with the literature, abstracts and skimming are used. The same points, fallacious or sound, are made again and again, and everybody is under too much pressure to take time off and attempt to sharpen and resolve issues.) Thus, the leading graduate schools are wedded to a "rigorous," specialized training, while short courses given by various agencies appear to be of very limited effectiveness. Perhaps the foundations could best promote the type of training for future advisers, although to do so they would themselves require the services of experienced advisers and a careful selection of candidates. It is possible, however, that the services of past members of the Council of Economic Advisers might be secured for the final screening and preparation of programs that the foundations could in turn fund in universities. Or apprenticeship training for advanced and mature students might be provided by such agencies as the CEA itself, the OECD, or the National Planning Association.

Sponsorship

Little can be said of one of the most important of all factors bearing on the acceptability and implementation of advice—sponsorship in the host country. The ideal situation from the adviser's point of view is to have access to a person who is receptive, influential, and effective in securing action, and who has a tenure sufficiently prolonged to permit him to push the implementation to a point where the policy or new institution becomes self-sustaining. Unfortunately, such ideal conditions rarely exist; compromises must be accepted and chances taken. Unless a sponsor fulfills at least some of the conditions just mentioned, however, there is a strong probability that time and money will be wasted. This judgment applies with even greater strength to large missions organized for the purpose of making comprehensive country studies. A report unsponsored by influential individuals and agencies, addressed to the government at large, will almost certainly result in no action.

A fortunate series of circumstances or accidents may bring together a good team of advisers and administrators that may chalk up some notable achievements. But the case studies considered here suggest that such happy developments are largely in the nature of accidents. Since, in democratically organized LDCs, the policy formulators—the president, ministers, and heads of agencies—change rapidly, and since the same is true of advisers, the prospect of a good combination being made or maintained for any length of time is not bright. The only organizational clue to this problem is provided by a consideration of the advising process in countries like Great Britain and the United States, where, while advisers may be mistaken in individual policies, they have at least been well trained and have had to match and defend their views against those of others in the profession. Unfortunately, such background and professionalism tend to accompany rather than to precede development.

Thus, while organizational changes may enhance the possibility that advice to LDCs may be both improved and accepted, too much should not be expected from this source. In general, policy in the macroeconomic field will depend on the ability and willingness of the chief executive to choose good administrators and advisers. Development is necessary to enhance the chances that appropriate advice will be sought, offered, and followed. But development itself is dependent, to a degree, on the adoption of appropriate advice. Organization and procedures have a role to play but in turn are dependent upon the general cultural and educational level of the country concerned.

16
THE APPRAISAL OF ADVICE: CRITERIA AND MULTIPLE OBJECTIVES

Multiplicity of Objectives

Until very recently and still in the overwhelming majority of cases, economic growth has been an important objective of policy. However, adherence to this objective is rarely wholehearted, and it must share its position with a number of others, of which perhaps the most important are better distribution of income and expenditure, greater price stability, and fuller employment. (Distribution as an objective may in turn be treated arithmetically, or in terms of "absolute" and "relative" poverty, or in terms of regions or even nations rather than of individuals.) All these are undoubtedly worthy ends, but the greater the number of objectives of policy, the greater the danger that they will offset and cancel out each other.

All of the success stories among developing countries have possessed in common a dedication to growth stronger than prevailed in, for example, Colombia. Indeed, at one point, growth in Colombia acquired a bad connotation, and the stated objective became better distribution. Whether or not as a consequence, a serious recession promptly occurred, and for a time there was neither growth nor better distribution.

Some policies to promote better distribution may be compatible with the promotion of economic growth, and some may not be. Economic growth may alleviate both relative and absolute poverty of the masses, or it may alleviate absolute poverty but not relative.[1] Attempts by the state to transfer purchasing power from the richer to the poorer may accomplish its objective without interfering with growth. Or it may not. In the case study on tax reform in Chapter 11, the "reform" paradoxically worsened distribution and probably slowed, for the time being, the rate of growth. In this particular case, the objectives explicitly stated were to improve distribution within and between income groups and to raise revenues, rather than to encourage growth.

In another measure to improve distribution by working through the price mechanism, the state tried to stimulate agricultural productivity in general, restrain mobility, and increase competition among the rural poor. Perhaps the problem here is better treated under faulty theory. But setting prices to restrain the rise in the cost of living clearly can be in conflict with growth in output and employment. In such cases, the objectives of price control are usually stated to be to prevent the abuse of monopoly and excessive profits, but evidently it is extraordinarily difficult from month to month to set prices at a point where investment is encouraged but "monopoly profit" is not permitted. If the objective of price setting is to provide a support price to avoid losses to agriculturalists and keep up production, again, a fine balancing act between supporting prices and keeping down the cost of living is required.

A serious conflict frequently occurs in the management of exchange rates. They have been set for long periods at levels that require rationing and controls and have discouraged non-coffee exports, although the promotion of exports has always been a stated objective. Unfortunately, it conflicts with the other objective of restraining the rise of internal prices. In monetary policy, the objectives of stable prices and promotion of production and employment in specific fields have almost continuously been in conflict. The usual result has been excessive monetary expansion and rising prices, with no consequential increase in production and employment. In real terms, that is, after correction for inflation, interest rates have generally been negative, and this has made both stability and growth difficult. This is also the familiar conflict between the objectives of control of money and control of interest rates. "Keeping interest rates low," once a means to an end, is now defended as an objective in itself, as is "setting money growth targets." There has been interminable confusion between the immediate impact of more loanable funds on interest rates and the longer range increase in interest rates resulting from inflation and the resultant rise in demand for loanable funds. On occasion, monetary policy has been motivated by the desire to meet the credit needs of specific sectors ("productive credit control") or, on other occasions, to assure equality in rates for different classes of borrowers.

The promotion of fuller employment has frequently been unnecessarily in conflict with the attainment of a high rate of growth, largely because of the means chosen to achieve it, as when labor-intensive techniques are adopted even where they were clearly uneconomic. Conflicts of objectives closely akin to this are those between output and the correction of regional disparities in income and between the objective of growth and that of decentralization, where the outcome is further confused by the intermixture of private and social benefits and costs.

Still another conflict may arise between the objective of rapid growth through measures facilitating the transfer of technology and full employment and the objective of retaining control by nationals over all types of enterprises. Nationalist sentiment is often far stronger than the desire to be more efficient or to gain foreign markets.

Subtle differences in objectives can create equally disruptive confusion. In the field of housing, for example, providing a single family "home of one's own" for a few may outweigh providing better than existing housing for a larger number of people. In the only case of cities-within-cities that was actually launched in Colombia, it was proposed that over half the housing in very valuable land within a ten-minute walk of the center of a city of 400,000 (Bucaramanga) be of a space-extravagant, single-family type. The same problem is widely evident in farm programs, where ownership becomes an end in itself.

In the discussion of the rural poor, it was noted that even the choice of crops to study for the purpose of improving productivity was influenced—and weakened—by considerations of equity. If it is pointed out that higher yielding varieties of a particular crop may benefit richer farmers, the crop would probably be discarded for another for which increased productivity may be less important and more difficult to attain, but which is grown mainly by very poor farmers.

Demographic control, under various names, has become a national objective but rarely is so strongly held as to be placed in opposition to the policy of restraint of migration or decentralization. The objectives of decreasing pollution, improving the environment, and conserving resources likewise generally lose out in conflicts with other objectives or with private interests.

A fairly recent policy objective that has generated a considerable amount of emotion is the elimination or lessening of income differentials between the richer and poorer countries. This leads less to suggestions for policies within the LDCs than in what they propose should be done by the more affluent countries under the general heading of the New International Economic Order. This usually takes the form of greater pressure for loans and for more favorable treatment of actual or potential exports of the LDCs by the OECD countries. This particular objective, however, does not appear, at least for the time being, to be in conflict with other objectives of LDCs.

A factor influencing advice and policy formulation is the failure to assign reasonable relative quantitative importance to qualitative considerations. This is particularly serious in relation to the multiplicity of objectives. A common example can be found in the reluctance to allow the exchange rate to fall with a relative rise in prices because it "tends to cause inflation." If imports are 10 percent of GDP, a fall of 10 percent may (very roughly) tend to raise internal prices by 10 percent of 10 percent, or 1 percent. But a 10-percent fall in the exchange rate may be critical for many exports and hence the growth in GDP.

For obvious reasons, doing something for depressed regions is a popular issue or objective in most countries, including those in the more developed category. The British government has been seeking to influence employment and population location since World War I, with a notable lack of success but at considerable expense.

Setting negative rates "to reduce costs" may result in a misallocation of resources as well as a reduction in saving. Again in Colombia, despite the constant assertion of lack of capital, a law forces the distribution of the major portion of profits in dividends "in the interests of the less well-to-do shareholders"! Migration to the cities is alleged to reduce agricultural output. How much? What if the rural opportunity cost of the "surplus" labor is zero? Examples could be multiplied. A related form of the same source of error is to list the pros and cons of a course of action in which an insignificant consideration appears to acquire weight equal to what should be the conclusive factor.

This list of objectives, while not exhaustive, probably includes the leading objectives of policy in LDCs. In some cases, the objectives need not be mutually exclusive, and the problem may be in the choice of means or in faulty theory. In the cases studied here, it has become apparent that a large number of objectives, along with the failure to think through and establish priorities and attempt to reconcile differences, can easily lead to stalemate and to loss of effective action. Again, the success stories have been characterized by stronger dedication to fewer objectives, with a greater reliance on the forces of a market economy to promote and attain the subsidiary objectives.

Recently, Paul Streeten argued persuasively that the primary objective of development is a fuller life, which implies the satisfaction of basic human needs (or the removal of absolute poverty).[2] I think, however, that there is a big gap between the relief of dire poverty and the attainment of a fuller life, and I would like to interpose the more difficult requisite of first acquiring that degree of control over environment that characterizes what we have agreed to call the more developed countries. A serious additional difference is that Streeten appears to feel that meeting basic needs necessitates resort to a direct attack, and he is inclined to downgrade the contribution of growth and mobility. All this serves to emphasize the "basic" need for sharpening and clarifying issues.

Subjective Versus Objective Criteria

One hesitates to call the mix of personal, political, and purely emotional considerations objectives of policy, but certainly they are a source of motivations closely akin to those provided by what I have described above as objectives. Insofar as they constitute ends of policy and enter into policy formulation, they are relevant to the theme. They offer, in addition, explanations of why advice directed toward increasing efficiency is so often disregarded.

Policy is more often motivated than one would like to think by the personal consideration of popularity, sometimes identified as a "political consideration" from which, generally, there is no appeal. There would be no harm in this if popularity and soundness corresponded. Unfortunately, on matters of economic policy there appears to be a perverse relationship. Likewise, as noted already, there is the political necessity of every incoming government to produce a new plan. There are just not enough correct answers to justify the constant juggling of priorities.

A macro policy is frequently rejected or weakened because it may benefit Mr. X who is already "making too much money" or provides loans for people who are already wealthy. The converse is also true, of course. In Colombia, for many years, interest rates for mortgages were maintained at unreasonably low levels because most influential people were borrowers. The fact that this led to inadequate savings and funds for mortgages was not attributed to the low rates, and to change this situation required a terrific struggle. Even after the change, the influence of borrowers fairly quickly reasserted itself.

Not all objectives, of course, can be based on grounds of efficiency or be subjected to the test of the results shown on the "bottom line." Yet, when more subjective criteria are involved, the field becomes as open to the demagogue as to the skillful manipulator of words for praiseworthy purposes. Little economic discussion and probably no discussions of national policies are free from the dangers arising from the use of imprecise and value-charged terms. We may be opposed to "monopoly" or "the concentration of economic power" but in favor of "the rationalization of industry to withstand foreign competition"; in favor of "competition" but against the "unbridled," or "cutthroat" varieties; in favor of mobility and free choice of occupations but opposed to "the depopulation of the countryside"; opposed to "middlemen" but in favor of "orderly marketing"; opposed to "hoarders" but in favor of more "storage facilities"; in favor of "efficiency" but opposed to "the trickle-down" process. "Labor-intensive" techniques are good, and "labor-wasting" techniques bad. It is good to utilize low-paid labor, but reprehensible to "exploit" it by paying only the going wage. One can favor "growth," but not, of course, "growth mania." "Small is beautiful," "bigness is a curse," and "we must build from the bottom up," not from the top down.

The injection of personal values has appeared in most of the case studies in this book. The first World Bank mission talked of "basic human needs" and the necessity of an "attack on poverty." The arguments for the integrated steel plant at Paz del Rio were largely noneconomic; the most telling argument was the need to "do something" for a depressed area and to use "national raw materials." In discussions of the rural poor and urban living conditions, the language becomes most value-charged; it is difficult to consider the merits of alternative approaches dispassionately. Foreign advisers generally deplore the existence of "tenant farmers," "sharecroppers," and "landless laborers"—even though on occasion they are much better off than owners of tiny plots—and generally recommend the redistribution of land with or without compensation. Long after the great bulk of the people in the United States lived in or around large cities, the presumed social superiority of the quality of life in small towns and rural regions was generally accepted as a fact or as part of the folklore it was unwise or not politic to question. It is curious that the rise in urban land values, much more marked than in the case of rural land, has not been denounced, with consequent proposals for expropriation of the "unearned increment." The general tendency has been to deplore the rise in land values but to advise decentralization as a solution.

The Colombian Planning Agency's chief interest in 1971-1974 was in using building as a leading sector to give impetus to growth, and, to this end, housing, urban policy, and saving to supply funds for mortgages were all essential parts of the package. But the concern of AID was not in all of this but rather that the new savings institutions be "mutual" and that strict limits be placed on the cost of housing to be financed. If the subject were the establishment of priorities in the objectives of development, it is unlikely that the fostering of mutual savings rather than joint stock institutes would rank very high. And yet, in the eyes of one aid agency, for a period in 1972, the creation of mutual institutions was ranked above growth and employment. Although the help of the agency was consequently dispensed with, the succeeding government also downplayed growth and was critical of the sector's failure to utilize more fully private savings for "social" ends. For this reason, the government reduced the incentives to save through this channel.

One can hardly expect or ask that advisers and formulators of policies should not have personal values and that their values should never be reflected in their language. For example, my one-time choice of the term "the net federal contribution to purchasing power (or incomes)" to describe what others might call a cash deficit was deliberate and was hailed by a subsequent writer as a masterpiece of semantics.[3] One can only hope that in time a general rise in objective and critical habits of thought will make it more difficult to sway actions solely by appeal to emotions.

Subjective considerations need not refer only to causes and beliefs. They may be intensely personal. The desire to have one's name associated with a reform or at least to receive credit for it in some circles is certainly a powerful and pervasive motivation and may explain why one reform or policy is praised and another opposed. (This may explain why one may influence one's students but only rarely one's colleagues.) For many years in Colombia, a newly appointed minister was expected immediately to announce "a complete reorganization" of his prospective ministry, accompanied by "vast" reforms. However, "sweeping," "far-reaching," and "comprehensive" reforms are rarely as effective as less ambitious changes and improvements.

The basic misconception of Truman's Point Four aid program was that people in developing countries were anxious to be more efficient; all that was necessary was to tell and show them how to be so. This ignored, of course, a host of other objectives and motivations and helps to explain the frustrations and disappointments of aid agencies. But the aid agencies themselves have accorded little study to the conflicts that so easily arise from the multiple objectives of growth, equality, and the satisfaction of basic human needs.

17
THE APPRAISAL OF ADVICE: THEORY AND FACTS

The role of theory and factual data as criteria in the appraisal of the effectiveness of advice is the focus of this chapter, which argues that frequent sources of error and of inappropriateness of advice can be found in faulty theory and incorrect or irrelevant factual data. Contrariwise, appropriate advice must rest on "good" theory and a more or less correct understanding of the relative magnitude of environmental variables.

Difficulty of Determining the "Correctness" of Theory

If economic theory is understood as a generalized explanation of the functioning of the economic system in terms of causal sequences, motivations, and incentives, using the accepted tools of analysis, practically all policymakers are also theorists, whether or not they think of themselves as such. Likewise, the diagnoses of problems implicit or explicit and the proposed solutions or policies rest on theory. Generally, when a person distrusts theory in general or states that something is all right in theory but does not work out in practice, he means that he disbelieves one theory but accepts another, which he calls "in practice."

The social sciences' inability to demonstrate the correctness of a given theory is a more serious problem. Naturally, this applies equally to advice, which is also based, at least in part, on theory.

Many things are always happening at once. To disentangle one out of various possible causes and assign it a quantitative value and establish its certain relation to an effect is rarely possible. In much of macroeconomic policy, the only final test or criterion of effectiveness is whether a sufficient number of leading scholars in the discipline are convinced that the logical argument and the quantitative evidence available establish a presumption of "reasonableness"—and reasonableness is a matter of opinion. Possibly the most depressing episode bearing on the point was afforded by the near consensus of opinion on the advisability of balancing the U.S. national budget in the years 1930-1938 and the tenacity with which such a view was held despite all the arguments to the contrary. These arguments were so strong that, later, "demand management" through fiscal management became an accepted tool of macroeconomic policy, finally passing the test of "reasonableness."

The evaluation of case histories for this book furnishes an almost continuous exercise in theory, usually controversial. The prevailing lack of consensus, it seems, arises not only from use of different factual data but also from different interpretations of the data and, much more distressingly, from differences of opinion on causal sequences and on motivations. When differences go so deep, "reasonableness" is of limited value. When economists can be cited on both sides of an issue, their authority is correspondingly lowered, and the policymaker is free to follow his own inclinations.[1] That policy formulation is more an art than a science is thus attributable not only to differences in personal values and objectives, but also to the unreliability and misuse of statistics, disagreement as to the relevancy and correctness of assumptions, and, most unfortunately of all, differences in the handling and interpretation of theory itself. A measure of agreement can often be reached only when all the truly interesting and significant variables are impounded in *ceteris paribus*. When they are not so impounded, as in the actual world of events, either differences of opinion appear or we become guilty of what Paul Streeten has called "the fallacy of illegitimate isolation" in neglecting other and relevant variables and alternatives.[2]

Economic Discipline and Judgment

Arthur Okun[3] has pointed out some attitudes and qualities possessed by economists that peculiarly fit them to contribute to policy formulation—a lively awareness of choice both in alternatives and opportunity costs; an almost ingrained inclination for the incremental or marginalist approach as, for example, what extra costs and benefits arise from extra efforts; a tendency to weigh public against private interests; a preference for the roundabout rather than the direct approach in attempting to resolve problems;[4] and an awareness of and respect for the efficiency of the pricing mechanism in general in the allocation of resources. Above and beyond these characteristics is the intangible and almost indefinable element of judgment. There are times and circumstances when direct action is preferable to indirect; when opportunity costs are zero (or activity is costless in overall terms); when the average or aggregate may be more meaningful than the margin; and when the pricing mechanism may make for faulty allocation of resources.

The term "judgment" suggests a characteristic of a disciplined mind in which the terms of reference or universe of discourse are kept constantly in the fore; the relevance of assumptions to the argument and to the facts is constantly and almost instinctively checked; and the consistency of empirical data is subject to constant checking so that inconsistent data become immediately suspect. An example of the last case is afforded by data purporting to show a high income elasticity of demand for foodstuffs. Except in cases of the existence of actual and chronic hunger, it would be well to regard the high elasticity data with profound skepticism. Lost in what have been described as "thickets of algebra" or carried away by generous feelings of indignation, some economists and advisers are liable to disparage or even forget these simple characteristics of their discipline.

Most nonscientific discussions follow the lines of free association, in which one thing leads to another and the universe of discourse constantly changes. Unfortunately, even the most "scientific" economists are not always immune to this habit even when dealing with important problems. Personal values rear their heads, and suddenly the nature of the problem undergoes an abrupt change; previous discussion becomes irrelevant. This is perhaps one reason why conferences or workshops, or even discussions in scientific and professional journals, fail to resolve issues or to sharpen them so that points of difference can be identified. These remarks have particular relevance to the task of evaluating advice, for there is no authority to which the evaluator can appeal. He is forced to rely on his own judgment, which, naturally, is influenced by his own personal values. Generally acceptable theory is based on certain assumptions, is cast in the form of tendencies, and makes use of such crutches as "other things being equal." In its application to policy, the crutches may be dispensed with, the assumptions questioned, and the tendencies held to be offset by extraneous factors.

Thus, the chief difficulties confronting an economic adviser, in the application of theory to specific cases and specific countries, lie in the necessity of keeping in mind the objectives of policy, the reliability and relevance of the data, the political and administrative feasibility of the proposed advice, the time element, the internal consistency of the various policies being advocated, and, all the while, taking care that the theory involved can be defended in the discipline and yet made intelligible to the layman. Certainly the task is difficult, indeed much more difficult than being a good theorist. A good adviser cannot afford to let himself become exclusively absorbed in theory. Rather, like a driver in heavy traffic, he must be alive to many things going on around him.

The Importance of Underlying Assumptions

In offering advice based on theory, the assumptions underlying the theory are often forgotten. An example would be the allocation of *existing* resources under the principle of comparative advantage. A more dynamic view might stress the dangers of monoculture and the prejudice to more diversified exports and to an industrial base, or to development in a wider sense of the term. The point is discussed in Chapters 2 and 3.

Examples of the Use of Theory in Advising

A few illustrations of the use and abuse of theory may serve to illustrate these rather general remarks. Most of the advice designed to improve the condition of the rural poor seems to rest on faulty theory—that, for example, a generalized increase in physical productivity will in itself lead to a generalized increase in agricultural income; that the relief of hunger and the relief of poverty are the same thing; that the work of middlemen and intermediaries is unproductive; that there is insufficient employment outside of agriculture to "absorb surplus labor" and sufficient employment cannot be created (the implicit assumption being that nonfood needs are saturated or cannot be made effective); and that some technical improvements require more labor and are "good," while others displace labor and are "bad." Advisers here seem to ignore the basic economic concepts of mobility, competition, elasticities of supply and demand (both of price and income), productivity in its various senses (physical and value, per unit of area and per unit of labor), the interplay between factor proportions and cost per unit (or relative scarcity), and the fallacy of composition. In addition, certain valid assumptions on motivations and incentives are not made—that under conditions of competition between many small units, supply is relatively insensitive to a downward movement of prices but responds rapidly to an upward movement; that because of farm ownership and difficulty of adjustment to new surroundings, mobility is too low and supply may continue excessive, in relative terms, for long periods; and that family planning is likely to be less effective among the rural poor than among other classes.

In addition to the use or nonuse of theory, recourse may or may not be had to supporting facts—the universal experience of all countries now classified as more developed and to the experience of most LDCs, where the growth of agricultural productivity in terms of physical output per worker has outrun the growth in demand so that labor has remained abundant and low paid; the experience of the Mexican land reform and of the land reform imposed in Japan and Taiwan and Korea that resulted in excessive fragmentation of holdings; and the revolution in cotton growing in the United States and the spur given to technical advances by the growing scarcity and rising cost (remuneration) of farm labor. Thre is no evidence in any country that a *generalized* reduction in agricultural costs leads to a *generalized* increase in income. The rise in farm incomes per capita in the United States, where the advances in output per worker have been most spectacular, has borne no relation to such advances but rather reflects the drastic absolute and relative decline in the farm population so that labor has become less abundant. Even so, the rise has been low in relative terms. The slow growth in demand for foodstuffs per capita, especially in terms of calories, is a universal phenomenon except, perhaps, at actual hunger levels. The fall in urban fertility rates in developing countries is becoming marked.

The highest rise in sectoral wages in this century in the United States has occurred in a field in which the increase in physical efficiency has probably been least—domestic service. This was owing entirely to market forces making for great relative scarcity in such labor. The relatively high income of medical doctors is another illustration of scarcity arising from somewhat different causes.

In all of these cases, the facts can be explained in terms of basic economic theory, particularly price theory. That faulty theory and advice based on that theory should be so widespread and persistent is probably explicable in terms of personal values and the presence of actual hunger, and even, on occasion, starvation, which influences judgment. Moreover, the widely held view that labor cannot be "absorbed" outside agriculture stands in the way of a highly efficient agriculture, the use of labor to produce other things, and effective family planning.

The same inadequacy of theory is evident in the widespread advice to intervene in the resource allocation field to provide incentives to use less efficient and more labor-intensive techniques. There is no basis in theory that makes the volume of employment dependent upon capital formation or distribution of income. Capital formation has to do with factor proportions and the output per man, and distribution of income with the composition of demand for goods and services from a given sized income. The lack of any particular relationship between "industry," capital formation in "industry," and employment in general or in 'industry" has been demonstrated again and again but seems to make little impression.

One cannot help feeling either that proponents of labor-intensive methods do not wish to examine the evidence or that they believe that because a machine can "displace" some workers, many machines can displace many workers—the fallacy of composition again. A third possibility is that because of imperfection in the market mechanism, more intensive use of labor might also be more efficient, that is, more profitable, but to study all mixes of factors in all industries and firms within industries from this point of view would be a herculean task.

As pointed out at length earlier, radically differing advice to relieve the condition of the rural poor can be explained in terms of differing diagnoses of the problem, one stressing excessive immobility and another low physical productivity.

A theoretical approach that had and has many adherents, and underlies the overall advice of the 1970 World Bank Mission report, the IMF, and the Harvard group in Colombia, seeks to stimulate production by removing presumed constraints on supply either of domestic savings or of foreign exchange for imports. It takes for granted the existence of sufficient demand to ensure full employment and rising output as flowing from the insatiability of wants, but it assumes that there is a deficiency or gap in capital formation, usually resulting from a deficiency in exports and/or borrowing. This is a logically consistent theory. Its weakness, it appears to me, lies rather in its assumptions and in the failure to explore alternatives.

The difference in viewpoint comes out clearly in the success stories cited above (Chapter 14). Were the very high rates of growth due to the success in removing the exchange constraint on domestic production by large exports and imports, or did the rapid growth in exports and in the internal market extend the size of the market and permit the economies of scale that made possible an even faster growth in exports? Or putting the question slightly differently, as these cases were characterized by rapidly growing savings and capital formation, did the savings precede and cause the growth in capital, or did the growth in markets make profitable and possible a rise in both capital formation and savings? Since the process was simultaneous, it is difficult to settle the matter by econometric techniques. One is forced back to one's sense of reasonableness and judgment on the nature of the motivations and causal sequences involved.

In any case, perhaps enough has been said here to indicate the supremely important role of theory in the formation of macroeconomic policy. A mistake in theory can be extremely costly in loss of overall production and growth, with the loss compounded through the years.

Use of Theory in Determining Incidence of Policies

In almost all problems having to do with incidence—that is, who really pays taxes and increased costs and who really receives the benefits of subsidies or increased productivity and what is the mechanism involved in a market economy—a knowledge of theory is indispensable. Economists are not in full agreement even on pure theory here, as the mechanism may not function as postulated and the process is lengthy. Almost everyone would say without hesitation that a tax on corporations falls on or is borne by the shareholders. But if the tendency under competition is for the rate of profits on investment to tend to equalize and this applies to profits *after* taxes, then the burden of corporate taxes is passed ahead to consumers and back to wage earners, and the incidence of a corporate tax is the same as the incidence of a sales tax. The mechanism works through variations in the flow of new investment to where it can earn the highest returns after taxes. But a newly imposed tax *may* actually fall on shareholders (or a reduction redound to their benefit) since the transfer mechanism takes time to operate.

Another illustration may be drawn from urban land. A tax on buildings may in time (through consequent variations in supply) be passed along to tenants, but a tax on land, where the supply is fixed, may remain on the owners. Similarly, a rise in land values is held to accrue almost exclusively to owners. But if it leads to a cessation of building for rental purposes, expenditures on upkeep, and a growing gap between what can be earned on buildings and on other investments, and the supply shrinks, the freeze is eventually repealed and the tenants pay much more. However, it is a most inequitable and, for the community, costly process.

One of the most difficult matters to understand is the uneven incidence of inflation. Everybody either gains or loses, but in different degrees. There is a profound conviction among all workers that they lose and that only they lose. But a strong union can protect itself, and all savers in fixed obligations, large and small, lose. In any case, the net impact of inflation is undoubtedly to increase inequality within income groups by creating arbitrary transfers and to affect the allocation of new resources.

A lay minister of finance obviously needs advice on all matter of incidence, but unfortunately the answers may appear so obvious to him that he does not know that he needs advice. Even if he has a well-trained economist as adviser, the answers he may get may seem unsatisfactory, as they often depend on the time element involved, the degree of competition, and the mobility of capital. A person who expects straight, simple answers may well become impatient.

In the case of advice on a wide variety of specific projects in which cost-benefit analysis may be possible and the basic criterion is efficiency, the role of the theory may be assumed by accountancy and the correctness of projections. Even in such cases, however, noneconomic objectives may overrule the criterion of efficiency. In some projects, such as the provision of a good infrastructure of roads or public services, the benefits may be difficult to determine because they are widely diffused, they may be multiplied by subsequent economies of scale, and political considerations may be responsible for low direct returns. Here cost-benefit analyses must be supplemented by wider considerations of theory, and the evaluation may, in the end, turn on the judgment of the evaluator.

Dangers of Piecemeal Applications of Theory

Probably the strongest criticisms of policies in the present study have been directed against the faulty theory underlying many sectoral programs and the failure to study and adopt more embracing alternative policies to better accomplish the same objectives. It is too easily forgotten that sectors and their problems are arbitrary divisions of a single economy. Such divisions are necessary for administrative convenience, but the government must have its antennae in good working order to catch the repercussions of a sectoral policy and to ensure that alternative solutions are given a full hearing. This task appears to be peculiarly appropriate for a central planning agency or council of advisers.

The dangers of excessive specialization or fragmentation do not apply only to governments. The World Bank, the various agencies of the United Nations, and the bilateral aid agencies have become such huge organizations that specialization has become a necessity. However, this specialization of agencies, departments, and divisions militates against an overall view and prevents the establishment of priorities, and consequent violence may be done to the "seamless web." For a period in the early 1970s, the sectoral programs of AID in Colombia, reflecting the personal values and opinions of a very few people, expanded to a relatively very large figure (US$100 million a year) which, with the accompanying counterpart or peso-matching requirements, resulted both in an allocation of resources and budgetary deficits that would not otherwise have occurred. This period was succeeded by a drastic winding down of the whole sectoral program, but the further consequences of deficits and inflation and debt remained.

Nor are the universities immune from the dangers of excessive fragmentation of subject matter. This is naturally reflected in the excessive specialization of most potential advisers as well as graduate students from LDCs—excessive, that is, from the point of view of overall policy formulation and advice.

The resolution of a sectoral problem will sometimes lead to the resolution of many other problems. A good metropolitan urban design, with appropriate financing, would in itself exert beneficial influence on a number of other sectors, just as a relatively successful monetary policy would act to obviate the need for a host of ad hoc price controls and other measures to stabilize prices. But the theoretical overview is indispensable to identify and concentrate on the "key log" in such a log jam.

Generally, the danger lies in tackling too many problems simultaneously or in spreading oneself too thin, a defect easy to see in retrospect but difficult to avoid in the press of events. Some problems must be deliberately put aside in order to devote sufficient effort to the solution of more important ones. The problems set aside must not, however, include essential parts of the package of macroeconomic policies. The selection of issues is one of the most difficult and important decisions for an adviser.

Economic Theory Versus Development Economics

There is no "development economics"; there is only economic theory applied to different sets of circumstances in different countries, more and less developed. Different levels of administrative efficiency and different levels of poverty, absolute and relative, may affect judgments about the choice of policy but do not justify the assertion that economic theory may be applicable to, say, the United States but not to India.

Although there is perhaps no statement that is more generally accepted than that less developed countries are "capital poor," the scarcity of capital is relative. If growth is slow and wages are low, it may not pay to use more capital per worker, so that capital may be relatively more abundant than in rich countries! Capital accumulation and use per worker are probably the result rather than the cause of rapid growth. In the success stories of developing countries, rapid growth made it profitable to devote more of the labor force and capital equipment to the expansion of productive capacity without a decline in consumption. In fact, the growth in consumption was a factor in making it profitable to increase saving and investment in absolute and often in relative terms. Differences in policies recommended may quite legitimately turn on differences in values and political feasibility without violating any economic principles. Extreme poverty may justify a policy of making the possession of private automobiles more costly, changing the design of metropolitan areas to minimize transport difficulties, and diverting the real rise in urban land values to social purposes, but there is nothing in such measures that is inconsistent with accepted economic theory.

Even the economists who would accept the validity of economic theory for the countries of Latin America are hesitant to apply it to, say, India. The Indian government's earlier attempts to force investment in heavy industry are cited as a conclusive demonstration that agriculture must be given preference over industry. I have nowhere seen it argued that if final *demand* for nonagricultural goods increased rapidly so that it paid to devote resources to meeting this demand, overall growth would not benefit. If new crop varieties and cultures existed that would permit 10 percent of the Indian work force to produce the actual harvests, would it be regarded as a blessing (per economic theory) or a disaster, as the attitude of the work-spreaders implies?[5]

Faulty and Misused Data

Data are naturally far less reliable in LDCs than in countries with better administration, and foreign scholars are particularly apt to give too much credence to local information. In the absence of unemployment benefits, figures of unemployment derived from random sampling are highly suspect. Figures of "disguised" unemployment are virtually worthless. In Colombia, there are no statistics on current building expenditures, and the figures cited are not complete and are derived from building permits, which may or may not be followed by building that may or may not go according to schedule. Data on all common crops grown by small farmers are highly suspect as well as data derived from income tax returns or from answers to census sample questionnaires, where people may believe that it is to their interest to understate incomes, sales, and values of various kinds. Figures that started their career as mere guesses acquire, in successive incorporations, an aura of completely unmerited reliability. Data on cattle population and slaughterings are most unreliable, and most cattle exports from Colombia are clandestine and unreported. The only statistic confirming Colombia's often cited status as the world's leading exporter of narcotics is a suspiciously large figure of sale of foreign exchange in payment of "services," and a suspicion that "legitimate" exports are overstated. Thus, all figures must be checked for reasonableness and consistency, and impressions may on occasion be more reliable than official statistics. The misuse of data is another frequent source of error. A common example is the comparison of basic wage scales with cost-of-living data to conclude that wage and salary earners as a class are receiving a decreasing real wage. Since the real GDP per capita is rising, this would indicate a very substantial annual growth in the proportion of the national income going to property owners. It is highly unlikely that this could occur year after year as the proportions would soon assume fantastic relations. One would have to check for fringe benefits, participation rates, and understatement of earnings before accepting such a conclusion.

Misuse of data is frequently combined with lack of conceptual precision. For example, savings deposits are often added to checking accounts to obtain an aggregate called M_2, so that excessive monetary expansion and inflation seem to result from a growth in saving. Despite constant discussion of inflation and the general practice of "deflating" current figures in terms of money to arrive at "real" figures, writers continue to talk of high interest rates (nominal) when they (the rates) are actually negative, which makes nonsense of the capital allocation and factor proportion functions of the interest rate. Other writers treat a rise in food prices as evidence of inelasticity of supply and propose great campaigns to increase production, when the rise may only reflect rising monetary demand.

The same carelessness in the handling of factual data is evident in the sweeping generalizations that abound in the literature, such as that the poor are getting poorer, impoverishment is worsening, and inequality is growing.[6] Such concepts are extremely difficult to quantify in a single country, and in most cases, they appear to be based on selected countries in Southeast Asia. The picture of less developed countries in general is sufficiently somber, and growth rates are so generally below potential that there is no need to distort the facts, even on the grounds that the need for action justifies some distortion.

18
THE APPRAISAL OF ADVICE: FEASIBILITY AND IMPLEMENTATION

The term "feasibility" is imprecise and may have the connotation of either acceptability or workability. An adviser on conditions to be attached to a loan may not have to worry overmuch about the acceptability of his advice to the prospective recipient of the loan, but he must consider its workability. A "pure" adviser, however, must use persuasion. He cannot afford to offer too much advice, however workable, that is unacceptable, or he may find that he is no longer asked to give any.

Unfortunately, in economics, the dice seem to be loaded against sound advice, and it is difficult to make generalizations on its acceptability. What is sound is rarely popular or in accord with conventional wisdom or "common sense," and a president can do much to ensure that he will or will not continue to receive a variety of viewpoints. The growing elimination or departure of critics of the Vietnam war from Lyndon Johnson's presidential circle makes it only too clear that Johnson did not welcome critical advice. Franklin Roosevelt, on the other hand, encouraged the expression of differences. What some critics of Roosevelt called poor administration was actually a policy of ensuring that when choices had to be made between alternative policies—and there are always alternatives—he had the benefit of knowing what the pros and cons might be in advance.

One has to keep in mind that an executive's term is short and that in the multitude of present problems he cannot be expected to give much weight to a policy that will only show results in the long run. Although it is sometimes possible to stress the credit that will redound in the future to an action that may win no votes today (particularly with new institutions or laws), this is rarely true in the case of the many day-to-day decisions that cannot be considered in any way as future monuments.

Feasibility as "workability" involves a similar kind of judgment. The recommendation of the ILO missions that labor-intensive techniques should be used for open unemployment, quite apart from the very questionable theory involved, is clearly unworkable if applied on any extensive scale. It would require an intensive study of the methods employed by thousands of establishments (since techniques and processes differ even within an industry), with access to reliable records of costs, earnings, and profits—a veritable bureaucratic nightmare. Presumably, the decisions would be enacted by decree and would then require enforcement, with the necessity of current studies to keep abreast of new techniques in all establishments. Perhaps the excess labor would be absorbed in attempting to carry out the recommended policy.

So far as it is known, no government has seriously attempted this project. Lip service is paid to it, and, occasionally, in the past, it has been invoked in arbitrarily chosen cases. For example, it is considered one of the criteria used in granting import licenses for machinery and equipment, and in Colombia licenses have been denied the importation of cotton-picking combines (but not rice-harvesting combines). If a government wished to take the advice seriously, all it would have to do would be to prohibit agricultural tractors or hoisting machinery in the construction of multistoried buildings. Indeed, the possibilities are infinite if the only object is to create employment.

We have seen that the less developed a country is, the less it is in a position to execute policies calling for a high degree of administrative and technical expertise. A corollary to this is that for less developed countries, when a choice is possible, better execution of a policy will probably result if market forces can be used. One ILO mission advised the government of the Philippines to relocate industries in rural regions to supply employment, supplementing that provided by agriculture. This again was not only bad theory, since it totally ignored the economies of scale, but it was completely unworkable. It showed a lack of understanding of the reasons why industries locate where they do, and an equal lack of interest in efficiency and in the use of cost-reducing practices.

A favorite recommendation is the creation of model small-farm communities, which, it is hoped, will be copied elsewhere. The creation of a single model community is probably workable if it is (1) well chosen and (2) heavily subsidized. But even if such an individual effort should prove successful, this does not mean that it could be copied successfully in less-favored locations or with no financial help. The general experience is not encouraging.

It is not enough for advice to be feasible; ideally, it should propose the best of various feasible alternatives. When the site and services solution to the urban housing problem is proposed, the cited alternatives are shanty towns or overcrowded tenements. (See Chapter 10.) The case is clinched by income studies that purport to demonstrate that x percent of the families cannot afford conventionally built, well-serviced, and well-located housing. Here there is a failure to think in marginal or incremental terms. The margin is to be found in the net number of additional families per locality per year. The problem is not x percent of total families, but whether demand and financing can be found for a number of units equal to or preferably in excess of the *increment* in family units. While the site and services solution is feasible, a return to theory shows that it may not necessarily be the most feasible of alternatives.

An interesting incident during the site and services housing program illustrates another of the many factors involved in assessing feasibility. A local low-cost housing agency in Bogotá had been entrusted with the granting of loans for the purchase of materials. It was found that a very substantial number of the target group did not apply for loans. A private investigator, upon inquiring, found that an official had for some reason inserted a requirement that the applicant had to present, among a host of documents, evidence either that he had completed his military service or that he had been excused. Many could not comply with the requirement. Thus, the feasibility of a given project may depend on elements as wholly divorced from theory as personalities, bureaucracies, and accidents.

There appears to be no general rule that applies to the advance determination of feasibility of economic proposals. The policymaker must use his best judgment and attempt to assess the judgment of his advisers. A most helpful safeguard, however, is the use of an advisory group, even though this device may slow the process of decision, and the outcome still depends a good deal on the group's composition.

An otherwise feasible policy should be reconsidered if its implementation is doubtful. If, for example, tax administration is already at a low level, a highly complicated tax proposal or a drastic increase in rates will almost certainly fail, as did the tax "reforms" of 1974 in Colombia. (See Chapter 8.) Theoretically feasible and acceptable at least to the chief policymaker, the poor state of tax administration made implementation difficult. Paradoxical as it may seem, greater equity and revenue may in certain circumstances be obtained by lowering the rate of progression until better administration is obtained. Laws do not depend on enforcement. Rather, adequate enforcement depends on widespread acceptance of the law. This was one of the main lessons that could have been learned from the attempt, in the United States, to prohibit people from drinking. The net result of the effort was not a decline in drinking but rather a notable decline in the integrity of the enforcement machinery and the conversion of millions of otherwise law-abiding citizens into law-breakers.

In creating a new system for financing building in 1972, much credit should be given to the time and effort spent on its implementation. Indexation of savings and loans on a daily basis was new and apparently complex, but by initially permitting not only limited subscription of capital by existing financial institutions but also even the use of their quarters and staff, the system was quickly and successfully established. The initial decrees were limited to the bare essentials; the central government board was kept small, and the enforcement of decrees was entrusted to the experienced banking superintendent. The comprehensive tax changes of 1974, on the other hand, greatly increased the workload on an already overburdened government office, which militated against efficient enforcement of the changes.

A frequent sequence in policymaking that ensures poor implementation begins with the adoption of a requirement that most people regard as unfair and onerous. They resort immediately to evasion or avoidance. The authorities then pass other decrees or regulations designed to plug loopholes. The enforcement of these creates a heavier load on the public administration and the private sector, which leads to more avoidance with greater impunity. Yet more requirements are proposed to plug the new loopholes—and so on. It may take a year for someone to secure a building permit as more and more detailed information is requested. Large urbanizers, on the other hand, and certain influential individuals may secure permits in a month or less. The inference is clear: when such poor implementation is likely, a policy, however justified in theory and in fact, is *not* feasible.

The theme of implementation bears upon the burning issue of the indirect versus the direct attack on poverty. The direct attack characteristically implies dealing directly with millions of very poor people, and the probabilities are that it will be poorly administered. A particularly distressing case in Colombia may serve as a final illustration. For years the prices of gasoline for motors and of gasoline and propane gas for cooking were fixed at extremely low levels, with predictable results on exploration and wasteful use. Finally, the losses to the government petroleum company were so heavy that prices had to be raised, but this was offset by subsidies to owners of buses, as public transportation rates were also maintained at a low level, and the price of gasoline for cooking was maintained at a lower level than the price of gasoline for motors. The first consequence was evasion. Cooking gasoline was then colored blue, but the public found that it still paid to mix "white" and "blue" gasoline and to sell it on the side or for other uses. Hence, the supply of the cheap gasoline for cooking dried up and at every gasoline station could be seen long queues of very poor people standing for hours, each person with his individual container and frequently with babies or small children that could not be left at home. The margin of profit to the proprietor was fixed so low that he had no interest in expediting the service or in selling more "blue" gasoline. Thus, a "direct" policy to aid the very poor created, by 1978, conditions that only further embittered their lives.

19
THE APPRAISAL OF ADVICE: CONCLUDING REFLECTIONS

The Lack of Consensus

One of the conclusions that emerges from a consideration of the cases studied here is the ineffectiveness of the scholarly organization in gaining a consensus on the cumulative experience of less developed countries. There is a widespread impression that conditions differ so widely between countries that each must be treated as a special case, that what is appropriate for Brazil is inappropriate for Colombia, and particularly that what is appropriate for Latin American countries is inappropriate for Southeast Asian or African countries.

Common patterns of development exist not only among the developing countries but also between the more and the less developed. The insatiability of wants, the powerful drives of economic incentives and penalties, the deprivation effect, the linking of technical efficiency with profitability, the influence of rising incomes and educational levels on size of families and participation levels—these and other elements that all countries have in common create a strong presumption that economic theory is not national and that similar economic policies, adjusted to varying quantitative and qualitative differences, will probably yield similar results.

A rent freeze may be expected to reduce building for rent wherever it is imposed. Protecting savings from inflationary erosion will likely result in increased savings wherever it is practiced. An expansion in the money supply at a rate substantially in excess of the growth of real output may be expected to result in a rising price level in all countries where prices are free to move. The income elasticity of demand for foodstuffs is low in all countries except, possibly, the very poorest. That the degree to which it pays to specialize or to borrow new technology is dependent on the market is not peculiar to any country. The differences between, say, Japan and Britain in the late nineteenth century did not prevent Japan from following, overtaking, and finally surpassing Britain in economic growth. The impulses to the leading sectors underlying the spectacular development of Singapore are open to most countries as well as to city-states. The spectacular upsurge in South Korea since the mid-1960s was not an inevitable consequence of American aid but of policy. A common explanation of Brazil's economic advance is that it is "a continent in itself." But so it was for a hundred years before 1966.

The point is that all countries called "developed" have shared certain patterns, and all countries with rising per capita real income share experiences which, if continued, create patterns that will more and more closely resemble them. Developing countries should therefore be able to adopt policies to hasten the process of development, and the history of other countries should provide a rich storehouse of experience on which to draw. Yet, little effort is made to study this experience. The international agencies cannot escape some measure of responsibility for the consequent loss of time and effort, the repetition of mistakes, and the failure to adopt successful policies.

Closely related to the failure to learn from successes is the failure to learn from past failures. The inability of economists to sharpen, clarify, and dispose of issues is particularly regrettable. Most of the theory dealt with in this work has been discussed many times, and some fallacies have an ancient lineage. In part, this is doubtless due to the reluctance of distinguished economists to insist on what they regard as obvious, and in part, to a reluctance to be critical of the work of friends or colleagues. Whatever the reason, the result is a great deal of lost motion and needless repetition of errors which find their way into policy recommendations. In other cases, there can be legitimate differences of opinion. The problem in such cases is not to expose fallacies, but to expose and discuss underlying assumptions and to attempt to reach agreement, as in the issue of the exchange constraint on growth versus the constraint exercised by inadequate demand. Recently (1977), there have been encouraging indications that a group in the World Bank has begun to study the lessons to be derived from the more successful cases of growth.[1]

The Transfer and Acquisition of Technology

The transfer and adoption of more efficient ways of doing things and the conditions favoring such adoption and transfer have received surprisingly little attention in the past. The importance of the topic has been so lost in the multiplicity of objectives that advanced technology has even become suspect. There is much discussion of "appropriate" technology, which has acquired almost a peculiar connotation of *not* enabling fewer people to produce more in agriculture and industry. There is more concern with the "displacement" of labor than with its increased productivity, more with the dangers of foreign investment than with its benefits in making accessible technology and markets, more with decentralization and "balanced" regional development than with economies of scale, more with the accumulation of capital than with the technological processes associated with capital accumulation. Indeed, it is hardly an exaggeration to say that technology has penetrated many developing countries in spite of, rather than because of, their governments' policies.

The dilemma is this: the poorer the country and the lower the demand, the less it pays to specialize or to use better techniques and consequently the less incentive there is for the transfer of technology. But the growth in gross and per capita income, and hence the growth in demand in a real sense, depend on greater productivity. To foreswear technical advance in less developed countries is to foreswear economic growth. The poorer the economy, the greater the need to increase production per capita in another sense of the term.

In mixed economies, the incentive to specialize in skills, in firms, and in the use of capital equipment is provided by a growth in demand in real terms and in the size of the market. The market, whether domestic or foreign, again illustrates the interaction between size and growth. The larger the production, the greater the incentive to specialize and use more capital equipment per worker, the lower the costs, and the greater the possibility of controlling quality and of meeting delivery schedules.

The implications of the argument are various. One is that in order to have a firm basis for financing the transfer of technology, we must be concerned with the rapidity of growth and not just assume that technique will in itself bring it about. Without the initial growth, it is difficult to justify the use of advanced techniques and advanced training, without which, however, high rates of growth in productivity cannot be attained unless by the export of raw materials for which there is a large and growing demand, like oil. A second implication is that the appropriateness, in economic terms, of a technique depends on the constantly changing size of the market much more than on new inventions or improvements. For developing countries, every enlargement of the market makes it economic to utilize *known* techniques which were not economic previously. What is appropriate, therefore, depends in large measure on how rapidly the market is growing. It is a relative and not an absolute concept.

A third implication is that it is probably necessary, first, to resolve the issue of productivity *versus* employment. If it can be demonstrated that there need not be a conflict and that a rapid rise in productivity per worker is perfectly compatible with a continuous growth in employment, the way will be cleared for the adoption of labor-saving techniques as rapidly as it becomes profitable to do so. There would be no conflict between economic and social goals.

Note that the argument applies as much to training as to techniques and machinery. Unless jobs open up rapidly for trained people, which in turn depends on the stage and rapidity of growth, they will either go abroad or drift into other occupations, and the investment in human resources will be largely lost. Furthermore, scientific training is but one facet, though an important one, of the general transfer of technology, which extends down to simple implements and easily acquired skills.

The stock of accumulated knowledge is enormous, and much of it is relatively free. How rapidly and how massively it can be bought, borrowed, or obtained as a gift depends in very large part on internal institutional arrangements and on the growth in the size of the market. In both of these aspects, developing countries in all stages of growth can do much to accelerate the process: in a dynamic sense, therefore, economic policy (and consequently advice) should be directed toward setting in motion the trends toward increasing returns or the economies of scale. This, it has been argued here, requires a positive effort, for growth has, for good reasons, a tendency to continue along existing tracks and at current rates, making the initial breakthrough to a higher plateau of growth of paramount importance.

The Interaction of Advising and Stage of Development

A new economics of development is not necessary, nor, for most LDCs, is massive financial assistance or loans. Policies that look toward a continuation of subsistence farming, a low degree of urbanization and continued high birth rates, and the promotion of the "informal" sector are looking backward rather than forward. In general, macro advice that is most appropriate should seek to make the fullest and most remunerative use of the most abundant resource of LDCs—the human resources. This criterion would lead to policies to improve labor mobility and labor utilization, both in the domestic and foreign markets—to urbanization, industrialization, and declining birth rates.

The current tendency for the number of foreign economic advisers to decline and the passing of the big missions and comprehensive country program reports do not for a moment mean that foreign macroeconomic advice has ceased to be important. What it does mean is that the influence will be exerted more through conditions attached to loans (and the types of loans favored) and through books, articles, and foreign training of nationals at a graduate level. The linkage of advice to policy will be more indirect and difficult to detect. This places an increased responsibility on national advisers to modify and adapt theories and policies to domestic requirements and on the advisers in international lending and technical assistance agencies to ensure that the leverage exerted by the offer of loans and grants is really used in the best interests of the countries concerned.

The ability to identify appropriate advice and the adoption of better macroeconomic policies depend on the background, training, and cultural characteristics of the formulators of policy. It would be unreasonable to expect that these individuals would not be a representative cross-section of the class from which they were drawn—in most LDCs this class is fairly well defined and not large. There is no mechanism to ensure that only the best trained or the most conscientious of that class will formulate policy. Therefore, we reach the sobering conclusion that, as a general rule, improvements in policymaking and in administration will be limited by the capacity, training, and dedication first of the upper class, and, to a slightly lesser extent, of the larger middle class. A corollary is that expenditures on training, especially abroad, and on creating attitudes favorable to better domination and control of the environment will prove highly productive over a period of time.

The acceptance and implementation of advice will continue to be mainly dependent on its assumed impact on the fortunes and interests of the policy formulators. It is too much to expect that progress in development can change human motivations in this respect. However, with the growth of a more informed and critical public opinion, what can be hoped for is that there will be a tendency for decision-makers to identify their personal interests more with the longer term interests of the community and to give more weight to the probable judgment of history. Hence, it is to be hoped that with progress in development, more appropriate advice, as a rule, will be offered, accepted, and in its turn will further that progress. Fortunately, there can be beneficent as well as vicious circles.

The relatively poor record of macroeconomic advisers in the past thirty years in large part arises from the nature of underdevelopment itself, as I have defined the term. The relative lack of dominance over the social, economic, political, physical, and demographic environment provides a formidable barrier to the acceptance of appropriate and feasible advice. There are, of course, conscientious and able presidents and ministers, but their ability to bring about fundamental improvements in the short period usually available to them is strictly limited. It would seem to be simple to streamline a procedure in the interests of greater efficiency, but those who have tried quickly find themselves in a morass where one thing depends on another which depends on another, and it seems an insuperable task to cut through to an efficient operation. For a minister or head of agency to make an enduring contribution to the greater efficiency of an agency is a gigantic task for which, even if successful, he would receive little credit. Other activities promise much surer harvests. Greater efficiency threatens specific jobs and on this score will be effectively, if silently, opposed until the would-be innovator's patience is exhausted and/or he departs for a more peaceful life.

One of the claims that might be made for the definition of development adopted herein is that it calls attention, for the purposes of appraising economic advice, to a difficulty inherent in the nature of the subject. Less control over environment means that those policies that depend for their success on efficient management on the part of the state are probably inappropriate or at least have less chance of being implemented successfully.

The basic economic theory is applicable to all market or mixed economies; specific policies may or may not be, depending on the degree of control of environment that exists. This is a painful dilemma, since it means, in effect, that it is precisely in those countries where certain policies may be most needed that they cannot be recommended because the economy does not yet possess the degree of control called for. Because this may not be conceded by the country in question, there is a common tendency to undertake policies which, for successful implementation, require a degree of state administrative efficiency far beyond that which exists, and a tendency on the part of advisers to recommend such policies.

This dilemma can be resolved in various ways. One is to seek out alternative policies to accomplish an objective and to recommend the one policy that makes the least demand on the bureaucratic machinery. This may, on occasion, place the adviser or policymaker in the position of appearing to favor a second-best policy. Another is to carry out sweeping administrative reforms. But since the inefficiency basically reflects the state of the society, this approach will probably be ineffectual. A third way is to reduce the number of objectives and to place the greatest emphasis on stimulating growth through the private sector in the hope and expectation that growth will in itself bring about changes that will lead to greater control. This last course, however, may be contrasted with the number of redistributive and regulative policies in actual operation in the more advanced societies and may be rejected as retrogressive.

Generally, the poorer a society, the less dominance it has over its environment in all its aspects and the poorer the distribution of income because of lax administration and low tax tolerance, low mobility, and masses of unskilled workers. These conditions severely restrict the feasibility of many policies that are in use and that may have contributed to better distribution in more developed countries. They are particularly applicable to measures that call for dealing directly with great numbers of people.

A reasonable hypothesis to explain the fairly high correlation between high per capita incomes and better distribution is that high and rising incomes bring in their train a higher degree of efficiency and civic sense. Hence, they have a tendency to heighten the feasibility of various measures to improve distribution. This applies particularly to measures designed to lessen inequality in incomes from ownership. The main economic force tending to lessen inequality in incomes from work is mobility, which, thus, is both a cause and a consequence of higher per capita income. This may also throw some light on why there are so few success stories. The nature of underdevelopment tends to perpetuate obstacles to its solution. The choice for advisers and formulators of policy is not as simple as is often stated: growth *versus* distribution. Advising requires a delicate balancing of the ideal and the practical for a particular society at a particular moment, and it is in this obscure and difficult area that advisers may legitimately differ.

These sobering reflections do not mean that greater dominance or control is unattainable. The fact that there are constant complaints, which provoke promises of sweeping reorganizations, is itself a hopeful sign, even though few of the reorganizations seem to result in greater efficiency. What it does mean is that development is a painfully slow and difficult process. One can see very little progress from day to day, and often one only sees retrogression.

Nevertheless, over a generation, marked progress has occurred. As emphasized again and again in this book, there are powerful forces that are tending to bring about great transformations in society. To make his work more fruitful, a macroeconomic adviser should try to identify those forces and to shape his advice to further rather than obstruct them. By so doing, he can take some comfort in the thought that time will be on his side. The forces that encourage growth also encourage development, and the cultural characteristics that impede growth are yielding to those that promote it. Growth facilitates more advanced training for increasing numbers, which is an indispensable condition for attaining greater development.

Dominance over environment is a qualitative and relative concept. To make the transition from a less to a more developed category gives no assurance that the dominance will be sufficient to resolve all problems that are confronting and will confront the more developed countries. The problems themselves appear to be growing in magnitude and difficulty. The goal of making the transition to a "more developed" state is highly worthwhile and indeed necessary, but it is not a guarantee of enduring well-being, nor is it an assurance that emerging problems on a world scale will be satisfactorily resolved. In short, "development" in the sense of dominance over environment is a moving goal that keeps retreating as we advance, but even so it is highly worth the effort both for more and for less developed countries.

20
AFTERWORD: TOWARD
A THEORY OF ECONOMIC
ADVICE-GIVING

An understanding of the interrelationships among the concepts that underlie and condition advising is necessary for the construction of a theory of economic advice-giving. Many of the basic concepts examined below have been brought into focus as a result of my examination of economic advice to developing countries in general. These concepts and their implications for policy constitute the basic materials from which generalizations about economic advice-giving can be drawn.

Basic Concepts

The terms "economic theory," "economic policies," "growth," and "development" are the source of endless confusion. As used here, economics as a science is that part of the explanation of the functioning of a society in the production and distribution of goods that, in the words of Karl Popper, has not (as yet) been disproved. But since controlled experiment and "proof" are difficult, explanations differ in degree of accepted validity. There are a few "laws," a respectable corpus of accepted theory, generally used tools of analysis, and many hypotheses. However, this state of uncertainty, so different from mathematics, does not mean that economics is not a science and must necessarily be normative. Economics attempts to explain things, not to advocate them. In itself, it has no goal or objective other than explanation. A lot of ink has been expended on this subject, largely as a result of a failure to distinguish between theory and policy. The latter, policy, can be concerned with goals and objectives, can be normative, and can differ with different writers and different countries.

Disagreement about policy matters occurs not only in terms of logic and fact, as in theory, but also in terms of goals, which imply personal values and, even worse, because more subtle and difficult to recognize, in terms of goals as they relate to time. Some writers go further and feel that theory itself is colored by values, but this appears to be using terms in different senses. An explanation of the functioning of a system rests on certain assumptions about behavior. It assumes that most people desire a larger income than they have and that for this reason wants, as a whole, are insatiable. It assumes adherence to some "rules of the game": sufficient personal and property security and a system of justice and enforcement sufficient to permit people to plan ahead. In a market or mixed system, it assumes a belief in a degree, at least, of private property. The desire for higher incomes provides the incentive to produce and the criterion of success. The rules of the game may be more or less favorable to the attainment of higher income.

It is important to distinguish between such underlying assumptions and personal values. In her excellent and stimulating discussion of these matters, Joan Robinson uses the terms "ideology," "conscience," and "values" to argue that theory is necessarily colored by values.[1] But these terms are themselves value-charged and a bit misleading. I suggest that if, instead, the term "culture" is used (in its sociological sense of a set of beliefs, attitudes, and customs), economic theory can accept a prevailing culture as providing the rules of the game and as such providing also its basic assumptions. It can do so without the observer himself necessarily becoming involved as favoring or disapproving of the culture. The culture may be more or less favorable to "efficiency," which provides the rationale of economic activity and the criterion of success of a "well functioning" system in a purely neutral and non-normative sense.

Admittedly, it is difficult to be a completely detached observer of a particular culture (especially one's own!), but it has been done, and the social sciences, insofar as they are sciences, make the effort.

An economist may be impatient and even personally disapproving of some aspect of a culture that is prejudicial to efficiency, but this attitude need not prevent him from describing and discussing the aspect in neutral and nonvalue-charged terms. All that is required is an awareness of the distinctions between basic assumptions or rules of the game and values, and between economic theory and policy. Policy may rest upon or appeal to theory, but it is conceptionally different. Policies entail choices, not theory.

This leads us to "development." The term offers a curious case of constant use with rarely an attempt at definition. There is no question that it is value-charged. Virtually all writers are in favor of "development" and more and more of it.

But what development is remains a bit of a mystery. One difficulty is the fear of wounding the sensibilities of what people call "less" developed, or "lesser" developed, "underdeveloped," or "developing" countries. (The last is the preferred term, but all countries are presumably "developing.") That growth alone is not a sufficient criterion for development is suggested by the reluctance to include newly oil-rich countries in the "more" developed category. Occasionally, the meaning of the term is confused with its own "objective," variously stated to be well-being, or better distribution, or well-being of the poorer half, or the satisfaction of basic human needs or of basic material needs. Despite this confusion and uncertainty, there is surprising unanimity when it comes to classifying countries into the "more" or "less" developed categories.

After wrestling with the problem for many years, I finally decided that the distinction is qualitative; that the countries we have agreed to call "more" developed are characterized by the possession of a more or less common degree of control or dominance over their economic, social, political, demographic, and physical environment that enables them to adopt more or less appropriate responses to problems as they arise. Such a definition seems to add a depth and significance absent in a mere enumeration of characteristics— high standard of living, better distribution, urbanization and industrialization, low birth rate but high life expectancy, high literacy and high rate of advanced education, social security, and so forth. It enables us to characterize the New England of the eighteenth century as being a more developed country, although the standard of living was low and life was hard. It also permits us to say that the United States lost its more developed ranking in the Great Depression when, for a period, it was completely unable to cope acceptably with its major problems. It seizes, socially, upon the most important characteristics that countries we agree to call more developed have in common, as well as those we still include in the less developed category. The culture of the United States and Japan differs in many respects, but both countries give an impression of being better able to cope with emerging problems than do, let us say, Bangladesh and Uganda. The truly significant difference between the most and the least developed countries is not the standard of living but rather the difference in the degree of domination of environment they appear to possess.

In short, this definition is functional. It focuses attention not on symptoms but on causes. A characteristic of lack of domination (or less than acceptable domination) is its pervasiveness, extending as it does to so many spheres of life. Furthermore, any particular evidence of lack of control may be duplicated in more developed countries. It is in the number and pervasiveness of such evidence that the difference lies. It is important to keep in mind that the distinction is relative, not absolute. The new definition emphasizes the enormous difficulty of the task of raising the level of development, since it directs attention to the culture itself and to its manifestations in many different sectors. It is not just a matter of monetary policy, or trade policy, or rate of growth, or government organization and level of administration, but of all of these and *many more*. Anybody who has spent much time in a developing country can attest to the baffling nature of the problem, which seems to be everywhere. The solution of one difficulty rests on the solution of another, which requires the solution of a third, and so on. The country abounds with intertwined vicious circles, and the truly difficult thing is where most effectively to break into them. Very frequently, the solution to a specific problem may not be very difficult. But to win acceptance of it and to assure adequate implementation may require a host of changes which would entail profound alterations in the culture.

By its nature, a culture is a tenacious thing, yielding only reluctantly to change, which usually arises from developments outside itself. People who are about to play an active part in community decision-making are themselves the product of a particular culture. Even though that culture has undergone some modification in their own youth, the general story seems to be that they will, after a certain age, resist further modifications. The history of growing domination over environment—development—is a history of a prolonged rearguard action fought by an establishment with a prevailing set of beliefs and attitudes. With a change in the environment, it is not reasonable to expect profound changes in the culture from one generation to another. Yet, a change in the environment may require or at least can be greatly accelerated by a change from within. The culture of a rural, more or less self-subsistence community is obviously more resistant to change than one well on the way toward industrialization-urbanization. The tremendous rate of cultural change experienced by all the more developed countries in the twentieth century is obviously associated with technological and economic changes and may be contrasted with the much slower rate of change in the nineteenth century, and even slower rates in the eighteenth or seventeenth centuries.

So we arrive at the biggest and most difficult circle of all—the interrelation of culture and development itself. If a people with a particular culture has, to date, shown itself to possess less than acceptable domination of environment, how can the degree of change that seems necessary to accelerate the process of development and the date of transition from a less to a more developed category be brought about?

The Relation of Economic Growth to Development

Fortunately, there are countervailing forces that favor development. Before discussing them, it is necessary to say a few words on the relation of economic growth to development. Growth does not automatically give control over environment, but it is, I believe, a necessary, if not a sufficient, condition. It creates the surplus over the bare necessities of life; it permits the great transformations in living styles that all the countries we call developed have experienced; it gives time for wider and more intense secondary and ad-

vanced education; it improves distribution both directly and indirectly, both through market forces and because better distribution of an increased product encounters less resistance than
redistribution of existing wealth or a low and static income. There
appears to be a high correlation between incomes, education, and
smaller families. The importance of growth has been questioned
because it was thought to be identified with welfare, which is an
even more elusive and difficult concept. But if the focus is shifted to
the more definite concepts of domination and survival, the necessity or at least desirability of growth is more readily grasped. The
fact that growth in itself creates problems of survival is a matter of
real concern, especially for the more developed countries looking
to the future. Here our concern is with the less developed countries,
which need to deal with the problems created in part by growth but
which would in any case exist.

If, therefore, economic growth is a condition for and can promote development, the prospect brightens considerably because the
growth process itself is cumulative and self-perpetuating unless
checked by powerful forces. This arises from Adam Smith's dictum
that specialization or division of labor is limited only by the size of
the market, and, of course, division of labor is a powerful factor
making for greater productivity per capita. Many years after Adam
Smith, Allyn Young amplified the early concept of division of labor
to include specialization by firms and roundabout or capitalistic
methods of production[2] and, incorporating Marshall's external
economies of scale, how a growth in the market in real terms
creates economies both internal and external to the firm and so
promotes production, the extension of the market, and still more
production.

Thus, opposed to forces that tend to perpetuate underdevelopment (such as an excessive rate of population increase, obstacles to
mobility, obstacles to the use of capital imposed by excessively low
wage rates, and so forth) are forces making for growth. To the importance given the size of the market in making increased specialization and increased use of capital profitable may be added the rate of
growth of the market (in physical terms). Hence, even if a country
is poor and its internal market is small, if the rate of growth can be
accelerated, this will in itself speed up the rate at which it pays to

become more technical and will further the growth process, and, by stimulating growth, will make conditions more favorable for development.

These cumulative and self-perpetuating characteristics of economies of scale, broadly interpreted, work mostly in unplanned fashion through the forces usually referred to as "the market," by daily making it profitable to adopt (or adapt) known techniques that were not profitable with a smaller volume of output. It helps to explain the emphasis placed by businessmen on extending not only their sales but also their share of the market. Even where the internal economies of scale may not be so noteworthy (as in agriculture), external economies (such as the internal combustion engine, chemicals, fertilizers, and drugs) increase productivity. The process is so pervasive, depending as it does on the almost universal desire to increase earnings, that it is taken for granted and rarely figures in national planning. Even where government action facilitates external economies of scale (roads, communications, and so forth), it is usually justified and defended on other grounds. Occasionally, governments attempt to alter the factor proportion mix, but this is usually done in the mistaken idea that the market will not assure employment and that work should be spread. Rarely indeed does the government consciously push labor-saving techniques.

I am here speaking of trends. Market forces do not move smoothly and evenly, and individuals do make mistakes. But the same is true of centrally planned government operations. For one thing, rarely is a public official held personally responsible for a misallocation of resources or for a policy that may adversely affect growth. In the market, the penalty for misjudging the demand, or for a less profitable combination of factors than those adopted by a competitor, may be very serious indeed. In any case, apart from publicly produced goods and services, the major job of determining what goods will be produced by what methods, where, in what volumes and qualities, and by what combination of factors must depend on profit considerations and individual motivations. It is through such calculations and motivations that market forces (the "unseen hand") operate. This does not mean that calculations and motivations may not be influenced by public policies on either side. All it means is that all countries, including developing countries, can rely on the existence of market forces that, in the absence of adverse events or policies, exert pressure toward cumulative growth.

The Significance of Patterns of Development

In recent years, considerable work has been done on patterns of growth and development as more and more quantitative data have become available for comparative analysis. As a result, broad patterns common both to more and less developing countries have emerged. The early appearance of a surplus in agricultural production, the great transformations from predominantly rural to predominantly urban living and from predominantly agricultural to predominantly industrial and service activities, the fall in the birth and population rates of growth, increasing participation in the work force, more diversified foreign trade, higher and longer education, better distribution—this general pattern reappears again and again. Where it does not, there is generally little growth per capita (except in new oil-rich countries) and little development.

This suggests the existence of common forces at work: the mostly silent but highly persistent adoption of more efficient ways of doing things, the tendency toward common patterns of elasticities of demand that make it more and more profitable to expand manufactured goods and service of all kinds relative to foodstuffs, great movements of people in response to economic possibilities to increase incomes. As much of this pattern is unplanned and indeed is often deplored, the fact that it occurs again and again and from day-to-day in all countries we call more developed and in the more successfully developing countries again attests to the tremendous strength of what are usually referred to as market or natural forces. At any given time in any given country, attention is likely to be concentrated on problems and policies, particularly on what governments are expected to do. Yet, the great transformations of societies generally owe little to government policies, and on occasion, they even proceed in spite of policies. Making a living and making profits are usually considered distinct from government policies. The major part of production—what is produced, where, in what quantities and qualities, and at what relative prices—is a by-product of the business of making a living. This is true to such a degree that a highly successful businessman may be and often is economically literate. The economy performs with little understanding by those whose activities make it function.

Conflicting Circles

Development may be viewed as taking place in a vast battlefield in which there are many forces making for stagnation or recession, economically speaking, and many for growth with its accompanying beneficent effects. This way of viewing the process helps to explain what otherwise appears inexplicable—the persistence of growth despite a host of policies and events inimical to it. In the period 1950-1970 in Colombia, for example, the exchange rate was chronically overvalued; the birth rate and the rate of population growth were extremely high (over 3 percent), though declining in the later years; the level of government administration was low; official government policy was opposed to labor mobility (migration from the countryside); and little encouragement was given to foreign investment. At one point for some years, economic activity virtually ceased in parts of the country because of political unrest and lawlessness. Yet, throughout the period, growth remained positive in both gross and per capita terms. The experience attests to the strength of the market forces.

This statement should not be understood as a blanket endorsement of such forces. The same forces create great inequality, especially in income from ownership. Through bribery and drawing away the abler young managers, the private sector impedes the efficient operation of the public sector. The planlessness of the larger cities, which typically reflects a surrender to private pressures, is particularly regrettable. What should be noted, in as neutral a manner as possible, is that the force of the market is a fact. It cannot be pushed aside by any policy. As a fact, and as a powerful and continuing drive toward increased efficiency or the search for profits, it can be put to use.

Some Implications

1. Development is not a state subject to quantitative measurement, but rather a demonstrated capacity to adopt more rather than

less appropriate policies to the solution of problems as they arise. This capacity permeates all aspects of life and is infinitely more significant than the possession of natural resources or the presence or absence of specific policies or characteristics.

2. In the widest sense of the term, development reflects the prevailing culture of a country. If a country is in the less developed category, it is probable that the particular culture is, or was in the past, inimical to a higher degree of development.

3. Progress toward a more developed stage probably requires quite profound changes in the prevailing culture, and there are strong resistances to such changes.

4. Changes in culture for the most part flow from exogenous shocks, events, or developments. One of the chief of these is economic growth, which generally brings in its train profound changes in habits, attitudes, customs, and training. For better or worse, economic growth enforces its own discipline and forces changes in the rules of the game.

5. Insofar as growth depends on the adoption of appropriate policies, growth is dependent upon development, just as development is generally dependent on growth.

6. The circle growth-development is not a closed one, however, as growth can proceed in part independently of development.

7. Given some minimum rules of the game and a fairly general desire for higher income, the transfer of more efficient techniques responds to the growth in the market, and growth thus begets growth.

8. While "growth tends to beget growth" is valid as a general statement, it appears to apply to the rate of growth as well.

9. The generalized pattern of development, exhibiting common transformations in styles of living and in economic growth, suggests that the basic minimum conditions exist very widely.

10. But the less developed a country and the lower the rate of growth, the more difficult it is to break the vicious circles of poverty-underdevelopment-poverty, and the less inducement there is to adopt and transfer more efficient techniques.

11. Hence, the key or strategic initial target in a very poor country is the attainment of a high rate of economic growth.

12. Policies that require a high or even a medium degree of effi-

ciency in the public sector are less likely to be successful than the fostering of conditions that initially favor market forces. The fall in the birth rate, better distribution, higher educational levels, and so forth are all favored by a high rate of economic growth and, indeed, generally depend on it as a necessary condition.

13. The less developed a country, the greater the need to satisfy basic human needs and lessen inequality. But the less developed the country, the greater the danger that giving top priority to these objectives will tend to extend the period of underdevelopment. This is a cruel paradox, but it apparently exists and follows from the argument of this paper.

14. The appropriateness of advice to developing countries must be judged not only from the viewpoint of the correctness of theory but also from the level of development attained. The less developed a country, the less appropriate, as a general rule, is advice requiring a high degree of efficiency, honesty, and dedication in the public sector.

15. Similarly, financial aid is likely to be more effective the more it supplies the infrastructure and contributes to external economies. The more it relies on a *direct* attack on poverty by dealing directly with millions of very poor people, the less likely it is to be effective in bringing about the changes in culture and styles of living essential to development.

16. Therefore, advice and aid are likely to be more effective the more they facilitate and promote these transformations and reinforce rather than obstruct natural or market forces. There are, of course, exceptions to this generalization that have been stressed in the literature, but it nevertheless appears valid as a general rule. The greatest contribution a government of a developing country can make to development is the initial adoption of policies that lead to a sustained period (ten years or more) of high economic growth.

NOTES

Chapter 1

1. It was recently estimated that some 80,000 persons from member countries of the Organization for Economic Cooperation Development are engaged in this activity, down from 100,000 a few years ago. United Nations, "World Plan of Action for Application of Science and Technology to Development," 1971, p. 39.

2. Robert Asher, *Development Assistance in the Seventies* (Washington, D.C.: The Brookings Institution, 1970), p. 16.

3. For a useful summary of resolutions and declarations of various groups of LDCs, see Marshall Wolfe, "Approaches to Development, Who is Approaching What?" *Cepal Review* (First Half 1976). The *Cepal Review* is available through the United Nations.

4. Lester Pearson, ed., *Partners in Development, A Report of the Commission on International Development* (London: Praeger, 1969).

5. The roster of scholars who participated in this effort is impressive. Most, however, were specialists who assumed no responsibility for the overall recommendations drawn up by the ILO staff in an official statement on "Employment, Growth and Basic Needs" (1976), Geneva.

6. Jan Tinbergen, coordinator, *RIO: Reshaping the International Order: A Report to the Club of Rome* (New York: E. P. Dutton and Co., 1976).

7. John White, *The Politics of Foreign Aid* (London: Bodley Head, 1974).

8. It has often been remarked that growing social discontent, or at least its vocal expression, frequently accompanies an improvement in conditions rather than the reverse. It is possible, therefore, to interpret the current discontent as an indication of progress, though probably this argument will not carry conviction with many.

9. Everett Hagen, *The Economics of Development* (Homewood, Ill.: Richard D. Irwin, 1968), p. 14. Hagen's general orders of magnitude have recently been con-

firmed in Irving Kravis, Alan Heston, and Robert Summers, "Real GDP Per Capita
for More Than One Hundred Countries," *Economic Journal* (June 1978).

10. That, at least, is the implication one draws from Table 4 in Kravis, Heston, and
Summers, "Real GDP," where in most cases the "real" growth rate of LDCs (relative
to the rate of the United States) is lower than the "normal" growth rate (again
relative to the United States).

11. Kravis, Heston, and Summers, "Real GDP," pp. 239-241.

Chapter 2

1. This is close to earlier definitions by Arthur Lewis and Marshall Wolfe,
although Lewis linked control directly to growth, while I prefer to link it to development and to make growth one of the conditions. Arthur Lewis, *The Theory of
Economic Growth* (London: Allen and Unwin, 1955), p. 421; Marshall Wolfe,
"Preconditions and Propositions for Another Development," *Cepal Review* 4
(1978).

2. Jacob Viner, *International Trade and Economic Development* (Glencoe, Ill.:
The Free Press, 1950), p. 127.

3. Lauchlin Currie, ed., *Operación Colombia* (Bogotá: Cámera Colombiana de
Construcción, 1961) and *Accelerating Development* (New York: McGraw-Hill,
1966), p. 20.

4. Wolfe, "Preconditions and Propositions," treats these and other problems in
the current attempt to single out the "absolute poor" as a target group for special
attention.

5. Arthur Okun, *The Political Economy of Prosperity* (New York: W. W. Norton and Co., 1970), p. 125.

6. Lauchlin Currie, "Needs, Wants, Wellbeing and Economic Growth," *Journal
of Economic Studies* 2, No. 1 (May 1975): 47-59.

7. Departamento Nacional de Planeación, *Las Cuatro Estrategias 1971-74* ["Guidelines for a New Strategy"] (Bogotá, 1972).

8. See P. D. Henderson, "Two British Errors," *Oxford Economic Papers* (1977),
pp. 159-205.

9. Robert Asher, *Development Assistance in the Seventies* (Washington, D.C.:
The Brookings Institution, 1970), p. 53.

10. T. J. Byres, ed., *Foreign Resources and Economic Development: A Symposium on the Report of the Pearson Commission* (London: Frank Cass, 1972).

11. Lester Gordon and Associates, *Report on A.I.D. Strategies* (Washington,
D.C.: The Brookings Institution, 1977).

12. Ibid.; statistical appendix by William Cline.

Chapter 3

1. Allyn Young, "Increasing Returns and Economic Progress," *Economic Journal*
38, No. 152 (December 1928).

2. Ragnar Nurkse, *Problems of Capital Formation in Underdeveloped Countries*

(New York: Oxford University Press, 1953). Lectures given in 1951. By 1962, there had been eight impressions of the book.

3. Samuel A. Morley and Gordon W. Smith, "Managerial Discretion and the Choice of Technology by Multinational Firms in Brazil," Rice University Program in Development Studies, Paper No. 56, Fall 1974, state that "with remarkable regularity, scale emerged as the overwhelming determinant of machine choice and labor use." Quoted in Werner Baer, "Technology, Employment or Development: Empirical Findings," World Development 4, No. 2 (1976), pp. 121-130.

4. Lauchlin Currie, "The Exchange Constraint: A Partial Solution," Economic Journal (December 1971): 886-903. At the time, the recommended shift was from automobiles to buildings. Since then, the possibilities of substituting for petroleum products have been widely discussed.

5. As an example of this approach, see C. Hsieh, "Approaches to Fixing Employment Targets in Development Plans," International Labour Review 97, No. 3 (1968): 277-296; reprinted in Richard Jolly, et al., eds., Third World Employment (Harmondsworth, Middlesex, England: Penguin Books Ltd., 1973), pp. 385-401. See also Ian Little, Tibor Scitovsky, and Maurice Scott, Industry and Trade in Some Developing Countries (New York: Oxford University Press, 1970), pp. 86-92, where it is argued that "growing unemployment" is attributable largely to capital-intensive techniques and to excessive expansion of "capital-intensive sectors."

6. Current discussions are reminiscent of the fallacy of "the wages fund doctrine" which insisted that wages were paid out of a fixed capital stock rather than out of current production. This analogy was pointed out to me by Roger Sandilands.

7. George Beier, Antony Churchill, Michael Cohen, and Bertrand Renaud, "The Task Ahead for Cities in Developing Countries," World Development, May 1976, p. 409.

8. Economic Report of the President to the Congress (Washington, D.C.: U.S. Government Printing Office, 1977), p. 224.

9. Ibid., p. 203.

10. Ibid., p. 237.

11. Ibid., p. 194. The distinction between goods and services is not very meaningful in itself, but does serve to indicate the excessive emphasis placed by many writers on "goods."

12. The point is that in order to sell the increased output of capital-intensive sectors, there must be a real exchange. Increased manufactured goods are exchanged, to a large extent, for increased services. Increased services did require substantial additional labor. Werner Baer argues that "it is quite likely that the growth of large-scale capital-intensive industrial units generates more service employment . . . than labor-intensive industry." "Technology, Employment or Development," p. 130. Yves Sabolo makes the same point in "Les Tertiaires" (Geneva: ILO, 1974).

13. Towards Full Employment: A Program for Colombia (Geneva: ILO, 1970).

14. Members of the medical profession, for example, are highly paid, not because they have had a long and costly training, but because that training and the other requirements to practice have reduced their number, thereby reducing competition.

15. Contrast a recent ILO document in which it is stated that a redistribution of

income should change the composition of demand and "induce a shift in the pattern of production toward goods, which in many cases are more suitable for production on a relatively small scale. This may tend in turn to generate higher levels of productive employment, to the extent that this new product mix is characterized by greater labor intensity." *Employment, Growth and Basic Needs* (Geneva: ILO, 1976), p. 50.

16. This was the justification advanced in the early and academically respectable article of A. E. Kahn, "Investment Criteria in Development," *Quarterly Journal of Economics* 65, 1951.

Chapter 4

1. Although the plan was foreshadowed in "Operation Colombia" (see Chapter 6), no mention was made of this; it had been long out of print, and in general the plan was accepted as being new.

2. For comparison of the Plan of the Four Strategies, which stressed growth, and the subsequent plan To Close the Gap, which stressed distribution, see John Sheahan, "Aspects of Planning and Development in Colombia," Technical Paper Series No. 10, Institute of Latin American Studies (Austin, Tex.: University of Texas Press, 1977).

3. Allyn Young, "Increasing Returns and Economic Progress," *Economic Journal* 38 (December 1928): 518-542.

4. Nancy and Richard Ruggles, *Demographic and Economic Change in Developed Countries*, National Bureau of Economic Research (Princeton, N.J.: Princeton University Press, 1960), pp. 155-193.

5. Taken from the National Accounts, Banco de la República, Bogotá, published annually in the *Review of the Banco de la República*.

6. For a comparison with Brazilian and Chilean systems, see R. J. Sandilands, "Monetary Correction and Housing Finance in Colombia, Brazil and Chile," "La Corrección Monetaria, Cuatro Estudios," Cuadernos del ILPES, No. 24 (Santiago, Chile, 1976).

7. Some US$200 million at the 1972 rate of exchange.

8. I have gone into some detail on the process because there must be very few cases in which an adviser is called upon to play such an active role in implementing such a highly controversial policy. There was literally no person in the country with experience of indexation, and a good deal of theory had to be translated into a workable system.

9. Discussed in Chapters 10 and 11.

10. National Accounts, prepared by the Banco de la República, available annually in the *Review of the Banco de la República*.

11. Calculations in the National Planning Agency, 1980, distributing annual rates of growth by quarters.

12. Albert Berry, "A Positive Interpretation of the Expansion of Urban Services in Latin America, with Some Colombian Evidence," *Journal of Development Studies* (January 1978): 210-231; Gary S. Fields, "Lifetime Migration in Colombia: Tests of the Expected Income Hypothesis," *Population and Development Review* 1, No. 2

(June 1979): 247-266; Samuel H. Preston, "Urban Growth in Developing Countries: A Demographic Reappraisal," *Population and Development Review* 5, No. 2 (June 1979): 195-216.

13. The advisory responsibilities of the previous board were formally transferred to the monetary authority in 1976.

14. Generally, new vested interests take the form of a new public agency, but one created by enlisting private interests may prove stronger.

Chapter 5

1. As related to me a few months later by Emilio Toro, then executive director of the World Bank for Colombia.

2. The Kemmerer missions of the 1920s were specifically to set up central banking, budget, and accounting systems for a number of governments and usually included putting them firmly on the gold standard. The next modern mission was by the United Nations to Bolivia, which followed that of the Bank to Colombia by a few months.

3. The Fund subsequently regretted this collaboration, and I had considerable difficulty including recommendations on exchange in the report because the Fund felt that recommendations should not be made in a Bank publication. Later, the agencies collaborated more smoothly.

4. International Bank for Reconstruction and Development (IBRD), *The Basis of a Development Program for Colombia* (Washington, D.C., 1950; and Baltimore, Md.: Johns Hopkins University Press, 1952, 1953). Hereafter cited as World Bank Report, 1950.

5. Making the mission head responsible for the report was one of the innovations and resolved a difficulty. The alternative was a series of unrelated monographs, or a highly circumspect "official" document, as otherwise it would probably never have gained clearance.

6. The report probably influenced subsequent Bank attitudes in both of these areas. Doubtless, the Bank would in time have stressed both social programs and macroeconomic concerns with monetary, fiscal, and exchange policy, but as a "Bank" it could easily have devoted much more attention exclusively to fundable projects in the beginning.

7. World Bank Report, 1950, p. 288.

8. The outstanding success of the combined work of the mission, report, and committee was in the field of transport.

9. In the light of subsequent attitudes and approaches espoused by the Bank, I am less confident than I was at the time that greater participation in macro planning is to the member country's interest.

10. Edward Mason and Robert Asher, *History of the World Bank* (Washington, D.C.: The Brookings Institution, 1973).

11. The smoothness of the Bank's relations with Colombia at the beginning may be contrasted with its disastrous relations with Brazil. A criticism of the Brazilian episode can be found in Mason and Asher, *History of the World Bank*, pp. 657-665.

12. Actually, one of the members of the committee was attached to the aviation monopoly and strongly opposed the recommendations of the report in this field but did not secure the support of other members.

13. An additional explanation of its effectiveness was the emphasis on transport, which unified the country in economic terms and contributed to the enlargement of the market and the consequent reaping of the economies of scale. This also happened to be a popular field and encountered little opposition, although the bulk of the expense was borne by the country and its taxpayers.

Chapter 6

1. August 20, 1952.

2. Letter from Emilio Toro, then council president, to Robert Garner, August 26, 1952, asking for and specifying the work of seven advisers.

3. IBRD, "An Appraisal of the Development Program of Colombia," Washington, D.C., June 1962.

4. Exceeded in some respects by the Harvard-sponsored mission to Pakistan, which started in 1954 under the aegis of the Graduate School of Public Administration, but also with the support of the Ford Foundation.

5. Ray Vernon, director, "Report on the Activities of the Development Advisory Service," Harvard University, June 1, 1962-June 30, 1963.

6. The text refers to the later history of CONPES. It did not function under President Valencia.

7. John Sheahan, "Rival Approaches to Planning," November 1963, in files of DNP, p. 5.

8. Memorandum for the files of the Ford Foundation, May 26, 1965, reviewing the history to that date.

9. In the personal communication to the author, he stated: "I occupied an office adjoining that of Edgar Gutiérrez, had direct access to him without passing through a secretary, attended most of the coordinating meetings with heads of division . . . ," October 17, 1977.

10. A similar emphasis was apparently preferred by the Rockefeller Foundation. At a social meeting, I once remarked to the head of the Rockefeller agricultural work in Colombia that I wondered why they did not do more research on native pasture grasses. He replied with considerable heat that they were in Colombia not to do genetic research but to train Colombians.

11. Albert Berry to William Cotter, August 25, 1969. Comments on Grant to Harvard University. (Files of Ford Foundation.)

12. HDAS Progress Report, March 1970, p. 15. (Files of Ford Foundation.)

13. Communication to the author, October 16, 1977.

14. This view is held by Albert Berry, Memorandum in Ford Foundation files, August 25, 1969.

15. It is surprising that nothing that might be called a Harvard Position on Development came to light in the course of this study. One might have thought that in working the same field in various developing countries, a recognizable point of

view would have developed, as appeared to be the case with Chicago advisers and Chicago-trained economists in the more southern part of the continent.

Chapter 7

1. I did not realize the inflationary consequences that could result from a devaluation badly carried out, as in 1962.

2. IBRD, *Bank Operations in Colombia* (Washington, D.C., 1972), p. 20, and Annex Table 1.7.

3. All the figures in this paragraph were taken from IMF, *International Financial Statistics* 1972, Supplement, pp. 120-122.

4. Unfortunately, most of the rich mine of material built up by the IMF over the years is unavailable for analysis by scholars.

5. Article VIII of the agreement asks that members supply all the economic information required by the IMF, and Article XIV authorizes consultations.

6. J. Keith Horsefield and Margaret G. de Vries, *The International Monetary Fund, 1945-65: Twenty Years of International Monetary Cooperation* (Washington, D.C.: International Monetary Fund, 1969), Vol. 2, p. 169. Canada adopted a floating rate as early as 1950.

7. My main sources are documents of the IMF and an excellent paper by Eduardo Wiesner, "Devaluación y Mecanismo de Ajuste en Colombia," *Banca y Finanzas* 159 (March 1978).

8. The Fund's reasoning in granting standby arrangements during this period is ably described by Margaret de Vries in *The International Monetary Fund 1966-1971: The System Under Stress* (Washington, D.C., 1976).

9. For the political aspects, see R. L. Maullin, "The Colombia-IMF Disagreement of November-December 1966: An Interpretation of Its Place in Colombian Politics," Memorandum RM 5314-RC, The Rand Corporation, Santa Monica, Calif., June 1967.

10. One result of the exchange crisis of 1966 was unintentional. Apparently, the president originally intended to use CONPES as the vehicle for the determination of exchange policy, and there were frequent and long discussions on the subject up to the end of 1966. But the growing complexity of the problem led the president to entrust part of the negotiations to the Colombian ambassador in Washington, to see representatives of international agencies himself, and to appoint subcommittees on which DNP (the Planning Agency) was not represented. This established a pattern and diminished the role of the Planning Agency in this vitally important field, as the position of DNP has always been less influential in the Junta Monetaria than in CONPES.

11. Quoted in Minutes of Meeting of CONPES, January 3, 1967.

12. For a more sympathetic appraisal of the role of monetary correction in Colombian capital markets, see Robert Barro, "Monetary Correction, Capital Markets, and Open-Market Operations in Colombia," *Journal of Economic Studies*, New Series, 2, No. 1 (May 1975): 1-9.

13. Even when the ceilings are observed, it appears, as remarked above, that the

ceilings are not well or not effectively chosen, and the expansion continues unchecked.

14. Based on only end-of-year figures and omitting government deposits in the central banks, the rates of growth in 1971-1974 were, respectively, 11, 24.4, 29.9, and 19.5 percent, and for 1975 and 1976, 27.8 and 34.7 percent, respectively.

15. "La Política Monetaria y el Nivel de Precios," *Revista de Planeación y Desarrollo* 5, No. 2 (Abril-Junio 1973 [actually published February 1974]).

Chapter 8

1. *Bases para una Reforma Tributaria en Colombia* ("Musgrave Report"), Bogotá, 1969, pp. 28-30. Some of the projections and assumptions for these figures appear questionable.

2. Ibid., p. 231.

3. Revista Banco de la República, January 1974.

4. Rodrigo Manrique, *Las Reformas Tributarias en Colombia 1886-1974*, Instituto de Estudios Colombianos (Bogotá, 1977). Compiled from data in Informes Anuales de la Contraloría General de la República.

5. When those lines were written, the country was on the threshold of the really stiff inflation of the 1970s, and the salaried workers in 1978 were still subject to steadily rising rates on a real income scale.

6. The Musgrave Report, p. 238.

7. Manrique, *Reformas*, pp. 34-36.

8. Antonio Hernández Gamarra, "Deficit Fiscal, Política Monetaria y Distribución del Crédito," in *El Mercado de Capitales en Colombia*, Banco de la República, 1974, p. 77.

9. Unfortunately, he was a "bond" man, not a monetary theorist, and his visit was short and ineffectual.

10. Manrique, *Reformas*, p. 57.

11. Enrique Low Murtra and Marco Tulio Ruiz Suárez, *Manejo de la Política Económica Colombiana, 1974-78*, Fundación de Investigaciones y Estudios Económico-Sociales (FINES) (Bogotá, June 1978), p. 16.

12. Jaime Bueno Miranda, "El Concepto del Ingreso Fiscal en la Legislación Colombiana," in *La Estructura Fiscal Colombiana* (Bogotá: Pontificia Universidad Javeriana, 1978), p. 71.

13. In December 1977, some relief was given for "illusory" capital gains, but nothing for earned incomes.

14. By the Government Statistical Agency, DANE Boletín, January 1975 and subsequent issues for the cost-of-living index.

15. Enrique Low Murtra, in a seminar of FINES, Bogotá, June 1978, amplifying a paper in *Cifras y Letras*, Bogotá, March 1978, pp. 2-7. The same findings were made by Bueno, "El Concepto," pp. 36, 37, who also found that tax administration had been adversely affected, p. 39.

16. Manrique, *Reformas*, p. 57.

17. Perry, *Estructura Fiscal*, p. 261.

18. Bueno, "El Concepto," p. 40.

19. R. Musgrave, *La Tributación y el Desarrollo Económico*, pp. 23, 25-26.
20. See note 4, "Cuadro 1.4."

Chapter 9

1. Strictly speaking, the law, as stated by Engels, applied to different-sized incomes at a given time. It appears legitimate, however, to extend it to cover intercountry comparisons and demand for foodstuffs per capita over time.
2. This pattern can be seen clearly from an examination of the comprehensive cross-country data in Hollis Chenery and Moises Syrquin, *Patterns of Development 1950-1970* (Oxford: Oxford University Press, 1975) (for the World Bank).
3. All farm and population figures for the United States are derived from *Economic Report of the President 1977* (Washington, D.C.: U.S. Government Printing Office), pp. 290-292. The *Report* for 1979 does not modify the conclusions of the text (pp. 287-291).
4. Edward Denison and William Chung, *How Japan's Economy Grew so Fast: The Sources of Post-War Expansion* (Washington, D.C.: The Brookings Institution, 1976), pp. 84, 151, 225.
5. Ibid., p. 38.
6. See, for example, Yujiro Hayami, *A Century of Agricultural Growth in Japan* (Minneapolis: University of Minnesota Press, 1977), p. 228.
7. Lauchlin Currie, *Accelerating Development* (New York: McGraw-Hill, 1966), pp. 73-74. The factual material was drawn from James Street, *The New Revolution in the Cotton Economy* (Chapel Hill, N.C.: University of North Carolina Press, 1957).
8. *Economic Report of the President 1979*, pp. 184, 287.
9. *Economic Report of the President 1977*, pp. 193, 291, 292. For the early history of more developed countries, the following rates of growth figures in agricultural output have been cited: France, 1.3 percent per year (1825-1834 to 1855-1864); Germany, 1.9 percent (1816-1861); Sweden, 1.7 percent (1861-1865 to 1891-1895). Hayami, *A Century of Agricultural Growth*, p. 211.
10. Hayami, *A Century of Agricultural Growth*, p. 71, attributes the growing mechanization of farming in Japan to rising agricultural wages.
11. Jorge García García, "Is Food Security Important for Colombia?" Paper presented at IFPRI-CIMYT Conference on Food Security, El Batan, Mexico, November 21-23, 1978, and published in the *Revista de Planeación y Desarrollo* 11, No. 3, Bogotá, 1979.
12. Currie, et al., *Resources, Population and Growth: Colombia 1950-2000* (Bogotá: Instituto de Estudios Colombianos, 1977), Chapter 7.
13. Another solution, favored by some writers, is the establishment of agroindustries in rural areas. The idea is attractive, and there are some successful examples, especially in Israel. Success appears to be particularly dependent on leadership, however. In most developing countries, this is in scanty supply, and the loss of the economies of scale offered by larger cities is particularly felt. The best possibilities in this direction, unfortunately, are offered by highly developed coun-

tries with excellent transport and communications facilities. As a solution for mass rural poverty in LDCs, it appears to offer little hope.

14. As was done recently by Thomas Balogh, "Failures in the Strategy against Poverty," *World Development* 6, No. 1 (January 1978): 11.

Chapter 10

1. The advice generally offered and discussed here can be found in the various sector papers on urban housing published by the World Bank and in a long article by four staff members of that institution. See G. Beier, et al., "The Task Ahead for Cities in Developing Countries," *World Development*, May 1976.

2. See Currie, "The Interrelations of Urban and National Economic Planning," *Urban Studies* 12, No. 1 (February 1975): 37-46.

3. See Leland S. Burns and Leo Grebler, "Resource Allocation to Housing Investment: A Comparative International Study," *Economic Development and Cultural Change* 25, No. 1 (October 1976): 103.

4. Currie, et al., *Resources, Population and Growth*, Chapter IX. (Calculations were made by Homero Cuevas.)

Chapter 11

1. Letter from S. S. Kirmani of the Bank to the head of DNP and the mayor of Bogotá, September 1, 1971.

Chapter 12

1. This is condensed from a much longer version prepared by Roger Sandilands.

2. Actually, an earlier study by the American Rolling Mill Company in 1944 had made an adverse recommendation.

3. Koppers Company Inc., *Informe Sobre Paz del Rio S.A.*, Bogotá, February 1961.

4. P.D. Henderson, "Two British Errors," *Oxford Economic Papers* (1977), pp. 160-205.

5. Ibid., p. 185. In an effort to make this point, Henderson's study of the two costly British errors in allocation of resources remarked that the loss equaled the total amount spent in research and development expenditures in all British universities at the 1975 rate (£200 million a year) for a twelve-year period.

6. For a similar finding, see IBRD, "Bank Operations in Colombia: An Evaluation" (The Christopher Willoughby Report, unpublished, 1972), pp. 100-107.

7. J. King, *Economic Development Projects and Their Appraisal* (Baltimore, Md.: Johns Hopkins University Press, 1967), pp. 524-525.

Chapter 13

1. Currie, et al., *Resources, Population and Growth: Colombia 1950-2000* (Bogotá: Instituto de Estudios Colombianos, 1977).
2. Compare the articles in Berry, Fields, and Preston cited in Chapter 4.

Chapter 14

1. *World Bank Atlas*, 1977, p. 8.
2. Hugh Patrick and Henry Rosovsky, eds., *Asia's New Giant* (Washington, D.C.: The Brookings Institution, 1976), p. 407. The growth in exports was from US$2,011 million in 1955 to US$36,840 million in 1973.

Chapter 15

1. Sir Alec Cairncross, *Essays in Economic Management* (Albany, N.Y.: State University of New York Press, 1971).
2. Alan Peacock, "Giving Economic Advice in Difficult Times," *The Three Books Review* (March 1977): 14.
3. Many details of this episode are revealed by Stephen Fay and Hugo Young in two long articles in the *Sunday Times* (of London), May 14 and May 21, 1978, "How the Hard Money Men Took Over Britain." It is significant that many of the details were obtained from American rather than British sources.
4. Henry C. Wallich, "The American Council of Economic Advisers and the German Sachverständigenrat: A Study in the Economics of Advice," *Quarterly Journal of Economics* 82, No. 3 (August 1968): 349-379.
5. Ibid., p. 378.
6. James Tobin, former member of the CEA, feels strongly that the chief executive needs the opinions of full-time professional advisers who are an integral part of his administration but not of any Cabinet department. He feels that the location in the Executive Office of the President is both sufficiently removed from the White House staff and close enough to the president and independent of any other official, to serve this purpose. James Tobin, *National Economic Policy* (New Haven, Conn.: Yale University Press, 1966), p. 202.

Chapter 16

1. For a good summary of the conflicting and contradictory empirical evidence on this point, see Paul Streeten, "Editor's Introduction," *World Development* 6, No. 3 (March 1978): 242-243. However, his selection was heavily weighted on the side of distribution. For an excellent discussion of the more theoretical issues involved, see Arthur M. Okun, *Equality and Efficiency: The Big Trade-off* (Washington, D.C.: The Brookings Institution, 1975).

2. Paul Streeten, "Basic Human Needs," *Millennium* Special Edition, Autumn 1978, pp. 29-45.

3. Rendigs Fels, ed., *The Second Crisis of Economic Theory.* Note especially the contribution by Alan Sweezy, "The Keynesians and Government Policy, 1933-1939" (Morristown, N.J.: The General Learning Press, 1972), p. 118.

Chapter 17

1. As Michael Posner, formerly deputy chief economic adviser to the British government, remarked, "It was relatively easy to secure acceptance of advice when there existed a consensus. The difficulty was that such consensus was lacking on most of the really important issues."

2. Paul Streeten, "Economic Models and Their Usefulness for Planning in Southern Asia," Vol. 3, App. 3, in Gunnar Myrdal, *Asian Drama* (New York: Pantheon, 1968).

3. Arthur M. Okun, *The Political Economy of Prosperity* (New York: W. W. Norton and Co., 1970), pp. 4-6.

4. "The man in the street knows that the penicillin designed to cure his sore throat is not injected into his throat; but he does not have similar experience with the flow of economic medicine through the body politic." Ibid., p. 5.

5. This discussion of theory is perhaps best illustrated by a little anecdote. Many years ago Jacob Viner, noted for his caustic wit, was attending a meeting in the Department of Agriculture and was elaborating a theoretical point. One of the participants remarked that "in Agriculture, we don't take much stock in theory." Viner, without a moment's hesitation, shot back, "That is interesting. What do you use in place of thinking?"—an answer that would occur to most of us only when the moment had passed.

6. For a discussion of the uncritical use of income distribution data in Kenya, see A. Hazlewood, "Kenya: Income Distribution and Poverty—An Unfashionable View," *Journal of Modern African Studies* 16, No. 1 (1978): 81-95.

Chapter 19

1. A group working under the direction of Bela Belassa. See "Export Performance in Developing Countries: A Comparative Analysis," World Bank Staff Paper, No. 248, January 1979.

Chapter 20

1. Joan Robinson, *Economic Philosophy* (Chicago: Aldine Publishing Co. 1962), p. 13.

2. Allyn Young, *The Economic Journal* (December 1928).

BIBLIOGRAPHY

This book is in part an appraisal of economic advice that has been given developing countries in the past thirty years and in part an effort to derive some generalizations on giving advice. There is a vast literature dealing with specific advice (studies, mission reports, articles, and so on), but few attempt to make overall evaluations. At appropriate places in the text, I have cited examples of what I have assumed to be representative of economic advice in general to developing countries. I have relied in part on the theories and strategies of growth and development to which I subscribe and which, naturally, provide a basis for my own evaluation of advice given. Sources of these views are also given.

In many cases, material used in the text was made available to me by the organizations mentioned in the text. For monetary and exchange advice by the International Monetary Fund, staff papers of the 1960s were made available to me, but unfortunately have not been published. I have been granted access to file material by the Ford Foundation; the International Bank for Reconstruction and Development and the Agency for International Development (both in Washington, D.C.) and the Instituto de Estudios Colombianos, the Fundación de Investigaciones y Estudios Economico-Sociales, the Banco de la República (whose National Accounts are available annually), and of course, the Departamento Nacional de Planeación (all in Bogotá) have allowed me access to materials in their files.

I have also consulted the *Economic Report of the President* (1977 and 1979, available through the U.S. Government Printing Office, Washington, D.C.) and, for the history of the International Monetary Fund, Margaret de Vries and J. Keith Horsefield's *The International Monetary Fund, 1945-65* and Margaret de Vries' *The International Monetary Fund, 1966-71* (Washington, D.C.: International Labor Organization, 1969, 1976).

Books

Asher, Robert E. *Development Assistance in the Seventies: Alternatives for the United States*. Washington, D.C.: The Brookings Institution, 1970.

Baer, Werner. *Industrialization and Economic Development in Brazil*. New Haven: Yale University Press, 1975.

_____, and Kerstenetzky, Isaac. *Inflation and Growth in Latin America*. New Haven: Yale University Press, 1970.

Bauer, P. T. *Dissent on Development: Studies and Debates in Development Economics*. Cambridge, Mass.: Harvard University Press, 1972.

Byres, T. J., ed. *Foreign Resources and Economic Development: A Symposium on the Report of the Pearson Commission*. London: Frank Cass, 1972.

Cairncross, Alexander K. *Essays in Economic Management*. Albany: State University of New York Press, 1972.

Chenery, Hollis, et al. *Patterns of Development 1950-1970*. Oxford: Oxford University Press, 1975.

Currie, Lauchlin. *Accelerating Development*. New York: McGraw-Hill, 1966.

_____, ed. *The Basis of a Development Program for Colombia*. Baltimore: Johns Hopkins University Press, 1950.

_____, ed. *Operación Colombia*. Bogotá: Camera Colombiana de Construcción, 1961,

_____, et al. *Resources, Population and Growth: Colombia 1950-2000*. Bogotá: Instituto de Estudios Colombianos, 1977.

Denison, Edward, and Chung, William. *How Japan's Economy Grew so Fast: The Sources of Post-War Expansion*. Washington, D.C.: The Brookings Institution, 1976.

Fels, Rendigs, ed. *The Second Crisis of Economic Theory*. Morristown, N.J.: The General Learning Press, 1972.

Galbraith, John K. *Economics, Peace and Laughter*. New York: Pelican Books, 1975.

Gordon, Lester, and associates. *Report on A.I.D. Strategies*. Washington, D.C.: The Brookings Institution, 1977.

Hagen, Everett E. *The Economics of Development*. Homewood, Ill.: Richard D. Irwin, 1968.

Hamilton, Ian. *The Moscow City Region*. Oxford: Oxford University Press, 1976.

Hayami, Yujiro. *A Century of Agricultural Growth in Japan: Its Relevance to Asian Development*. Minneapolis: University of Minnesota Press, 1977.

International Bank for Reconstruction and Development. *The Basis of a Development Program for Colombia*. Baltimore: Johns Hopkins University Press, 1952.

Jolly, Richard, et al., eds. *Third World Employment*. Middlesex: Penguin Books Ltd., 1973.

King, John A. *Economic Development Projects and Their Appraisal: Cases and Principles from the Experience of the World Bank*. Baltimore: Johns Hopkins University Press, 1967.

Lekachman, Robert. *The Age of Keynes*. London: Penguin Press, 1967.

Lewis, Arthur. *The Theory of Economic Growth*. London: Allen and Unwin, 1955.

Lipton, Michael. *Why Poor People Stay Poor: Urban Bias in World Development*. Cambridge, Mass.: Harvard University Press, 1977.

Little, Ian, et al. *Industry and Trade in Some Developing Countries: A Comparative Study*. Oxford: Oxford University Press, 1970.

Mason, Edward S., and Asher, Robert E. *History of the World Bank*. Washington, D.C.: The Brookings Institution, 1973.

Meier, C. M. *Leading Issues in Development Economics*. 2nd ed. Oxford: Oxford University Press, 1970.

Musgrave, R. A. and Gillis, M. *Fiscal Reform for Colombia*. Cambridge, Mass.: Harvard Law School, 1971.

Nurkse, Ragnar. *Problems of Capital Formation in Underdeveloped Countries*. Oxford: Oxford University Press, 1953.

Okun, Arthur M. *Equality and Efficiency: The Big Trade-off*. Washington, D.C.: The Brookings Institution, 1975.

_____. *The Political Economy of Prosperity*. New York: W. W. Norton and Co., 1970.

Papenek, Gustav, ed. *Development Policy, Theory and Practice*. Cambridge: Harvard University Press, 1968.

Patrick, Hugh, and Rosovsky, Henry, eds. *Asia's New Giant: How the Japanese Economy Works*. Washington, D.C.: The Brookings Institution, 1976.

Pearson, Lester, ed. *Partners in Development, A Report of the Commission on International Development*. London: Praeger, 1969.

Robinson, Joan. *Economic Philosophy*. Chicago: Aldine Publishing Co., 1962.

Ruggles, Nancy, and Ruggles, Richard. *Demographic and Economic Change in Developed Countries*. Princeton, N.J.: Princeton University Press, 1960.

Sandilands, Roger J. *Monetary Correction and Housing Finance in Colombia, Brazil and Chile*. Farnborough, England: Gower Publishing Co., 1980.

Stamper, B. Maxwell. *Population and Planning in Developing Nations: A Review of Sixty Development Plans for the 1970's*. New York: Population Council, 1977.

Stein, Herbert. *The Fiscal Revolution in America*. Chicago: University of Chicago Press, 1969.

Street, James. *The New Revolution in the Cotton Economy*. Chapel Hill: University of North Carolina Press, 1957.

Tinbergen, Jan. *RIO: Reshaping the International Order*. New York: E. P. Dutton and Co., 1976.

Tobin, James. *National Economic Policy*. New Haven: Yale University Press, 1966.
Viner, Jacob. *International Trade and Economic Development*. Glencoe, Ill.: The Free Press, 1950.
White, John. *The Politics of Foreign Aid*. London: Bodley Head, 1974.

Articles

Balogh, Thomas. "Failures in the Strategy against Poverty." *World Development* 6, no. 1 (January 1978).
Barro, Robert. "Monetary Correction, Capital Markets, and Open-Market Operations in Colombia." *Journal of Economic Studies*, new series 2, no. 1 (May 1975).
Beier, George, et al. "The Task Ahead for Cities in Developing Countries." *World Development* (May 1976).
Berry, Albert. "A Positive Interpretation of the Expansion of Urban Services in Latin America, with some Colombian Evidence." *Journal of Development Studies* (January 1978).
Burns, Leland S., and Grebler, Leo. "Resource Allocation to Housing Investment: A Comparative International Study." *Economic Development and Cultural Change* 24, no. 1 (October 1976).
Currie, Lauchlin. "The Exchange Constraint: A Partial Solution." *Economic Journal* 81 (December 1971).
———. "The Interrelations of Urban and National Economic Planning." *Urban Studies* 12, no. 1 (February 1975).
———. "The Leading Sector Strategy Model of Growth." *Journal of Economic Studies* (May 1974).
———. "Needs, Wants, Wellbeing and Economic Growth." *Journal of Economic Studies* (May 1975).
Fay, Stephen, and Young, Hugo. "How the Hard Money Took Over Britain." *Sunday Times* (of London), May 14 and May 21, 1978.
Fields, Gary S. "Lifetime Migration in Colombia: Tests of the Expected Income Hypothesis." *Population and Development Review* 1, no. 2 (June 1979).
García, Jorge García, "Is Food Security Important for Colombia?" *Revista de Planeación y Desarrollo* 11, no. 3 (1979).
Hansen, J. A. "The Leading Sector Development Strategy and the Importance of Institutional Reform: A Reinterpretation." *Journal of Economic Studies* (May 1976).
Hazelwood, Arthur. "Kenya: Income Distribution and Poverty—An Unfashionable View." *Journal of Modern African Studies* 16, no. 1 (1978).
Henderson, P. D. "Two British Errors." *Oxford Economic Papers* (1977).
Hsieh, C. "Approaches to Fixing Employment Targets in Development Plans." *International Labour Review* 97, no. 3 (1968).
Kravis, Irving et al. "Real GDP Per Capita for More Than One Hundred Countries." *Economic Journal* (June 1978).
Maullin, R. L. "The Colombia-IMF Disagreement of November-December 1966: An Interpretation of Its Place in Colombian Politics." Memo RM 5314-RC, The Rand Corporation, Santa Monica, Calif., June 1967.

Miranda, Jaime Bueno. "El Concepto del Ingreso Fiscal en la Legislación Colombiana (1978).

Morley, Samuel A., and Smith, Gordon W. "Managerial Discretion and the Choice of Technology by Multinational Firms in Brazil." Rice University Program in Development Studies, paper no. 56 (Fall 1974).

Myint, Hla. "Economic Theory and Development Policy." *Economica* 34, no. 134 (May 1967).

Peacock, Alan. "Giving Economic Advice in Difficult Times." *The Three Books Review*, March 1977.

Preston, Samuel H. "Urban Growth in Developing Countries: A Demographic Reappraisal." *Population and Development Review* 5, no. 2 (June 1979).

Revista de Planeación y Desarrollo. "La Politica Monetaria y el Nivel de Precios," 5, no. 2 (Abril-Junio 1973).

Sheahan, John. "Aspects of Planning and Development in Colombia." Technical Paper Series no. 10, Institute of Latin American Studies, Austin, University of Texas Press, 1977.

Stewart, Frances, and Streeten, Paul. "New Strategies for Development." *Oxford Economic Papers* (1976).

Stone, Richard. "Keynes, Political Arithmetic and Econometrics." Seventh Keynes Lecture in Economics, British Academy, Cambridge, April 1978.

Streeten, Paul. "Basic Human Needs." *Millennium*, Autumn 1978.

_____. "Editor's Introduction." *World Development* 6, no. 3 (March 1978).

_____. "The Limits of Development Research." *World Development* 2, no. 10-16 (December 1974).

Wallich, Henry C. "The American Council of Economic Advisers and the German Sachverständigenrat: A Study of the Economics of Advice." *Quarterly Journal of Economics* 81, no. 3 (August 1968).

Wiesner, Eduardo. "Devaluación y Mecanismo de Ajuste en Colombia." *Banca y Finanzas* 159 (March 1978).

Wolfe, Marshall. "Approaches to Development, Who is Approaching What?" *Cepal Review*, first half 1976.

_____. "Preconditions and Propositions for Another Development." *Cepal Review* 4 (1978).

Young, Allyn. "Increasing Returns and Economic Progress." *Economic Journal* 38, no. 152 (December 1928).

INDEX

About The Author

LAUCHLIN CURRIE is an adviser to the Departamento Nacional de Planeación in Bogotá, Colombia. His previous books include *Accelerating Development, Taming the Megalopolis,* and *Saving, Money Correction, and Building.*

6 --
26 --